ENDORSEMENTS

In *Wrestling with God*, Lessing and Steinmann engage some of the Old Testament's most challenging questions. They masterfully employ Scripture to interpret Scripture, illuminating difficult passages with theological depth and pastoral insight. With clarity and sober judgment, they sift through biblical evidence and draw faithful and relevant conclusions.

—**Paul Elliott,** professor of theology, Concordia University Irvine

Being separated from the Old Testament by time, geography, culture, and language makes understanding it a challenge. These Old Testament scholars engage perennial questions about the Old Testament by carefully examining biblical texts within their original settings, but also self-consciously as Christians. Whatever one's opinions on the authors' stances, they are to be commended for helping us read the Old Testament more closely and faithfully.

—**M. Daniel Carroll R. (Rodas),** PhD, Scripture Press Ministries Chair of Biblical Studies and Pedagogy, Wheaton College

Readers of the Old Testament are well aware that it contains many puzzling and even disturbing passages. In this volume, Lessing and Steinmann, two seasoned interpreters of the Old Testament, join forces to "wrestle with" some of the most difficult passages. Their thoughtful and reasonable responses to tough questions, including those posed by the violence depicted in the Old Testament and by its portrait of an angry and vengeful God, deserve careful consideration.

—**Robert B. Chisholm Jr.,** chair and senior professor of Old Testament studies, Dallas Theological Seminary

Lessing and Steinmann draw on their decades of teaching and writing on the Old Testament to address the most pressing questions the church asks when reading the Old Testament. Whether readers agree with all of their conclusions or not, *Wrestling with God* is an accessible guide that will force readers to wrestle with God in specific Old Testament texts and the entire Bible for the good of the church.

—**Andrew Abernethy,** professor of Old Testament, assistant dean, director of the MA in biblical exegesis program, Wheaton College

For most Christians, outside of a few familiar places, the Old Testament is a strange, intimidating land into which they dare not venture. Lessing and Steinmann serve as guides to this strange land that makes up three-quarters of the Bible. Their magnificent comprehensive treatment addresses every major misconception of the Old Testament in a way that is easy to understand. Even more helpful are the discussion questions at the end of each chapter, which allow the reader to deepen his or her understanding of the Old Testament and develop a fuller appreciation for God's Word.

—**Rev. Dr. Ryan M. Tietz,** associate professor of exegetical theology, Old Testament, Concordia Theological Seminary, Fort Wayne

Wrestling with God clearly comes from pastors who love teaching Bible studies. Rather than dodging the hard questions, this book takes them head-on! With clarity and conviction, Lessing and Steinmann offer us a delightful guide into the murkier parts of the Old Testament. Under the guise of addressing difficult passages, they sneak in a ton of biblical theology—teaching us who God is for us as our Creator, Redeemer, and Sanctifier—all through the prophetic witness of the Old Testament.

—**Rev. Dr. Geoffrey R. Boyle,** assistant professor of pastoral ministry and missions, Concordia Theological Seminary, Fort Wayne

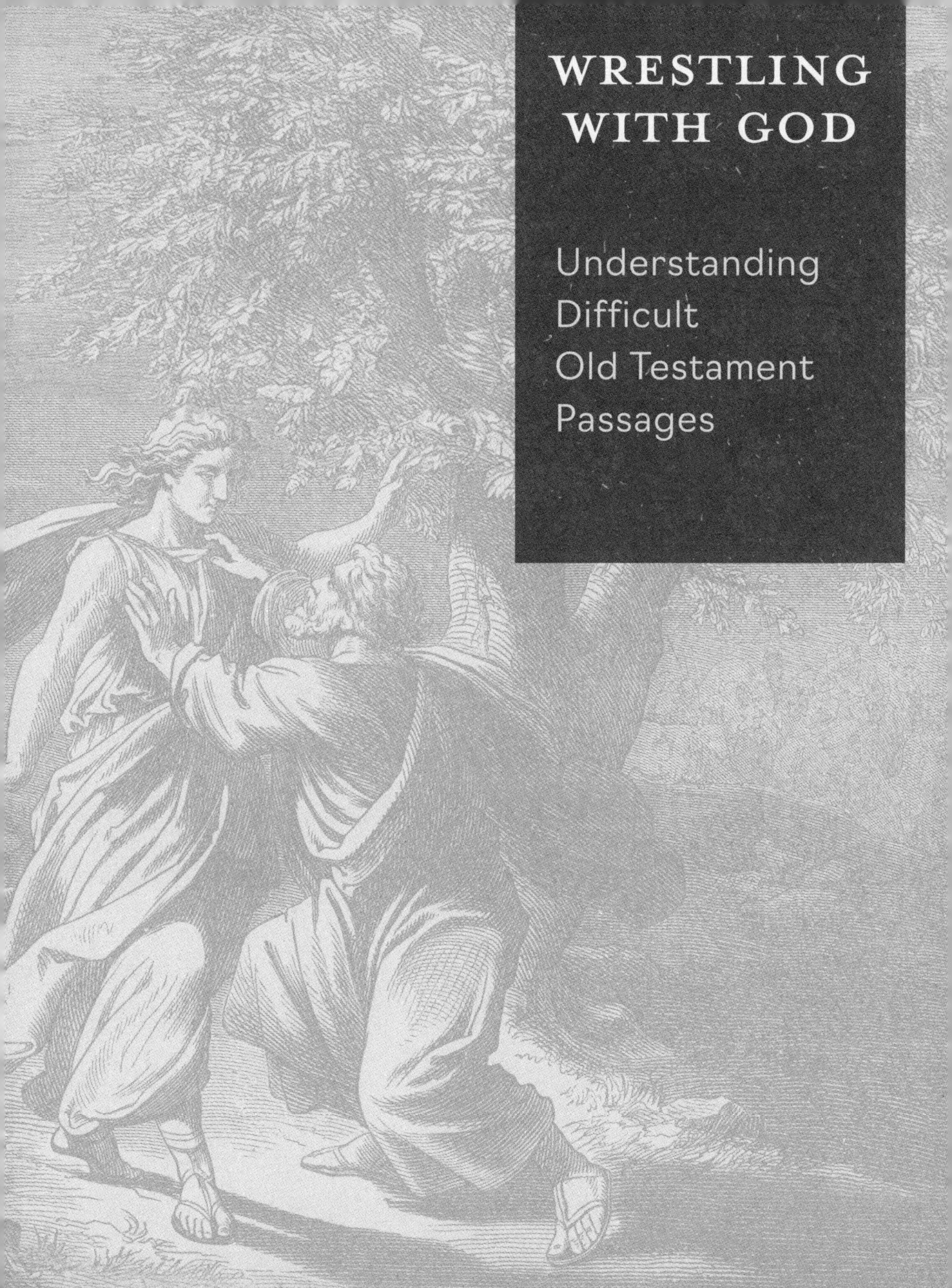

WRESTLING WITH GOD

Understanding Difficult Old Testament Passages

R. REED LESSING
ANDREW E. STEINMANN

WRESTLING WITH GOD

Understanding Difficult Old Testament Passages

R. REED LESSING AND ANDREW E. STEINMANN

Published by Concordia Publishing House
3558 S. Jefferson Ave., St. Louis, MO 63118-3968
1-800-325-3040 • cph.org

Manufactured in the United States of America

1 2 3 4 5 6 7 8 9 10 34 33 32 31 30 29 28 27 26 25

CONTENTS

PREFACE

WRESTLING WITH GOD'S WORD

Genesis 32 and Seeing God More Clearly

"Jacob called the name of the place Peniel." (Genesis 32:30 ESV)

There is much to love about the Old Testament (hereafter, OT). We marvel at its majestic account of creation in Genesis 1 and thrill to see Moses go toe-to-toe with stubborn Pharaoh in the book of Exodus. The OT features Israel's beautiful tabernacle and Isaiah's stunning prophetic predictions. And who among us isn't moved by David's beautiful psalms, especially Psalm 23? Other OT favorites include the practical applications in the book of Proverbs, as well as Solomon's down-to-earth wisdom in Ecclesiastes. But let's face it, the OT also includes a lot of strange names, strange places, and even stranger events.

After leaving the ark, Noah gets drunk. Abraham and Jacob—among other men—have multiple wives. Moses kills an Egyptian and ends up on the empire's most-wanted list. The book of Judges overflows with sordid stories of rape, mutilation, and murder. And how did some men live so long? Methuselah doesn't die until he's 969 years old!

The OT also incorporates prayers in which people scream and rage at God, insisting that He isn't doing His job right. How would that go over in our church services? And what about the times when God appears cruel and vindictive, or when the books of Esther and Song of Songs fail to mention His name?

While there are parts of the OT that resonate with light and beauty, a lot of it feels like clothing that doesn't fit or a movie that doesn't make sense or a recipe that doesn't go over well at Thanksgiving. We have to admit that there are a number of places where the OT feels like someone else's home decor that just isn't our style.

Need a few more examples? God changes His mind about having made people, then proceeds to destroy most of them in a worldwide flood (Genesis 6:6–8). Abraham is one hundred and Sarah is ninety when they have their first child, Isaac (Genesis 21:1–7). When Moses speaks to the Israelites about the Canaanites, he says, "Neither make a covenant with them nor show them mercy" (Deuteronomy 7:2). Elisha calls down two bears to maul forty-two children who mock him (2 Kings 2:23–25). Jeremiah laments that God has become like his enemy (Lamentations 2:4–5). And some of the books in the OT are so *long*. Isaiah has sixty-six chapters. Jeremiah, fifty-two. And the book of Psalms? One hundred and fifty! Little wonder Christians have sidelined the OT—"I can't relate to it, and I don't understand it. And to be honest, I have more than just a few problems with it."

Most Christians don't outright reject the OT. Instead, they pick and choose what they like and discard the rest. "I'll take four chapters in Genesis, eight in Exodus, and a sprinkling of psalms, proverbs, and prophets. You can have everything else—especially Leviticus and Numbers!"

Not content with picking and choosing some parts and rejecting others, some people completely dismiss Israel's Scriptures and argue that these texts are antiquated and irrelevant and contain nothing useful for Christians. That's what Marcion did.

In AD 138, Marcion moved from modern-day Turkey to Rome, where he began teaching that the OT God was different from the New Testament (NT) God. After all, Marcion argued, the God of the OT is angrier and more wrathful than the God of the NT, who in Jesus abounds with grace and mercy. The OT? It's full of violence and vengeance. The NT? It's full of compassion and salvation. End of discussion. There's no need for the OT!

Early Christian leaders like Irenaeus and Tertullian pushed back. They pointed out that Jesus didn't reject the OT (Matthew 5:17), that Paul taught that Israel's Scriptures were divinely inspired (2 Timothy 3:16), that the apostle endorsed these texts as sources of encouragement and hope (Romans 15:4). Based on these verses and others, in AD 144, the church rejected Marcion and his repudiation of the OT. The early church was convinced that it would be catastrophic to preach the Gospel of Jesus Christ apart from Israel's divinely inspired books.

Most Christians don't go as far as Marcion did, yet there remains a general distaste for the OT—an apathy for the Hebrew Scriptures. Churches don't officially renounce Genesis through Malachi, but they often don't see these books as important for faith and life.

Who among us hasn't scratched our head when we read about Moses slaughtering the Midianites or Jephthah sacrificing his daughter? Then there's the custom of taking off a sandal and giving it to another person to confirm a business partnership. There's even a book called Lamentations. Who needs that? We jettison the OT and go to what makes more sense—Jesus, Peter, Paul, John, and others. Who needs Abraham, Asher, and Aaron? Isn't the OT all Law and the NT all Gospel? And doesn't the NT supersede the OT anyway? My! The historical milieu, culture, and traditions in the OT are so far removed from our twenty-first-century lives; it's a chasm that simply can't be bridged.

The temptation, therefore, is to read the first three chapters in Genesis—rejoice in God's creation, mourn over Adam's fall, embrace the promise of a Savior—then skip the rest and get to Jesus. After all, what's there to lose? Much. Very much.

God's revelation in the OT makes up 75 percent of the Bible. To avoid three-fourths of what God says severely hampers our Christian life and witness. Reading only the NT, along with pieces and snippets of the OT, would stymie our understanding of our Savior. It's time to embrace the OT, learn from it, treasure it—yes, even love it.

That's why we wrote this book—to help you wrestle with some of the most difficult parts of Israel's Scriptures so that you come away with a better understanding of God's Word and a deeper appreciation for its role in your life. We intentionally use the word *wrestle* because growing in our knowledge of the OT takes time, effort, and determination.

Jacob should know.

You remember the story. Jacob steals Esau's blessing. Esau doesn't take it lightly. In fact, he vows to kill Jacob, who hightails it out of Canaan to live in Paddan-aram, or modern-day southeast

Turkey. Fast-forward twenty years, and now the two brothers are about to meet again.

Jacob's anxiety is off the charts. Can you imagine? Esau, his estranged brother, is coming to meet him with four hundred men (Genesis 32:6). This looks like an attacking army, not a welcome-home gathering for a cherished family member. That's why, after dividing his family into two camps, Jacob plans to spend the night alone—probably reiterating his earlier prayer to God (Genesis 32:9–12).

Suddenly, from out of nowhere, someone attacks Jacob. It's Christ Jesus in the form of a man, who will, in the fullness of time, take upon Himself the flesh of a man (John 1:14). Hosea 12:4 calls Him a Messenger, thus confirming that this man is Yahweh's Messenger, whom Israelites sometimes call God—because He is.

This God-man dislocates Jacob's hip. Then, He demands that Jacob release Him. Jacob replies, "I will not let You go until You bless me" (Genesis 32:26 ESV). The heavenly Wrestler, therefore, pronounces this blessing on Jacob: "Your name will no longer be called Jacob ["deceiver"], but Israel ["God has made right"], because you are right with God and with men you will prevail" (Genesis 32:28). Jacob's nemesis during the night turned into a promise keeper at the break of day. Jacob calls the name of the place Peniel, saying, "I saw God face to face" (Genesis 32:30).

What kind of God would wrestle with Jacob and allow Himself to be defeated by a mere mortal? The same God who allowed Judas to kiss Him, Peter to deny Him, Romans to arrest Him, the Sanhedrin to try Him, Pilate to condemn Him, soldiers to crucify Him, and Pharisees to mock and ridicule Him while He was hanged on a cross.

Thus, in both the OT and NT, this is the God who suffers for His people and gives them grace and mercy.

Jacob saw the woman's Offspring (Genesis 3:15), the wounded Victor, who, in the fullness of time, "came not to be served but to serve, and to give His life as a ransom for many" (Mark 10:45 ESV). He is the Lion and the Lamb of God, the Root and Offspring of David, and the bright morning star (Revelation 5:5–6; 22:16). The Messenger is God, who appears throughout the OT.

To see God and understand His ways in the OT takes some Jacob-like wrestling—but we're not alone. When Jesus was walking along the road to Emmaus with Cleopas and another man, He brought clarity to the Hebrew Scriptures (Luke 24:13–32). The Savior still illuminates the Hebrew Scriptures, even their strangest sections.

We invite you to wrestle with Israel's Scriptures and the God who gives them. After his wrestling match, Jacob was no longer Jacob—he was Israel. You, too, will be changed as you confront and contend with the OT's most challenging parts. The darkness of the night will yield to the light of a new day, and, just like Jacob, much more will become clear. This book is your Peniel.

Let's get started!

DISCUSSION QUESTIONS

1. Growing up, how were you taught to view the OT?
2. How does your church make use of the OT?
3. Take a look at this book's contents. What ideas are you most looking forward to wrestling with?
4. How do you, like Jacob at Peniel, anticipate seeing God more clearly through this study?

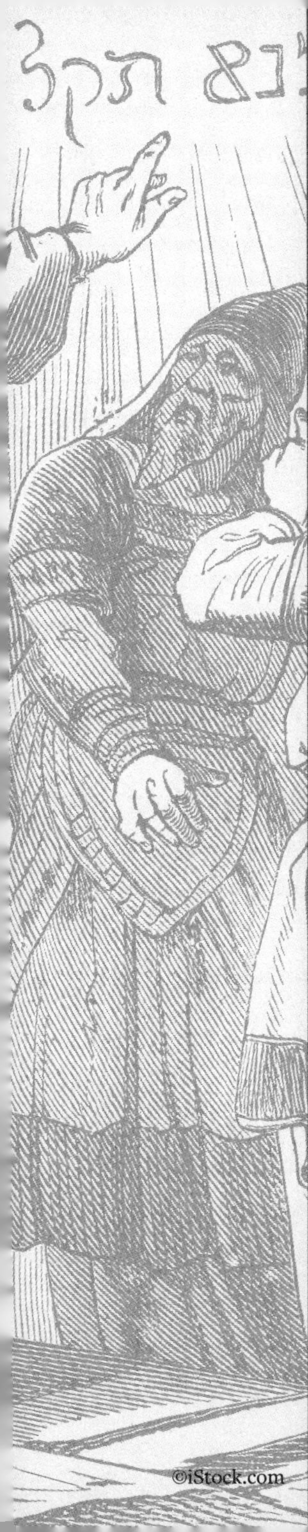

CHAPTER 1

WHAT MAKES PORTIONS OF THE OLD TESTAMENT SEEM SO DIFFICULT TO UNDERSTAND?

"[Paul's letters] contain some things that are hard to understand." (2 Peter 3:16)

Seeing a mountain and being on that mountain are two very different things. From a distance, you can see the mountain's shape, its relation to the surrounding landscape, its height, the tree line, and any clouds on its peaks. However, when you are on the mountain, you can see things that cannot be seen from afar—the change in flora as you ascend the mountain path, the animals that scurry along the ground and the birds that flit among the trees and bushes, the rocky landscape and sandy ridges that seem to pop out of nowhere as you come around a bend in the trail.

In some ways, our view of the OT is like viewing that mountain. We can only see it from a distance—a distance in time, culture, and language that is much greater than even the distance we have between us and the NT. Without specialized training in history and biblical languages, we face a challenge in getting a closer picture of the world of Israel in antiquity and understanding the Scriptures produced by the Hebrew authors. While learning history and languages can aid in getting a better understanding of the OT, even the most knowledgeable scholar will find some features of the text enigmatic and perplexing. Let's explore some reasons for this.

DISTANCE IN TIME AND PLACE

Literature coming from the distant past often contains features that are obscured by the passage of time. People who may have been prominent in their day can be forgotten by later generations. Examples of such persons in the Bible include Belshazzar (Daniel 5) and Pontius Pilate. At one time, there was such a lack of extrabiblical evidence for the existence of these men that some scholars proposed that the biblical authors invented them. Later archaeological discoveries of ancient inscriptions that mention Belshazzar and Pilate have proved the skeptics mistaken. However, this wrong turn in past biblical studies illustrates how distance in time from antiquity can obscure our knowledge of what the Bible is telling us.

On one hand, time obscures people and events from the past. Thus, it is often noted that there is little or no direct evidence outside the Bible for some very prominent events and persons in the OT, including the exodus from Egypt, the reign of King Saul, or the acts of Queen Esther. That, of course, does not mean that these events did not happen; it simply illustrates that we often have only the biblical writers' testimony to these events and no non-Israelite views with which to compare them. We cannot as easily place these crucial events in a wider context, as we might for persons or events for which we have extrabiblical information. For instance, we have a good amount of ancient historical material concerning Esther's husband, Xerxes, which helps us flesh out his character as we study the book of Esther.

On the other hand, a distant view can also serve to better put events in historical perspective. Some past events have appeared to be very momentous in that generation, but as time passes, those events may seem less significant. Therefore, events that are emphasized in the Scriptures may have held great importance for ancient readers but seem less important to us. For instance, the Israelite defeat of the kings Sihon and Og, who ruled territory east of the Jordan River, is obviously important to the authors of the OT—since it is mentioned nine times in six different books (Numbers 32:33; Deuteronomy 1:4; 29:7; 31:4; Joshua 2:10; 9:10; 1 Kings 4:19; Nehemiah 9:22; Psalm 135:11). Yet Sihon and Og are little known to many Christians today. The Bible mentions famous wise men in Solomon's day named Ethan the Ezrahite, Heman, Calcol, and Darda (1 Kings 4:31). Since their wisdom is compared to Solomon's, they must have been renowned in their day, and three of them may have been brothers (cf. 1 Chronicles 2:6; Darda in 1 Kings 4:31 is called Dara in 1 Chronicles 2:6). Yet, the Bible mentions Ethan only once more in Psalm 89, which might be an example of his wisdom. Moreover, we have no examples of the wisdom of Calcol or Darda. These men appear to have been important to the writer of the book of Kings, but they are merely a footnote in biblical history to us.

Places, too, can be obscured by time—even by only a few hundred years. How many people today know the location of Columbia, Losantiville, and North Bend, Ohio? They are now Cincinnati. What was Lugdunum in ancient Gaul? It is now Lyon, France. In a few cases, the Bible preserves the earlier names of places. For instance, the city of Dan in northern Israel was earlier called Leshem (Joshua 19:47). However, in other cases, the locations of places mentioned in Scripture are unknown, and sometimes hotly debated, such as the whereabouts of Sodom and Gomorrah or the city of Ai that Joshua and the Israelites destroyed. In a number of cases, it would be helpful to know the exact locations of these otherwise unknown cities to better understand the Bible's stories about them, but the passage of time has—at least for the present—prevented us from knowing.

Therefore, we should not be surprised that at times we struggle to understand the events, people, and places in the OT. Even a place as prominent as Jerusalem, which has been the subject of much archaeological digging for centuries, holds mysteries for us. Some places mentioned in Scripture to be in Jerusalem are still the subject of much speculation as to their exact location in antiquity.

DISTANCE IN CULTURE

The human culture that surrounds us and through which we interact with others affects us in ways that we often take for granted. Anyone who has traveled to a distant country has learned that other cultures and customs can be quite different from the ones we grew up in or now live in. At least we can inquire about these different present-day cultures and learn about them from living people.

It is not so easy when we encounter the ancient cultures of the OT. The Bible often contains references to customs or cultural assumptions that are quite different from ours. Moreover, while the several cultures of the ancient Middle East shared some features, like in our world today, they varied from place to place and time to time. The customs in ancient Egypt, Babylon, or Persia could be very different from those in Israel.

Israel's belief that there is only one God is something that we share with them and is common in the modern Western world. However, the general assumption among the other nations of antiquity was that there were many gods. Israel was surrounded by such beliefs, and it is not surprising that polytheism was a threat that continually tempted Israel. Therefore, we may shake our heads at how so many Israelites abandoned worship of the true God to worship the multiple gods of the surrounding nations. That is because it is difficult for us to see that there was a certain cultural allure that polytheism held in antiquity, and that made it much easier for Israel to fall into the sin of idolatry involving multiple gods than it is for us.

Other common customs and mores in antiquity may also appear quite foreign to us, especially those involving family and society. For instance, conventions about marriage can be altogether different than ours. One example is the expectation that a man would pay a bride-price to his future father-in-law to receive permission to marry the man's daughter (Genesis 34:12; 1 Samuel 18:25). Jacob, who had few possessions, negotiated a bride-price of seven years of labor to marry Rachel (Genesis 29:18). It is thought that the bride-price was supposed to be held in reserve by the bride's father and used to support her should her husband die. Note that both Rachel and Leah complained that their father had squandered the bride-price Jacob had paid (Genesis 31:14–16).

In some cases, a wife could be called a concubine, a custom that provided marriage for women from the lower strata of society or whose families were poor and needy. Concubines were wives and were sometimes simply called wives. For instance, Jacob's two concubines, Bilhah and Zilpah, are called wives in Genesis 37:2. Concubines, however, were obtained as wives without paying a bride-price, either because they had no living male relatives to demand one or because their family was of such low stature in society that no bride-price could be requested by the woman's family (as in the case of the very poor or slaves).

Inheritances were another custom that could be very different in ancient society. Normally, only sons inherited from their father; sons of concubines and other women to whom a man was not married were not expected to inherit anything unless their father had made provisions for their inheritance. That is why it was not shocking to ancient readers that the judge Jephthah, a son of a concubine, was exiled from his father's family (Judges 11:1–3), though that seems callous and coldhearted to us. On the other hand, we might miss the impact of Job's act of leaving inheritances to his daughters (Job 42:15). While we might find this expression of love for a daughter commonplace in our day, the original readers of Job would have seen this as an unusually magnanimous gesture. We might also not appreciate the in-your-face boldness of the request brought to Moses by the daughters of Zelophehad that they be allowed to inherit their father's portion of the Promised Land since they had no brothers and it might otherwise be given to more distant male relatives (Numbers 27:1–4).

These are just a few examples of how much distance in culture stands between us and the people of the OT. The writers of Israel's Scriptures often assumed that their ancient audience would understand their customs, norms, and institutions, and often felt no need to clarify them. Rare exceptions of explaining customs that fell out of use can be found (e.g., Ruth 4:7), but more often, the writers expected readers to have internalized the ways of society so that they would need no explanation.

However, we are positioned at quite a distance from the culture of ancient Israel. Our partial knowledge—or even ignorance—of some of the more obscure norms and expectations of society among the people of Israel and the surrounding nations places us at a distinct disadvantage when reading difficult or perplexing passages in the OT. While we can easily understand the major teachings of Moses and the prophets—and there can be no doubt about what the OT teaches concerning the essential doctrines of the Christian faith—there are times when some passages may seem enigmatic because of our lack of familiarity due to our distance in time from antiquity.

DISTANCE IN LANGUAGE

Another reason we are distant from the OT is language. At times, English and Hebrew can diverge in ways that appear unusual and are unexpected by modern readers. This is even true for readers whose native language is the Hebrew used in the contemporary state of Israel. Ancient Hebrew differs in a number of ways from modern Hebrew. Our human languages are not only a medium of communication but also an expression of our worldview, while simultaneously shaping our understanding of creation. Examples of this are words for colors. Most English speakers have learned to associate colors and their various shades with the visible light spectrum, as can be seen in rainbows. This is often memorized as seven basic colors: red, orange, yellow, green, blue, indigo, and violet. Thus, teal is often described as a greenish blue, and scarlet as a bright red with an orange tinge. Yet ancient peoples did not necessarily view colors by way of the visible spectrum of light. Colors were often viewed by association with the objects that produced them. Hebrew has a word that is often translated "scarlet" (*shani*; see Genesis 38:30; Joshua 2:18, 21). This word occurs at Isaiah 1:18 in tandem with another word for a kind of red color: "Although your sins are like scarlet, they will be as white as snow. Although they are crimson, they will be like wool." Isaiah uses the words *scarlet* and *crimson* as virtual synonyms. Yet, in English, crimson denotes a purplish shade of red that is distinct from scarlet. How is it that Isaiah sees them as synonymous? The key lies in the fact that both words are derived from the ancient manufacture of natural dyes from organic sources. In making such dyes, the shade of red could vary from batch to batch, and the color words do not signify a particular nuance of shade but the source of the dye.

A similar example can be found in the Hebrew names for plants and animals. Modern English speakers' words for living organisms are often determined by a Western, scientifically influenced classification that was not part of the worldview of ancient peoples. For instance, Hebrew has a word for large birds of prey: *nesher*. This word occurs twice in Proverbs 30:

> The eye that ridicules one's father and despises obedience to one's mother—may ravens of the valley pluck it out and young *vultures* eat it. (Proverbs 30:17)

> . . . the way of an *eagle* in the sky, the way of a snake on a rock, the way of a ship at sea, and the way of a man with a virgin. (Proverbs 30:19)

In just the space of three verses, the same Hebrew word is translated both "vulture" and "eagle" in most English versions (because of contextual factors). It is impossible to conceive of an English word that includes both eagles and vultures but not other birds of prey, such as hawks, falcons, and owls. For instance, the English word *raptor* includes both eagles and vultures but also encompasses other birds of prey that the Hebrew word *nesher* does not. For us, vultures and eagles are quite distinct both in appearance and behavior, but the same view of nature was not common among ancient Israelites.

Of course, English and Hebrew are quite different in other ways. In many instances, sentence structure in the two languages can be dissimilar. In grammar, Hebrew and English differ in a number of ways, including their views of tense (i.e., past, present, and future) and gender (i.e., masculine [he], feminine [she], and neuter [it]). At times, these differences are subtle and of little consequence, but in other instances, the divergence is significant enough to make certain Bible passages appear enigmatic for modern readers. Again, it ought to be emphasized that the plain passages of Scripture are little affected by this, and the OT's doctrine, especially Law and Gospel, are not called into question by our distance in language from the original authors and readers of the OT. For instance, the First Commandment unequivocally forbids all types of idolatry, whether in English or in Hebrew (Exodus 20:3; Deuteronomy 5:7). God as our Savior is the clear teaching of the OT, no matter what language we read the Scriptures in (see 2 Samuel 23:3; Isaiah 43:11; Hosea 13:4).

DISTANCE FROM THE INCARNATION: THE LIGHT OF JESUS ILLUMINATES THE OLD TESTAMENT SHADOWS

The OT contains many items that are made clearer by what we learn about Jesus in the NT. Paul refers to this as the OT's shadow that was being cast by Jesus: "Therefore, don't let anyone judge you with regard to food and drink or in the matter of a festival or a new moon or a Sabbath day. These are a shadow of what was to come. The body of Christ [cast the shadow]" (Colossians 2:16–17). Just as a shadow reveals some information about the object casting the shadow (such as an approximation of its size and shape), so do items in the OT, like those that Paul mentions—laws about food and drink, religious festivals, the holy days of the monthly new moons, and the weekly Sabbath days. They all reveal things about Jesus, who cast the shadow, but it is obviously easier to understand God's Word in Christ when we can see Jesus Himself rather than His shadow. Yet before Jesus took on human flesh, how were Moses and the prophets to describe the Savior who was yet to come and all the teachings He would make more understandable? They certainly prophesied about Christ in numerous ways so that the people of Israel could have faith in their Savior. (For more on this, see our book *The Messianic Message: Predictions, Patterns, and the Presence of Jesus in the Old Testament.*)

Yet it is difficult to describe in absolutely sharp focus something or someone that has yet to come. Imagine that you climb into a time machine and are transported back in time to see your great-great-grandparents. Suppose you want to describe to them many items and persons that are well known to us but unknown to them: a laptop computer, a mobile phone, the internet, the identity of a prominent world leader, the winner of last year's Super Bowl, or today's popular music. They would have no idea what a computer or the internet is. Most would probably never have used a telephone, much less a mobile phone. Today's world leaders might be quite different from the leaders just a few generations ago. And the Super Bowl would be completely unheard of, as would contemporary jazz, hip-hop, or rock music. Much of what you would try to describe would be by analogy—"these things are like . . . " And yet, no matter how well you describe them, your description would only provide a shadow of things to come in a future your great-great-grandparents would never see.

Thus, when we look back at the OT, we often see the shadows that are made clearer in the NT in the light of Jesus Christ. Even when Jesus was teaching His disciples during His ministry, they sometimes misunderstood because they had not yet seen His suffering, death, and resurrection (see Mark 9:31–32; Luke 2:49–50; 9:44–45; John 12:12–16). This indicates that, in some ways, we understand OT passages *better* than the original readers did. However, it also means that we struggle with the language of analogy and shadow that the OT writers employed because they could not refer to what would later be seen and revealed in the NT—the life and work of Jesus and all the implications of that work, which are so vital to the Christian faith from NT times to now.

While we will attempt in subsequent discussions to shed light on each of these features discussed in this chapter, we ought always to remember that even the most knowledgeable Bible scholar or the most learned theologian will struggle with some parts of the OT, because our knowledge of many of the things that separate us from the OT—including time, place, culture, and language—are only partially known to us. This much, though, is clear: "God's Word is our great heritage and shall be ours forever. . . . Through life it guides our way, in death it is our stay" (*LSB* 582).

DISCUSSION QUESTIONS

1. How does 2 Peter 3:16 not only summarize some of Paul's letters but also parts of the OT?
2. What do you wrestle with the most: OT history, places, culture, or language?
3. The Bible often describes some of God's revelations in Scripture as "mystery." How does a sense of not knowing everything we might like to know about God's Word help us better understand the greatness of God?
4. How does Colossians 2:16–17 help you understand parts of the OT?

©iStock.com

CHAPTER 2

WAS THE UNIVERSE REALLY CREATED IN SIX DAYS?

"How many are Your works Yahweh;
in wisdom You have made them all."
(Psalm 104:24)

"In the beginning, God created the heavens and the earth" (Genesis 1:1 ESV). These ten words are some of the most remarkable ever composed. In fact, Genesis 1:1–2:3, the story about how God created the world, ranks as one of the most stirring and majestic passages in all literature. Most striking is God's use of His spoken word to create. The expression "and God said" appears ten times between Genesis 1:3 and Genesis 1:29. God alone was active in the creation of the world—He didn't need assistance from anyone or anything. A number of other verses announce this stunning truth (Isaiah 40:26; 41:20; 42:5; 43:7; 45:7–8, 12, 18; cf. Psalm 148:5; Ephesians 3:9; Colossians 1:16).

Genesis 1 presents the six days of creation in a progressive and orderly way with the six days paired in two sets of three:

THE DAYS OF CREATION IN GENESIS 1		
DAY 1 *Heavens* empty, *light* created	**DAY 2** *Expanse of sky* separated from *sea*	**DAY 3** *Land* (dry ground) filled with plants
DAY 4 *Heavens* filled with sun, moon, and stars to *light* the sky	**DAY 5** *Expanse of sky* filled with birds; *seas* filled with creatures	**DAY 6** *Land* filled with animals and people

The narrative of the world's creation is more than a literary masterpiece; it's also one of the most hotly debated sections in the OT. Does a six-day creation account match what we know about the age of the universe? Is a Christian who believes in an old universe—say, twelve or thirteen billion years old—true to what Scripture teaches? Does our interpretation of Genesis 1:1–2:3 have an impact on our understanding of the rest of the Bible? And what's the relationship between the Bible and science? Are they on equal footing? Or does one have more authority than the other?

Christians have historically argued for a literal interpretation of the OT's creation account. These people are often called creationists. On the other hand, those influenced by Charles Darwin (1809–1882), who wrote *On the Origin of Species* (1859), maintain that Genesis 1:1–2:3 is symbolic, metaphorical, and without any historical veracity. They urge creationists to move on and embrace the science that has proven the Bible's creation story to be irrelevant. Many Christians have rejected macroevolution and defend the historicity of Genesis 1:1–2:3. Before we look closely at these verses, let's get some perspective. What's at stake in this debate?

CREATION AND EVOLUTION COMPARED

The following chart outlines the differences between creationists and Darwinian evolutionists.

CREATION	DARWINIAN EVOLUTION
God created the universe in six days.	The universe began billions of years ago.
God created the world from nothing by His word.	At some time in the distant past, there was nothing. A process known as vacuum fluctuation created what astrophysicists call a singularity. From that singularity, which was about the size of a dime, the universe began to expand.
People have a God-given image and are different from the rest of creation.	People are superior animals.

The purpose of life is to serve God.	The purpose of life is to survive.
People are responsible to God.	People aren't responsible to anyone.
People have infinite value.	People have limited value.
Life has meaning and purpose.	Life has little meaning or purpose.
There is a transcendent, personal God.	God only exists in people's minds.

While these two worldviews compete with one another for people's allegiance, it appears that Darwinian evolution won the day. However, consider this question: What's the probability of taking all the components of a space shuttle, placing them in a massive blender, and pushing the "on" button, then, after a few minutes, pushing the "off" button and presto—we have a perfect space shuttle? This seems highly unlikely, if not completely impossible. Darwinian evolution, though, would have us believe that the universe, infinitely more complex than a space shuttle, appeared out of nowhere—and all by accident.

Here are a few facts regarding the complexity of our world. Scientists estimate that there are between 1 and 10 million species of fungi, bacteria, and microscopic organisms. In addition, they calculate there are 900,000 species of insects; 250,000 species of flowering plants; 4,000 species of freshwater fish; 9,900 species of reptiles; and 4,300 species of mammals. And there are approximately 350,000 species of beetles in the world. To date, experts have identified approximately 1.4 million species of plants, insects, and animals. How many more until they finish? About 8 million more!

And all of this happened by chance? And life is completely random? And there's no Designer behind the design? Despite scientism and evolutionary philosophy, the advances of science—far from disproving that God created all things—demonstrate a deeply complex and amazing universe. The best evidence, however, for a Creator comes in Genesis 1:1–2:3.

THE DAY-AGE POSITION

There are several ways to interpret Genesis 1:1–2:3. We'll look at four of the most common explanations. The first is called the day-age approach. It's an attempt to harmonize the Genesis creation account with Darwinian evolution. This view sets forth several arguments.

First, day-age proponents interpret the Hebrew word for "day" (*yôm*) in Genesis 1:1–2:3 based on Psalm 90:4 (cf. 2 Peter 3:8): "A thousand years in Your eyes are like a day [*yôm*] that is gone by." When understood this way, "day" in the creation account denotes an era, an epoch, or a long period of time—comparable to a geologic age. Bolstering this interpretation, day-age advocates point out that "day" (*yôm*) in Genesis 1:5 and 2:4 clearly designates periods other than a 24-hour day.

Day-agers further their argument by contending that a gap of time exists between Genesis 1:1 and Genesis 1:2. That is to say, Genesis 1:1 describes God's initial creation, while Genesis 1:2 depicts creation's undoing and downfall. This theory is advanced with a particular translation of Genesis 1:2 that is not found in most English versions: "The earth became without form and void." Genesis 1:3–31 proceeds to describe creation's restoration after its ruination.

With these arguments in hand, day-age theorists conclude that the biblical account of creation is a metaphor for the evolutionary process. God created the basic natural elements and then let evolution carry out the rest of His work. This position is also called theistic evolution.

How should we respond? First, the six days in Genesis 1 are numbered and have evenings and mornings (Genesis 1:5). It's therefore incorrect to take the poetic expression "A thousand years in Your eyes are like a day [*yôm*] that is gone by" (Psalm 90:4) and conclude that Israelites couldn't differentiate between a figurative use of "day" and a literal use.

Second, the Third Commandment describes creation's six days as parallel to the days of human labor: "Six days you shall labor, and do all your work, but the seventh day is a Sabbath to Yahweh your God. . . . For in six days Yahweh made the heaven and the earth, the sea, and all that is in them, and rested on the seventh day" (Exodus 20:9–11). Because there aren't any gaps between the successive days in the human work week, it's not logical to argue that a long period of time exists between Genesis 1:1 and Genesis 1:2. The phrase "and all that is in them" (Exodus 20:11) further indicates that God didn't make anything after the first six days, and there was no gap between creating "in the beginning" and the "first day"—everything was created in six days!

The day-age interpretation of Genesis 1:1–2 is erroneous for another reason. The universe exists by God's word, not because He defeated chaos shortly after making everything. The depiction of matter as initially "without form and void" (Genesis 1:2 ESV) doesn't describe God's battle over unruly forces. Conflict with evil doesn't happen at creation. Evil enters the world in Genesis 3, through the wiles of Satan, after creation is finished.

Additionally, the grammatical structure of the Hebrew in Genesis 1:2 indicates that it's circumstantial information. The verse isn't continuing the narrative ideas from Genesis 1:1. The correct translation of Genesis 1:2 is the usual one: "The earth *was* without form and void," not *became*.

THE FRAMEWORK POSITION

Another way people understand Genesis 1:1–2:3 is by means of the framework theory. Just like the day-age scheme, this position also tries to harmonize the Bible's creation story with Darwinian evolution. How? The framework approach argues for a nonchronological view of creation's days. That is to say, the days in creation appear in a logical order, not a chronological one.

Adherents to the framework viewpoint appeal to the literary structure of Genesis 1—the first three days and the last three days are parallel. The "days," the argument contends, aren't twenty-four-hour periods but logical categories.

The reasoning goes like this: The first three "days" summarize creation's universality—light and darkness, water and air, land and vegetation. These are the major spaces in the world. The last three "days" sum up creation's particulars. The sun and moon, fish and birds, animals and people created in "days" four through six fill the spaces God made in "days" one through three.

One problem with the framework theory is a logical one—it holds that the two parallel sets of three days are a literary device primarily intended to demonstrate God's orderly creation and not intended to depict six actual days. However, this draws a false distinction between the literary aspects of Genesis 1, showing the orderliness of creation, and the text's chronological feature of six days, as if these features cannot coexist in one composition.

In addition, while the framework hypothesis places day one parallel with day four, day two with day five, and day three with day six, there are parallels that cut across these supposedly tight parallelisms. The lights in the sky (day four) are put in the heavens (day two). The sea creatures (day five) are put in the sea (day three). Humans (day six) are to rule the animals (days five and six). Thus, while the general framework of Genesis 1 as being two sets of three days demonstrates the orderly work of God in creation, it does not completely depict how God orders creation.

Those who follow the framework concept read against the plain sense of Genesis 1. It's a story that progresses, not a poem with two parts that symbolize the passing of long periods of time.

THE RELIGION-ONLY POSITION

Still another way to reconcile Genesis 1:1–2:3 with Darwinian evolution goes by the name religion-only theory. This approach suggests that the Genesis account has nothing to do with historical facts. Instead, the verses make two religious assertions: God created the world, and He created it beautifully for human habitation. Genesis 1:1–2:3, therefore, answers two questions: Who made the world? And why was it made? The issues are religious—who and why. Science, on the other hand, asks the historical question—how?

There's no doubt that Genesis 1:1–2:3, for the most part, focuses upon who and why. The passage chiefly makes theological statements. However, it also presents historical truth. The who and the why of creation appear in a story of how, with days, times, and specific details. Genesis 1:1–2:3 thus contains both theology and history, both literary beauty and factual statements. To read the creation account as teaching theology detached from history goes against the grain, assuming that the passage is a parable, a legend, or a myth. Yet what God has joined together—theology and historical claims—man must not separate.

THE YOUNG EARTH POSITION

Let's call the fourth way of looking at the creation account in Genesis the young earth position. This viewpoint doesn't try to reconcile Genesis 1:1–2:3 with Darwinian evolution. Instead, it advocates for a literal reading. Thus, the universe is thousands, not billions, of years old. Young earth proponents come to this conclusion because they believe there are no chronological gaps in Genesis 1:1–2:3—especially not between verses one and two.

What about the ancient fossils? Young earthers adopt what they call the flood geology—that is, the belief that fossil-bearing strata were laid down during the worldwide flood that happened at the time of Noah. Adherents of this belief also maintain that God fashioned the universe as fully functioning. Adam and Eve were created as adults, so the rest of the world was created as fully developed—fossils and all.

Because the genealogies in Genesis 5 and 10 list the age of each ancestor at the birth of his descendant, some young earth advocates add these numbers together to determine when the world was created—about six thousand years ago. It's better, however, to understand that these genealogical lists have gaps—they're selective, not comprehensive. If, in fact, they are all-inclusive, then, when the numbers are added, some who lived before the flood (e.g., Enosh, Kenan, and Methuselah) would have lived during Noah's era. Yet, we're told that Noah was the only righteous man of his day (Genesis 6:6–9).

There's more. Both genealogies in Genesis 5 and 10 list ten generations—as does the genealogy in Ruth 4:18–22. These features, along with extrabiblical genealogies that seldom go beyond ten generations, lead us to believe that the Genesis lists skip generations, making it difficult to gauge the number of years from creation to Abraham.

Thus, while we believe in a young earth that's thousands of years old, we don't embrace the idea that the world began on October 23, 4004 BC, as noted by some young earthers. Let's now consider Genesis 1:1–2:3 in greater detail.

GENESIS 1:1–2

An accurate interpretation of Genesis 1:1–2 doesn't allow for a gap of time between these verses and the rest of Genesis 1—a position some take to align the OT's creation account with Darwinian evolution. Any viewpoint that holds that Genesis 1:1 summarizes the creation account and that God begins constructing the cosmos in the next verse also believes that He didn't make everything out of nothing. Instead, this reading implies God used preexisting matter—a formless and void watery stew (Genesis 1:2).

However, the Hebrew verb translated "create"—appearing six times in Genesis 1:1–2:3—often denotes creating out of nothing. The verb comes forty-five times in the OT and exclusively employs God as its subject. And in every case, God never uses anything to create—although in some cases, He reworks things He previously created (e.g., Psalm 51:12; Isaiah 65:18). Hebrews 11:3 explains it this way: "By faith we understand that the universe was created by the word of God, so that what is seen was not made out of things that are visible" (ESV).

The Bible's first verse, then, recounts the actual divine act of creating the heavens and the earth—the totality of the universe, everything visible and invisible (cf. Colossians 1:16). Genesis 1:1 describes God's first act of creating an unformed, unfilled earth and the raw materials He would use to make everything else.

The storyline begins in Genesis 1:1 and continues in Genesis 1:3, when each succeeding sentence begins with "and [God]," then a verb:

- And God said . . . (Genesis 1:3)
- And He saw . . . (Genesis 1:4)
- And He called . . . (Genesis 1:5)

On the other hand, Genesis 1:2 begins with a conjunction and a noun: "And the earth . . ." This verse, therefore, makes a parenthetical statement that depicts the world following God's inaugural act of creation in Genesis 1:1.

The progression of events is as follows. First, God creates the unformed and unfilled heavens and earth (Genesis 1:1). Next, He begins to speak and bring things into existence. Genesis 1:2

essentially says, "Before we move on, here's a description of the initial state of the world after God created it and before He announced 'And let there be light.'" The first day of creation therefore begins in Genesis 1:1 and concludes in Genesis 1:5.

This interpretation rules out the understanding that Genesis 1:1 is a title and that creation begins with the preexisting matter in Genesis 1:2. It also rejects any notion that an indeterminate period exists between Genesis 1:1 and Genesis 1:5—the first day of creation.

DAY AND DAYS

Let's suppose we overhear someone saying, "Back in the day—1903 to be exact—it took Horatio Jackson and Sewall Crocker sixty-three days to drive coast to coast. They drove during the day." Though the word "day" has three different meanings in these two sentences, we have no problem understanding them. English speakers intuitively know that the first usage of "day" denotes an era; the second, twenty-four hours; and the third, sunup to sundown. Each of these three meanings is recognizable and common in English parlance. No one would argue that "day" has the same meaning in all three cases.

Welcome to the use of "day" (*yôm*) in Genesis 1–2. It has several different shades of meaning.

The word "day" first appears in Genesis 1:5a: "God called the light Day [*yôm*]" (ESV). Here, the term refers to daylight. It has the same meaning in Genesis 1:14 and 16. In these verses, a day is something less than a twenty-four-hour day, as the context makes clear.

The second time "day" appears in the Genesis creation account is in Genesis 1:5b: "There was evening and there was morning, the first day [*yôm*]" (ESV). This usage denotes a twenty-four-hour day.

A third use of "day" comes in Genesis 2:4: "These are the generations of the heavens and the earth when they were created, in the day [*yôm*] that Yahweh God made the earth and the heavens." Here, "day" indicates an unspecified amount of time that, in its context, refers to the first six days of creation.

Additionally, throughout Genesis 1:5b–2:3, the Hebrew word *yôm* denotes a twenty-four-hour day. Each of the six days of creation ends with the refrain "evening and morning." Of course, by asserting a twenty-four-hour day, we don't mean exactly twenty-four hours. Technically, a day is 23 hours, 56 minutes, and 4.09 seconds. The question at hand is, using everyday language, are the days in Genesis 1 literal days and equal to our days of the week today? The Bible says yes.

Those who want to cling to a semblance of biblical teaching and hold to Darwinian evolution maintain that since *yôm* is used in a nonliteral way in Genesis 2:4, this indicates the word is also imprecise throughout Genesis 1. It should therefore not be understood literally. However, this interpretation ignores the fact that in most cases in Genesis 1, "day" (*yôm*) is modified by a number and then followed by the refrain "evening and morning." Conversely, Genesis 2:4 employs the adverbial expression *beyôm*, which is best rendered "in the day." This nonliteral use of the word "day" (*yôm*) doesn't mean all the uses of the word in Genesis 1 are also nonliteral. Neither does it suggest that creationists are inconsistent in their interpretation of "day" (*yôm*) as literal in Genesis 1 but nonliteral in Genesis 2:4.

What about the expression "evening and morning" (Genesis 1:5, 8, 13, 19, 23, 31)? Or "seasons" and "years" (Genesis 1:14)? Throughout Genesis 1, the context requires that we understand these terms as descriptions of time, which is regulated by the movements of the universe. For instance, a year here means a period of roughly 365.2424 normal days and its parts—spring, summer, autumn, winter.

It's illogical, therefore, to maintain that the chronological terms in Genesis 1 are used in their common sense, denoting ordinary evenings and mornings and seasons and years, but "day" is not. It's incorrect to suggest that *yôm* in Genesis 1:5b–2:3 means anything other than a single rotation of the earth upon its axis.

GENESIS 1:3

This verse has confused people for millennia. Why does God create light on the first day and the sun on the fourth day? How should we understand that light (Genesis 1:3) and vegetation (Genesis 1:11) appear before the sun (Genesis 1:14–19)?

A compelling interpretation is that God knew people would worship the sun, moon, and stars, so He created light before the heavenly lights to show they aren't gods. In fact, they're small and insignificant compared to the Almighty, who creates light without them and makes plants without their assistance. Could it be that the sun's demotion demeans the worldviews of other ancient Middle Eastern cultures—especially Egypt—where it was worshiped?

GENESIS 1:5

Almost all English translations render the end of Genesis 1:5 with "the first day." However, a more accurate rendering would be "one day." In the remaining six days of creation, the Hebrew employs ordinal numbers (second, third, fourth, etc.). Why does Genesis 1:5 use the cardinal number one rather than "first"? "One day" means one (solar) day, which is how we are to interpret the following six days of creation.

THE SEVENTH DAY

Genesis 2:2–3 states, "On the seventh day [*yôm*] God finished His work that He had done, and He rested on the seventh day [*yôm*] from all His work He had done. God blessed the seventh day [*yôm*] and made it holy, because on it God rested from all His work He had done in creation" (ESV).

These verses are the source of another flash point because some believe divine "rest" is limited to a twenty-four-hour period, while others maintain that rest is ongoing—as stated in Psalm 95:11 and cited in Hebrews 3:11; 4:4; and 4:5. God, therefore, is still resting from His work (cf. Hebrews 4:9–11). However, if the seventh day is open-ended, then each of the six prior days would also be interpreted as open-ended, which is clearly not the case. Each ends with the notice of "an evening and a morning."

Moreover, Exodus 20:8–11 makes no distinction between the seven days which equal one week. These verses, along with Exodus 31:15–17, are the clearest commentary on Genesis 1:1–2:3 and mitigate all attempts to fit billions of years into Genesis 1—either between Genesis 1:1 and Genesis 1:2 or within the six days.

Additionally, the verses in Psalm 95 and Hebrews 3–4 don't teach that the seventh day continues. God's rest continues, but His creational activities as listed in Genesis 1:1–2:3 have ceased. The seventh day ended after twenty-four hours, just like the first six days—a fact stated twice in Genesis 2:1–2. Divine rest on the seventh day makes it clear that creation is complete.

WHAT'S AT STAKE?

What's at stake in this debate? Everything. If we don't take the days in Genesis 1:5b–2:3 as literal twenty-four-hour units of time, then we open the door for Darwinian evolution, and with it, the belief that for millions of years animals died and some became extinct. Next, we'd have to believe rock layers demonstrate that for hundreds of millions of years, before people were created, there were earthquakes, volcanoes, tsunamis, hurricanes, and typhoons. What do these two positions lead to? The idea that physical death and creational upheavals didn't come as a result of Adam and Eve eating the forbidden fruit. Instead, death and destruction are built into the order of the universe. They've been going on long before our first parents arrived on the scene.

The biblical witness, however, states that God made a perfect world. His flawlessness is celebrated with a seven-fold use of the term "good" (Genesis 1:4, 10, 12, 18, 21, 25, 31; cf. 1 Timothy 4:4). Creation was perfect, without strife, conflict, contention, disease, or death. To deny this is to deny the veracity of Adam and Eve's fall into sin (Genesis 3). Christianity sees death as a rude intrusion on life, "the last enemy" (1 Corinthians 15:26 ESV). The Creator didn't make people and animals to die. Death came as a result of sin, as is narrated in Genesis 3.

The central message of the Bible is that Christ Jesus came into the world to abolish "death and [bring] life and immortality to light through the gospel" (2 Timothy 1:10 ESV). The first Adam sinned, and the Second Adam, Jesus (see 1 Corinthians 15:45), was born to atone for the world's sin. This is what Paul teaches (Romans 8:19–23), and this is why the Father sent His Son—to reverse the curse and reconcile all things to Himself (e.g., Ephesians 1:10; Colossians 1:20). Any evolutionary scheme that includes millions of years of destruction and upheaval before Adam and Eve undercuts biblical teaching regarding the goodness of creation, humankind's fall into sin, and Christ's redeeming work.

Furthermore, those who promote Darwinian evolution, with science serving as their king, are unable to embrace biblical miracles. For, in addition to the miracle of a six-day creation, Moses parted the Red Sea (Exodus 14:21–23), the sun stood still (Joshua 10:12–4), Christ was born of a virgin (Matthew 1:18–23), and He died for the sin of the world (John 1:29). And don't forget the talking donkey, the floating axe head, Joshua and Jericho, David and Goliath, the feeding of the five thousand, Peter's escape from prison, and—supremely—Christ's resurrection from the dead, never to die again (Romans 6:9). If a six-day creation is unreasonable, then much of the Bible will appear unreasonable as well. And what's left of the Christian faith? Nothing.

CONCLUSIONS

The differences between the OT's creation account and Darwinian evolution are massive. Genesis 1 teaches that creation is Word-based. Macroevolution argues that it's random-based. The biblical worldview confesses meaning and purpose, beauty and dignity. Evolution offers chaos and disorder and the survival of the fittest, along with meaninglessness and purposelessness. Either the account in Genesis 1 is a myth, or it is history, albeit history written in a simple way to express profound truths. There is no middle ground. We take our stand with the OT. "Praise to the Lord, the Almighty, the King of creation!" (*LSB* 790:1). In doing so, we're not against science but only against scientific philosophies that try to eliminate God from creation, deny His existence, and attack the veracity of His Word.

DISCUSSION QUESTIONS

1. How does Psalm 104:24 summarize this chapter?
2. What have you been taught about the origins of the world?
3. When have you felt a tension between faith and evolutionary science?
4. What strikes you most regarding the differences between Darwinian evolution and the creation account in Genesis?
5. What have you learned about Genesis 1:1–2:3 regarding the meaning of the word *day*?
6. What might you say to someone who believes in Darwinian evolution?

CHAPTER 3

DOES THE OLD TESTAMENT TEACH US ABOUT THE HOLY TRINITY?

"Therefore go make disciples of all nations, baptizing them in the name of the Father and of the Son and of the Holy Spirit." (Matthew 28:19)

How do you describe something so new or different that there is no word for it yet? Sometimes, we do it by comparison: "It is like . . ." Other times, we give it a new name that describes it. When Alexander Graham Bell created a device that allowed two people to speak to each other when they were too far apart to easily hear one another, a name was needed for it. Something like it had never been seen before, so it was decided to call it a telephone. The word was coined by combining two Greek words: *tēle*, meaning "far," and *phōnē*, meaning "voice." Since then, we've created other similar words for new items: *television*, for "far seeing;" *internet*, for a series of *inter*connected *net*works; and *helicopter*, from the Greek *helikos* ("helix") and *pteron* ("wing").

Early Christians were faced with a similar challenge. How could they correctly refer to the one God who had revealed Himself as three coequal and coeternal persons in one divine substance? The church coined the Latin word *trinitas*, which means "three-ness" or "three occurring at once," to assert that the true God is three persons yet only one God (Deuteronomy 6:4; 1 Corinthians 8:4), the only God who exists (Deuteronomy 4:35, 39; 1 Samuel 2:2; 1 Kings 8:60; Isaiah 44:8; 45:5, 6, 14, 18, 21, 22; 46:9). The term *Trinity*, therefore, asserts the biblical mystery of the three divine persons while simultaneously professing the oneness of God, combining three and one without contradiction. Later in church history, in the early seventeenth century, Christians created another related word to express this truth—the adjective *triune*, a word that combines Latin roots *tri* (three) and *une* (one).

The revelation of God as three persons is so very clear in the NT, which explicitly mentions all three persons multiple times (e.g.,

Matthew 28:19; Luke 10:21–22; 2 Corinthians 13:14; Galatians 4:6; 1 Peter 1:1–2; 1 John 4:1–15). However, one can search in vain for a single OT verse that simultaneously mentions the triad Father, Son, and Holy Spirit using those names for the three persons. This might raise the question that is the title of this chapter: Does the OT teach us about the Holy Trinity?

While the full revelation of God's trinitarian nature is set forth ultimately in the NT, Moses and the other OT authors already spoke and wrote about the true God who is "three persons [who are] coeternal with each other and coequal, so that in all things . . . the Trinity in Unity and Unity in Trinity is to be worshiped" (Athanasian Creed, *LSB*, p. 320). Let's look at how the OT reveals the triune God.

PASSAGES IN WHICH GOD SPEAKS OF HIMSELF AS PLURAL

In three passages in the early chapters of Genesis, God is quoted as speaking about Himself in plural rather than singular terms:

- Then God said, "Let *Us* make humankind in *Our* image, according to *Our* likeness. They will rule the fish of the sea, the birds of the sky, the livestock, the whole earth, and the creatures that crawl on the earth." (Genesis 1:26)
- The LORD God said, "The man has become like one of *Us*, knowing good and evil. He must not reach out, take from the tree of life, eat, and live forever." (Genesis 3:22)
- "Come, let *Us* go down there and confuse their language so that they will not understand one another's speech." So from

> there, Yahweh scattered them over the face of the entire earth, and they stopped building the city. (Genesis 11:7–8)

Each of these passages occurs at a crucial point in the narrative of the earliest history of humans. The first depicts God's intention for people when He created them. The second tells us of God's intervention to prevent Adam and Eve from eating from the tree of life. The third tells us of God's involvement in confusing human languages, making it impossible for them to communicate with one another, thereby forcing them to fulfill His mandate that humankind should fill the earth (Genesis 1:28; 9:1). In each instance, God reveals Himself as "We" or "Us," although elsewhere the OT insists that there is only one true God. How should we understand this?

Some have argued that God is depicted here in a heavenly council scene similar to the scenes in the myths of ancient Middle Eastern pagan religions. In those scenes, a main god presides over a gathering of other gods. Of course, the OT is unanimous in ruling out the existence of other gods. So, instead, these scholars argue that God is depicted as presiding over a gathering of His angels. Appeal is often made to two passages: Job 1:6–12; 2:1–6, where the "sons of God" present themselves before Him, and 2 Kings 22:19–22, where God solicits His heavenly army for a plan to deceive King Ahab. There are two problems with this identification, however.

The first is that, unlike the presiding god in a pagan council of gods, the true God is not the first among equals. The angels are subservient to Him. Psalm 89:5–7 confirms this: God is among His heavenly council, where He reigns "awe-inspiring over all those around Him." Thus, in Job, the sons of God in the heavenly scene do not speak. They play only a background role in the scene where Satan presents himself before Yahweh. (The text of Job 1:6; 2:1 is not clear as to whether Satan is to be considered one of the sons of God or whether he is an intruder.) In 2 Kings, the angels offer plans to God, but it is God alone, not the heavenly council as a whole, that determines which angel's plan is best.

The second problem is that none of the "Us" passages in Genesis depict God acting in concert with the angels, which would be the implication of the use of the plural pronoun if it referred to a heavenly council. In these three passages in Genesis, God alone acts, and He does not delegate these missions to His angels.

Turning back to Genesis 1, after "let Us make humankind in Our image," we read "so God created humankind in *His* image, in the image of God *He* created him, male and female *He* created them" (Genesis 1:27). Humans were created in God's image, not in the image of God *and* His divine council. And this Creator God is both *Us* and *He*, both plural and singular. Note that the Creator of humans reverts to the singular *I* almost immediately when speaking to our first parents: "See, *I* have given you every green plant. . . . To every beast . . . *I* have given every green plant for food" (Genesis 1:29–30). Thus, the Holy Trinity is "Us" in internal dialogue but "I" when speaking externally to Adam and Eve.

Here we have the first depiction of the Holy Trinity in Scripture. While Genesis 1:26 does not tell us how many persons exist in the godhead, it reveals a multiplicity of persons that are the one true God.

Genesis 3:22 further reveals the triune God as "knowing good and evil." God notes that as a result of the first sin, humans have become "like one of Us" and also know good and evil. Once again, we should observe that the *Us* in this passage cannot be God and an angelic council since the Scriptures never depict God's holy angels as "knowing good and evil." That phrase is used elsewhere to denote the ability to determine autonomously what is acceptable or unacceptable, legally and morally correct or incorrect (Genesis 2:9, 17; 3:5; Leviticus 27:10, 33; 2 Samuel 14:17; Isaiah 5:20). (At 2 Samuel 14:17, David is described as able to discern what is good and what is bad "like the angel of God." In *The Messianic Message*, pages 35–37, we explored the identity of the "angel of God/Yahweh" as the preincarnate Second Person of the Trinity, not one of God's heavenly angels.) When Solomon prayed for the ability to discern good from evil, God granted him wisdom to govern through wise laws and decisions (1 Kings 3:9). Note that children, who are dependent on adults, do not possess this ability (Deuteronomy 1:39). In other words, when Adam and Eve ate the fruit, it bestowed on them the inclination to determine what is morally tolerable or reprehensible independent of God's will.

Finally, Genesis 11:7–8 records God's inner thought (*Us*) when He came down to see the tower building project at Babylon, and "Yahweh scattered them." Once again, Genesis identifies the *Us* as God, here called Yahweh. Moreover, we see humans attempting to autonomously determine what is good and what is evil. They sought good in making a name for themselves by building a tower with its top in the heavens in order to keep from being scattered. However, God had already determined that it would be a blessing for humans to spread throughout the earth (Genesis 9:7). By their knowledge of good and evil, people were defying God. However, the holy, triune God knew better, and He scattered them by confusing their languages.

These three passages in the early chapters of Genesis begin to reveal the Holy Trinity, though none of them tells us how many persons exist in the one divine unity that is God. That will be revealed in later books of the OT, including the other books of Moses. However, in light of later biblical revelation, we can see all three persons already at creation: the Father (Genesis 1:1), the Spirit (Genesis 1:2), and the Son (the divine Word; John 1:1–3, 14).

PASSAGES THAT SPEAK OF THREE PERSONS

Christian worship often begins with a trinitarian invocation: "In the name of the Father, and of the Son, and of the Holy Spirit." In Lutheran, Anglican, and Roman Catholic eucharistic worship, the service often ends with a blessing that is also trinitarian, but less obviously so. This blessing is drawn from God's revelation of His nature to Moses when He gave Moses instructions concerning the benediction Israel's priests were to use when blessing the people:

> Tell Aaron and his sons, "This is how you are to bless the Israelites. You should say to them: 'May Yahweh bless you and guard you. May Yahweh make His face shine on you and be gracious to you. May Yahweh look on you with favor and give you peace.' In this way they will put My name on the Israelites, and I will bless them." (Numbers 6:23–27)

As a sidenote, we observe that "look on you with favor" translates the Hebrew idiom "lift His face to you." In Hebrew thought, hiding one's face from someone is to deny them support and favor (see Deuteronomy 31:17–18; Psalm 30:7; 44:24). Therefore, when God lifts His face to look at His people, He is showing them His favor.

This blessing is a threefold mention of God by His holy name, Yahweh (often translated "the LORD"). The use of three blessings in one is no accident. In Hebrew, the first line is three words, the second is five words, and the third is seven words. In this way, it progressively reveals the God who is three persons in one divine being.

The first line magnifies God's creation and its gifts—gifts spelled out in Genesis 1, where God provides everything we need for our body and life. With its reference to God's face, Numbers 6:25 points to Christ's face, which—at His transfiguration—shined like the sun (Matthew 17:2). The third line of the Aaronic benediction concerns peace: "To set the mind on the Spirit is life and peace" (Romans 8:6). Peace is one of the Spirit's fruits (Galatians 5:22).

Moreover, God specifically says that this is the way that the priest would "put My name on the Israelites." God's name was to be used three times to place His name on Israel, a constant reminder of the threefold identity of the Trinity's persons. The unnumbered, plural *Us* of the early chapters of Genesis is now more specifically the three persons of the one divine Lord of the priestly blessing.

In Isaiah's inaugural vision, the threefold blessing of God on Israel was reflected back to God by the angels who praised Him. In this passage, we find the three persons referenced not only by a triple "holy" but also by God once again referring to Himself as "Us":

> In the year that King Uzziah died, I saw my Lord sitting on a high and lofty throne, and the hem of His robe filled the temple. Seraphim were standing above Him. Each had six

> wings: with two they covered their faces, with two they covered their feet, and with two they flew. And one called to the other: "Holy, holy, holy is Yahweh of armies! His glory fills the whole earth!"
>
> . . . Then I heard the voice of my Lord asking, "Whom should I send? Who will go for *Us*?" I said, "Here I am. Send me." (Isaiah 6:1–3, 8)

In mid-739 BC, Judah's king, Uzziah, died. This was a momentous event. Uzziah reigned fifty-one years—longer than any other king of Israel or Judah. His lengthy time on the throne lent a certain stability to the kingdom, and there would have been an understandable concern about the leadership of the new king, Jotham. Isaiah, however, was given a vision of the real king of Israel—Yahweh of armies, whose throne was "high and lofty" and whom the seraphim praised with a threefold "holy." This God is three times holy, even though He is only one Lord of armies.

Some have dismissed the triple repetition of the word *holy* as simply a way of emphasizing God's hallowed nature. As is sometimes done in English, an adjective or noun might be repeated to form an intensive in Hebrew (e.g., 1 Samuel 2:3, "proud proud" = "very proud;" 2 Kings 25:15, "gold gold" = "fine gold" and "silver silver" = "fine silver;" Ecclesiastes 7:24, "deep deep" = "very deep;" perhaps Proverbs 20:14, "bad bad" = "very bad"). An adverb can also be repeated for emphasis: "very, very" (as also in English) or "exceedingly" in Genesis 7:19, Exodus 1:7, and Numbers 14:7; also "around around" = "all around" in Ezekiel 42:15. However, there is no evidence for forming an intensive by employing an adjective three times consecutively in Hebrew as is done here at Isaiah 6:3.

Two possible cases for three consecutive nouns forming an intensive are Ezekiel 21:27 and Jeremiah 22:29. However, Ezekiel 21:27 is not an intensive but a repetition to emphasize God's unalterable judgment against Jerusalem: "I will make it a ruin, a ruin, a ruin" (see CSB, ESV, NIV, NRSV). Jeremiah 22:29 is probably a triple address at the head of an urgent call to gain the hearer's attention: "Land, land, land—hear the word of Yahweh!" In any event, the thrice "holy" of Isaiah 6:3 involves three adjectives, not three nouns. Moreover, this theory is contradicted by God's own words, which depict Him as a unity (*I*) with a plurality (*Us*) in verse 8. It is the triune God who sent Isaiah to prophesy to a people who would develop dull minds, deaf ears, and blind eyes (Isaiah 6:10).

Finally, we should note the correspondence of the triple "holy" of Isaiah 6 with Psalm 99, the only psalm that calls God holy three times. This psalm celebrates God as the king who reigned in Jerusalem between the cherubim in the temple. Verses 3, 5, and 9 call Him holy. While He is thrice holy, He has only one name—another three in one (Psalm 99:3, 5). This anticipates the baptismal formula Jesus would give His disciples. They were commissioned to baptize "in the name (singular) of the Father, and of the Son, and of the Holy Spirit" (Matthew 28:19).

Thus, several OT passages reveal that God is three persons in one divine unity. However, they do not reveal Him as Father, Son, and Holy Spirit. That is revealed elsewhere in the OT—a topic we discuss below.

PASSAGES THAT SPECIFICALLY NAME ONE OF THE PERSONS OF THE TRINITY

Have you ever misplaced an item and looked everywhere to find it, only to discover it in a place you had already looked several times? This can happen when you have a familiar item in a place where you do not expect it to be. Many times, we read the OT that way when it concerns the three persons of the Holy Trinity. We can read past the mention of one or more divine persons—the Father, the Son, or the Holy Spirit—without even realizing that they are mentioned. Let us look at a few of the passages in the OT that mention one person—or sometimes two persons—of the triune God.

GOD THE FATHER IN THE OLD TESTAMENT

For Christians who frequently profess the Apostles' or Nicene Creeds, God the Father is especially associated with creating all things—"the Maker of heaven and earth." Surprisingly, with the possible exception of James 3:9, there is no association of the Father with creation in the NT. Instead, consider these OT passages:

- Is this how you repay Yahweh, you foolish and senseless people? Isn't He your Father and Possessor? Didn't He make you and sustain you? (Deuteronomy 32:6)
- LORD, You are our Father. We are the clay, and You are our potter. All of us are the work of Your hands. (Isaiah 64:8)
- Don't all of us have one Father? Didn't one God create us? Why then do we act treacherously against one another, profaning the covenant of our ancestors? (Malachi 2:10)

Therefore, when the creeds call the Father "the Maker of heaven and earth," that description is derived primarily from the OT. While the Son and the Holy Spirit also participated in creating all things (Genesis 1:2; John 1:3), it is the Father who is notably singled out in the OT as Creator.

Moreover, as Isaiah 64:8 and Malachi 2:10 state, God the Father is the Father who has created us as His children. He is Father to His people who trust in Him, even if the ancestors of Israel do not acknowledge them as their children:

> Yet You are our Father, although Abraham does not know us and Israel doesn't recognize us. You, LORD, are our Father; Your name is our Redeemer from Ancient Times. (Isaiah 63:16)

More importantly, the First Person of the Trinity is the Father of the eternally begotten Son, and we see the Father speaking to the Son in two passages in particular. The first is Psalm 2:1–7:

> Why do the nations conspire and the peoples devise useless plots? The kings of the earth take their stand, and the rulers conspire together against Yahweh and His Anointed One: "Let's tear off Their chains and throw Their ropes off of us." The one sitting in heaven laughs; my Lord mocks them. Then He speaks to them in His anger and terrifies them in His wrath, "I have installed My king on Zion, My holy mountain." I will announce Yahweh's decree. He said to Me, "You are My Son; today I have become Your Father."

The psalm begins by noticing the rebellious conspiracy of the nations against "Yahweh and His Anointed One." They say, "Let's tear off *their* chains." Note the plural pronoun *their*. This is a rebellion against two persons. One of them is "my Lord," who states, "I have installed My king" and goes on to say that this king is "My son." Since the king is Yahweh's Son, Yahweh is His Father. Here we see God the Father giving His Son a commission to subdue all the nations and rule over them (Matthew 19:28; 25:31–32; Revelation 2:26–28; 12:5; 19:15). The Father also affirms His relationship with the Son: "You are My Son; today I have become Your Father." The Son is eternally begotten of the Father, a relationship that is affirmed again at Jesus' Baptism and transfiguration (Matthew 3:17; 17:5; Mark 1:11; 9:7; Luke 3:22; 9:35; 2 Peter 1:17).

The second passage is also in the book of Psalms. Psalm 110, a psalm of David, begins with the words of God the Father to His Son: "A declaration of Yahweh to my Lord: 'Sit at My right hand until I make Your enemies Your footstool.'" This verse is quoted five times in the NT, most notably by Jesus when He challenges the Pharisees on the identity of the Messiah. "If David calls Him Lord, how can He be his son?" Jesus asked (Matthew 22:45; see Mark 12:36; Luke 20:42; Acts 2:34; Hebrews 1:13). Of course, the answer is clear to those who know the Gospel story of Jesus: He is Son of the heavenly Father, the divine Second Person of the Trinity (David's Lord) and also the human descendant of David. In all these pronouncements about the Son, we hear the words of God the Father.

GOD THE SON IN THE OLD TESTAMENT

While there are many passages in the OT that prophesy about Jesus, there are only a few that mention Him as God's Son. Apart from Psalm 2, there is also the sage Agur's questions in Proverbs 30:4:

> Who has gone up to heaven and come down? Who has gathered the wind in His hands? Who has tied up the waters in a cloak? Who has established all the ends of the earth? What is His name, and what is the name of His Son—if you know?

Note that the creative work of the Father is highlighted before asking His name. God had revealed that name—Yahweh. But then Agur asks, "What is the name of His Son?" The name that the Son of God would bear—Jesus—was not revealed until God's angel revealed it to Joseph in a dream (Matthew 1:20–21). Nevertheless, Agur's words speak of two persons, the Creator Father and His Son—the First and Second Persons of the Trinity.

We can see all three persons of the Trinity earlier in Proverbs 8, which especially focuses on God the Son. In the opening verses of Proverbs 8, we meet Wisdom as a person who has the six Spirit-endowed attributes of the Messiah listed in Isaiah 11:2: wisdom, understanding, counsel, strength, knowledge, and fear of Yahweh. Then, in Proverbs 8:22–26, Wisdom claims to be God's possession from before the first of His acts—before creation. Finally, in Proverbs 8:27–31, Wisdom is present at creation, rejoicing in God's inhabited world. Here, Wisdom is the Son of God, who is endowed with the Holy Spirit's might and was a witness to the first creative acts of God the Father. (For more about Wisdom as the Son of God in Proverbs 8, see *The Messianic Message*, pp. 120–25.)

Other passages also highlight the divine nature of the Son that He shares with the Father, without calling Him "Son." One of them is Daniel 7:13–14:

> I continued watching in the night visions, and look! One like a son of man was coming with the clouds of heaven.

> He approached the Ancient of Days and was presented before Him. He was given dominion, and glory, and a kingdom. Every people, nation, and language will serve Him. His dominion is an everlasting dominion that will not pass away, and His kingdom is one that will not be destroyed.

Earlier in Daniel 7:9–10, the prophet related his vision of the enthroned God the Father, whom he called "the Ancient of Days." In that awe-inspiring vision, the Father's holy nature is highlighted by His white clothing and hair. His holiness is also shown by the fire of His throne and the fiery river flowing from Him. This holy fire can judge sinners (Daniel 7:11) and also purify His people (Zechariah 13:9; Malachi 3:2–3; 1 Corinthians 3:11–15).

When one like a Son of Man came before the Ancient of Days, He received an everlasting kingdom. The description "Son of Man" points to the incarnate Son of God, who took on human flesh to redeem the world. He will be the ruler of the everlasting Kingdom. Daniel indicates that this Son of Man is God in agreement with Psalm 145:13, which says of Yahweh, "Your kingdom is an everlasting kingdom; Your rule is for all generations" (cf. Daniel 6:26).

Thus, in Daniel 7, we see the Father and the Son revealed in their relationship to one another, and we learn of them as reigning together in an eternal kingdom (1 Corinthians 15:22–28). In this passage, we see two distinct persons—the Ancient of Days (God the Father) and one like a Son of Man (God the Son), who are two of the three persons in the one divine essence that is the only true God. In addition, Daniel 7 functions as a commentary on Psalm 110, giving a fuller picture of the inner-trinitarian relationship between the Father and the Son.

GOD THE HOLY SPIRIT IN THE OLD TESTAMENT

While there are few passages in the OT that speak of the First Person of the Trinity as "Father" or the Second Person as "Son," there are many passages that call the Third Person "the Spirit of God" or "the Spirit of Yahweh." The Spirit hovered over the surface of the waters as Creator (Genesis 1:2). The Holy Spirit is the one who "spoke by the prophets," as we confess in the Nicene Creed (see also Numbers 24:2; 1 Samuel 10:6, 11; 19:20, 23; 2 Chronicles 15:1; 20:14; 24:20; Micah 3:8). He is the one who empowered the leadership of Joshua and the Judges (Deuteronomy 34:9; Judges 3:10; 6:34; 11:29; 13:25; 14:6, 19; 15:14). The Spirit was among God's people Israel (Isaiah 63:11–14). The Holy Spirit also strengthened Israel's kings Saul and David (1 Samuel 11:6; 16:13). When God chose David to replace Saul as Israel's king, it was the Holy Spirit who left Saul and empowered David (1 Samuel 16:13–14; 18:12).

Moreover, the Holy Spirit is not simply an impersonal force of God but a person, with attributes that can only apply to a person. Note these passages in which the Spirit speaks:

- The Spirit of Yahweh spoke through me, His word was on my tongue. (2 Samuel 23:2)
- Then the Spirit of Yahweh came upon me, and He told me, "You are to say, 'This is what Yahweh says: That is what you are thinking, house of Israel; and I know the things that arise in your mind.'" (Ezekiel 11:5)

The Spirit also is described as a person who is capable of feelings and emotions:

- But they rebelled and grieved His Holy Spirit. So He became their enemy and fought against them. (Isaiah 63:10)
- House of Jacob, should it be asked, "Is the Spirit of Yahweh impatient? Are these the things He does?" (Micah 2:7)

The Holy Spirit is a person who needs no advice or counsel:

> Who has directed the Spirit of Yahweh, or who gave Him advice? (Isaiah 40:13)

Just as the OT depicts the relationship and interactions between the Father and the Son, so also it speaks of the Spirit's mutual work with the other persons of the Trinity. Thus, He participated in creation with the Father and the Son, making humans and giving them life (Job 33:4). Isaiah prophesied that the Spirit of the Lord would rest on the Messiah, the incarnate Son of God, the descendant of Jesse:

- Then a shoot will sprout from the stump of Jesse, and a branch from his roots will bear fruit. The Spirit of Yahweh will rest on Him—a Spirit of wisdom and understanding, a Spirit of counsel and might, a Spirit of knowledge and of the fear of Yahweh. (Isaiah 11:1–2; see Matthew 3:16; John 1:32)
- This is My servant; I strengthen Him, this is My chosen one; I delight in Him. I have put My Spirit on Him; He will bring justice to the nations. (Isaiah 42:1)

- The Spirit of the Lord GOD is on Me, because Yahweh has anointed Me to bring good news to the poor. He has sent Me to heal the brokenhearted, to proclaim liberty to the captives and freedom to the prisoners, to proclaim the year of Yahweh's favor, and the day of our God's vengeance; to comfort all who mourn, to provide for those who mourn in Zion; to give them a crown of beauty instead of ashes, festive oil instead of mourning, and splendid clothes instead of despair. And they will be called righteous trees, planted by Yahweh to glorify Him. (Isaiah 61:1–3; see Luke 4:16–21)

Finally, we should note that while we often think of the NT as speaking of the Holy Spirit dwelling with believers (see John 14:26; 15:26; 16:7), this was already prophesied in the OT as a gift of the Father and the Son:

- For I will pour water on the thirsty land and streams on the dry ground. I will pour out My Spirit on your descendants and My blessing on your offspring. (Isaiah 44:3)
- After this I will pour out My Spirit on all humanity; then your sons and your daughters will prophesy, your old men will have dreams, and your young men will see visions. I will even pour out My Spirit on the male and female slaves in those days. (Joel 2:28–29; see Acts 2:17–18)

Moreover, the Holy Spirit is mentioned more often than many readers of the OT realized. The term for "Yahweh's Spirit" appears twenty-seven times in the OT, while "God's Spirit" occurs sixteen times. He gives Joseph the skill to interpret dreams (Genesis 41:38) and gives Israel rest in the Promised Land (Isaiah 63:14). The Spirit imparts the skill necessary to excel in craftsmanship (Exodus 31:3; 35:31) and enables Balaam (Numbers 24:2), Saul (1 Samuel 10:10), Asa (2 Chronicles 15:1), Jahaziel (2 Chronicles 20:14), Zechariah (2 Chronicles 24:20), Micah (Micah 3:8), and Ezekiel (Ezekiel 11:5) to function as prophets. In fact, Peter reminds us that all of Yahweh's prophets were empowered by the Holy Spirit (2 Peter 1:20–21; cf. Nehemiah 9:20; Zechariah 7:12; 2 Timothy 3:16).

In the book of Judges, Yahweh's Spirit comes upon Othniel (Judges 3:10), Gideon (Judges 6:34), Jephthah (Judges 11:29), and Samson (Judges 13:24–25; 14:6, 19; 15:14–15). He descends upon Saul (1 Samuel 10:9–10; 11:6) but also leaves him (1 Samuel 16:14). Most importantly, the Holy Spirit empowers the Davidic Messiah to carry out His ministry (Isaiah 11:2–3).

At least thirty additional texts refer to the Holy Spirit with pronouns or other markers of the divine name. In these passages, we learn the following:

- Psalm 104:30—The Spirit renews the earth.
- Isaiah 30:1—God wants Israel's plans to be done through the Spirit, but often they are not.
- Nehemiah 9:20—Through His Spirit, Yahweh teaches people when they come out of Egypt.
- Numbers 11:17, 25; 27:18—God gives His Spirit to Moses, the seventy elders, and Joshua.

At one point, Moses even prays that all of God's people might have the Holy Spirit (Numbers 11:29), while David asks for God's "good Spirit" to lead him (Psalm 143:10). The Holy Spirit kills (Isaiah 40:7) and makes alive (Ezekiel 37:1–14).

CONCLUSIONS

When the NT speaks of Father, Son, and Spirit together, it is not innovative. In using those names for the three persons of the Holy Trinity, it draws on terms already laid out in the OT. In depicting Father, Son, and Holy Spirit as having one name (Matthew 28:19), and therefore being one divine essence, it is expanding on the OT depiction of God as both *I* and *Us*—a single God yet plural persons. And like the OT, the NT depicts the Trinity in Unity and Unity in Trinity as a mystery that can be described but cannot be explained. Instead, it simply presents the triune God "neither confusing the [three] persons nor dividing the [one] substance" (Athanasian Creed, *LSB*, p. 319). It is this God who spoke to Moses and the prophets, who led Israel through the wilderness, who calls us to be His people through His grace alone, and who will reign eternally in His everlasting kingdom. "Holy, Holy, Holy, Lord God Almighty! . . . Holy, Holy, Holy, merciful and mighty! God in three persons, blessed Trinity!" (*LSB* 507:1).

DISCUSSION QUESTIONS

1. How does Matthew 28:19 summarize this chapter?
2. Which surprises you most: what the OT teaches about the Father, the Son, or the Holy Spirit?
3. If we did not have the OT passages about the Holy Trinity, how would our understanding of God in the NT be impoverished?
4. Which passage about the Son in the OT is the most important in the NT?
5. What new appreciation do you have for Genesis 1? Numbers 6?

CHAPTER 4

WHY DID SOME MEN LIVE SO LONG?

"When the set time had fully come,
God sent His Son."
(Galatians 4:4)

History is important—at least, most schools think it is. It is hard to imagine a high school that does not offer courses in history, especially the history of one's own country. More inconceivable is a college that does not have a history department. At the postsecondary level, all kinds of history are taught, from ancient civilizations to modern ones, from the history of thought to the history of science, from the biography of various important people to the biography of nations and even genealogies. In addition to some practical reasons for all this interest in history at the academic level, there is also our innate curiosity about the past. What were people like? What great accomplishments and failures characterized their lives? What was important to them? How did their actions affect the future and even our own time?

The first eleven chapters of Genesis give us a whirlwind tour of the early history of humankind from the creation of our first parents to the birth and early life of Abraham and his brothers. Then the narrative slows, and we follow in more detail Abraham's later life and the lives of his son Isaac, grandson Jacob, and thirteen great-grandchildren (and even a few great-great-grandchildren). Those first eleven chapters move so quickly and are told in such broad sweeps of the remote ancient horizon that it is bound to call forth questions about some of the events that are given only in outline form. The most frequent questions concern the two genealogies in Genesis 5 and 11, where we encounter twenty men who appear to have had exceptionally long lifespans. Why did they live so long? Can the information about them be used to determine when God created the world and when He sent the great flood survived by Noah and his family?

LONG LIVES IN THE GENESIS 5 AND 11 GENEALOGIES

One question that those of us who teach OT are often asked is "Why did the people in the early chapters of Genesis live so long?" Beginning with Adam and going through Abraham's father, Terah, we are given the ages of nineteen men.

GENESIS 5	GENESIS 11
1. Adam–930 years	11. Shem–600 years
2. Seth–912 years	12. Arpachshad–438 years
3. Enosh–905 years	13. Shelah–433 years
4. Kenan–910 years	14. Eber–464 years
5. Mahalalel–895 years	15. Peleg–239 years
6. Jared–962 years	16. Reu–239 years
7. Enoch–365 years	17. Serug–230
8. Methuselah–969 years	18. Nahor–148 years
9. Lamech–777 years	19. Terah–205 years
10. Noah–950 years	20. Abraham–175 years

Many of the lifespans of those who lived before the great flood are extraordinary: Adam–930 years; Seth–912 years; Methuselah–969 years; Noah–950 years. Even after the flood, there are long lifespans: Shem–600 years; Shelah–433 years; Eber–464 years. Although the lives of the postdiluvian patriarchs decreased over time, Terah still lived an impressive 205 years at a time when the typical adult lifespan was 50 to 70 years.

There are a few features to note about these two genealogies. First, the years of life are much longer for those born before the flood than for those born after. Second, there is a steady decrease in lifespan over the years for those born after the flood. Thus, it would seem that people lived longer before the flood than after it.

However, we have to temper any observations by the knowledge that we have only ten generations with ten men before the flood (Adam to Noah, Genesis 5:3–32) and nine generations with nine men after the flood (Seth to Terah, Genesis 11:10–26; Abraham and his brothers are the tenth generation). Therefore, we have only one representative for each generation mentioned in these genealogies. We do not know that everyone was living as long as these men. In fact, we know from historical records such as those that speak of the lives of kings in Assyria, Babylon, and Egypt that most people in Terah's day were living much shorter lives than he did. The same applies for Abraham (175 years, Genesis 25:7), Isaac (185 years, Genesis 35:28), and Jacob (147 years, Genesis 47:28).

These are not just any genealogies. Unlike the genealogies given elsewhere in Genesis (e.g., Genesis 4:17–24; 36:9–19), these note the ages of each generation. Moreover, these are the men who are in the messianic line from Adam to Abraham, which would eventually lead to Jesus (see Luke 3:23–38). This may indicate that there was a special blessing of God on the nineteen men in the two genealogies. They were the bearers of God's promise to bring forth a Savior, which was given to Eve (Genesis 3:15) and later to Abraham (Genesis 12:3; 18:18; 22:18), repeated to Isaac (Genesis 26:4), and then given to Jacob (Genesis 28:14). It may well be that the long lives of these men were signs of God's favor to them since through them would come a blessing for all people. If this is the case, then we cannot extend the long lifespans of these men to their contemporaries, since they may have been living longer lives than others.

We should note that persons outside the ancestors of Jesus were sometimes blessed by God for their outstanding faithfulness and service to God and His people: Joseph (110 years, Genesis 50:22); Kohath, the father of the Levitical clan that produced Israel's priests (113 years, Exodus 6:18); Amram, father of Moses (137 years, Exodus 6:20); Aaron, Israel's first high priest (120 years, Numbers 33:39); Moses, the great prophet (120 years, Deuteronomy 34:7).

Thus, we can probably say the following about the long lifespans of the pre- and postflood ancestors of Jesus:

- We do not know that everyone was living as long as these nineteen men.
- It appears likely that people lived longer lives before the great flood, but how much longer cannot be determined.
- It also appears likely that lifespans were reduced after the flood until they came to the historic average natural adult lifespan of 50 to 70 years (with some living as long as 80, 90, or more, and others dying younger; see Psalm 90:10).

THE PURPOSE OF THE GENESIS GENEALOGIES

The genealogies in Genesis 5 and 11 are intended to link the messianic line from Adam to Abraham before the narrative of Genesis slows to give us important scenes from the lives of Israel's ancestors. However, since antiquity, there have been attempts to use these genealogies also for chronological purposes. Since the genealogies give us information about each man, including their ages at a critical point in each of their lives, as well as the length of their lives, it has been tempting to perform a bit of arithmetic and calculate the date of the flood of Genesis 7 or the date of creation based on these genealogies. However, it has also been recognized since antiquity that this approach presents a number of problems.

PROBLEMS WITH USING THE GENESIS GENEALOGIES FOR DATE CALCULATIONS

If the genealogies provide a way to calculate how long after creation someone was born, a number of peculiarities arise. In the genealogy of Genesis 5, such calculations would place Methuselah's death in the year of the great flood. Are we to assume that this oldest man in the OT drowned while Noah survived, or that God delayed the flood until Methuselah died in faith? In the genealogy of Genesis 11, such calculations would depict six ancestors of Abram, other than his father Terah—Shem, Arpachshad, Shelah, Eber, Reu, and Serug—as being alive when Abram was born. It appears preposterous on its face that Shem, who survived the flood, was still alive when Abram was born. Moreover, such calculations would require that Shem, Arpachshad, Shelah, and Eber were still alive when Abram left Haran for Canaan. In addition, all four men would still have been alive when Ishmael was born, while Shem, Shelah, and Eber would have been living when Isaac was born. Eber, in fact, would have been living as late as the birth of Jacob!

If that is not troubling enough, the presence of so many extremely old ancestors in Abram's day seems to fly in the face of Genesis 17:17, where Abraham doubted that a man 100 years old was vigorous enough to have a son. If Shem, Shelah, and Eber were still alive, and all were well over 300 years of age, why would Abraham have thought that a man of 100 years could not father a child?

Later, Esau assumed that Isaac was an old man and near death (Genesis 27:2, 41). From the information given in Genesis, it is possible to calculate Isaac's age at this time as 136 years old. Yet if Eber were still alive and well into his fourth century, and if Shem, Arpachshad, and Shelah had each lived over 400 years and died in recent memory, why would Isaac or Esau assume that after only 136 years, Isaac was near the end of his life?

Another factor that argues against viewing the Genesis 5 and 11 genealogies as continuous chains of father-to-son links is the placement of certain individuals in the line from Adam to Abraham using the important numbers seven and ten. (On the importance of the numbers seven and ten, see chapter 6.)

GENESIS 5	**GENESIS 11**
1. Adam	11. Shem
2. Seth	12. Arpachshad
3. Enosh	13. Shelah
4. Kenan	**14. Eber**
5. Mahalalel	15. Peleg
6. Jared	16. Reu
7. Enoch	17. Serug
8. Methuselah	18. Nahor
9. Lamech	19. Terah
10. Noah	**20. Abraham**

Many Bible readers are aware that Enoch, the righteous man who walked with God, is seventh in line from Adam (Jude 14). Noah, the righteous man through whom humankind survived the great flood, is tenth from Adam. When the line continues in Genesis 11, Eber, the man whose name is preserved in the word *Hebrew*, is in the honored fourteenth position—double seven—from Adam. Finally, Abram is in the esteemed twentieth position—double ten. These locations in the genealogies suggest something other than a strictly continuous chain of father-to-son links. Instead, the strategic placement of these individuals suggests that the Genesis genealogies are selective, that they skip over some generations in order to place certain men in positions of honor.

Still another problem for reading the genealogies as chronological information useful for dating creation comes from Genesis 11:10: "These are the family records of Shem: Shem was 100 years old, and he fathered Arpachshad *two years after the flood*." If this is taken to mean that Shem was 100 years old when Arpachshad was born, there is a problem. By the same assumption, Shem was born when Noah was 500 years old: "Now Noah was 500 years old, and he fathered Shem, Ham, and Japheth" (Genesis 5:32). If this means that Noah was 500 years old when Shem was born, it also means that Ham and Japheth were born that same year (and thus were triplets). Moreover, the flood took place when Noah was 600 (Genesis 7:6, 11) and ended when he was 601 years old (Genesis 8:13). Even if we are to assume that Shem was born at the end of the year when Noah was 500 years old, then Shem was at least 102 years old two years after the flood—and more likely, 103 years old (Genesis 11:10). Clearly, there is a problem with reading Genesis

11:10 as if Arpachshad was born when Shem was 100 years old. At the very least, there is a complication with reading Genesis 5:32 as if Shem were born when Noah was 500 years old. The arithmetic does not work, implying that these notices were never intended to be read as providing a way to compile an absolute chronology of the world in Abraham's day.

An even greater problem arises at Genesis 11:26: "Now Terah was 70 years old, and he fathered Abram, Nahor, and Haran." Genesis 12:4 notes that Abram was 75 years old when he left Haran, and this occurred after Terah died at the age of 205 years (Genesis 11:32; cf. Acts 7:4). Terah was actually 130 years old when Abram was born (205 – 75 = 130). Again, it would appear that either all three sons were born when Terah was 70 or Genesis 11:26 is to be read some other way. Yet from the information given elsewhere in Genesis, Abram was not born when Terah was 70 years old.

This has grave consequences for anyone attempting to read the Genesis 5 and 11 genealogies as continuous links in a chronological chain. The wording of Genesis 11:26 is a formula that is shared in almost every other instance of the reporting of a patriarch's age and the birth of a descendant in these genealogies. If one cannot read Genesis 11:26 as locating Abram's birth when Terah was 70 years old, one cannot reliably read any other of the twenty notices in the Genesis 5 and 11 genealogies that way, either.

Because of these problems—the appearance that many of Abraham's ancestors were alive in his day and later in Isaac's day, and the mathematical problems around the births of Shem's sons and Terah's sons—attempts were made in antiquity to overcome them. The ancient Greek version of Genesis preserves some of these attempts. The numbers were adjusted for many of the men in the genealogies. The age of Lamech, Noah's father, was increased so that the flood took place after the death of Methuselah. In Genesis 11, the numbers were changed so that Nahor, Abram's grandfather, was alive when Abram was born, but other ancestors had died. Both numbers and wording were altered for Terah to account for Abram's birth.

Modern English versions have attempted to solve the dilemma of the birth of Shem's sons and of Terah's sons by translating "*After* Noah was 500 years old" (Genesis 5:32; see ESV, NET, NIV, NRSVA) and "*After* Terah lived seventy years" (Genesis 11:26; see NIV, NRSVA). There is no reason to translate these verses this way other than the obvious problem caused by the perceived conflict concerning the births of Shem's sons and Terah's sons. But if Genesis 5:32 and 11:26 are to be understood as Noah fathering his sons sometime after he was 500 years old and Terah fathering his sons after he was 70, how are the genealogies in Genesis 5 and 11 to be understood when they use the same phrasing in Hebrew? Why are they translated "when (name) was (number) years old" when they employ the same expression as in Genesis 5:32 and 11:26? If one instance of this phrase is translated "after" instead of "when," then all could be understood as "after." If all these verses say that someone was born after their ancestor reached a certain age, then one cannot add all the ages to determine the date of the flood or of creation. Clearly, there is a problem with saying that the age given for the patriarch is the time when the descendant was born. That proposition does not hold for the births of Shem (Genesis 5:3) or Arpachshad (Genesis 11:11) or the birth of Abram (Genesis 11:26).

READING THE GENEALOGIES AS OTHER THAN A CONTINUOUS CHRONOLOGY

The solution to these problems lies in abandoning the notion that the genealogies are intended to give a chronology linking creation and the birth of Abram. To see how they might be understood as something other than strict chronologies, we must first examine the features of these two genealogies. Part of the dilemma is that because of the differences in the verb systems between English and Hebrew, it is difficult to translate the Hebrew verb in these genealogies, for instance in Genesis 11:14:

> Shelah lived thirty years and *fathered* Eber.

While that English translation leads readers to believe Shelah is the father of Eber, the Hebrew verb does not necessarily mean that. For instance, consider Deuteronomy 4:25:

> When you *have children and grandchildren*, and have grown old in the land, and if you act corruptly, make an idol in the form of anything, and do what is evil in the sight of Yahweh your God, angering Him …

The phrase "have children and grandchildren" uses the same verb as in the Genesis genealogies, but here it is translated "have," since one obviously cannot father grandchildren. The Hebrew verb does not mean to father children; it actually means "to cause someone to bear a child." (The verb is an H [Hiphil] stem of the root *yld*. While in the G [Qal] stem, this verb can mean "father a child," in the H stem, it is causative and means "cause someone to bear a child.") A man can start a chain of events that eventually causes a future generation to be born. Therefore, all that Genesis 11:14 tells us is that Shelah did something when he was 30 years old that led to the eventual birth of Eber. Eber may have been his son, his grandson, his great-grandson, or even a descendant in some later generation.

This same verb is used elsewhere to indicate a more distant future generation, not the immediate next generation. One example is Isaiah's prophecy to King Hezekiah after the king had courted the favor of Babylonian envoys by showing them his impressive palace. The prophet told Hezekiah, "Some of your descendants who will come from you, whom you *will father*, will be taken away, and they will be made eunuchs in the palace of the king of Babylon" (2 Kings 20:18). Here the verb translated "will father" is the same verb as in the genealogies in Genesis 5 and 11. However, these descendants were not Hezekiah's sons but were a later generation. Isaiah's prophecy was delivered to Hezekiah in 701 BC. The Babylonians first deported persons from the Judean royal court in 606 BC (Jeremiah 46:2–12; 2 Kings 24:1; Daniel 1:1–2). They would deport more Judeans in 597 BC (2 Kings 24:10–17; 2 Chronicles 36:10; Ezekiel 1:2) and again after Jerusalem's final fall to the Babylonians in 587 BC. Therefore, there were at least 95 years between Isaiah's prophecy and its fulfillment (701 to 606 BC), perhaps as many as 114 years (701 to 587 BC). Clearly, the descendants of Hezekiah who were made eunuchs in Babylon would have been his great-grandsons or even his great-great-grandsons. Thus, the verb *father* here skips over several generations and does not literally mean to father children but instead to cause future generations to be born.

DAVID'S GENEALOGY IN RUTH

It may seem strange to us that genealogies such as those in Genesis 5 and 11 might skip over several generations in this way, but that is not at all unusual in the Bible. For instance, consider the genealogy of David (Ruth 4:18–22). This genealogy begins with Perez and ends with David. Perez was one of the two sons of Judah by his daughter-in-law Tamar (Genesis 38:27–30). With information given in Genesis and elsewhere in the OT, it is possible to date the birth of these twins to about 1877 BC. David's birth can be dated to 1039 BC. That is a span of 838 years in which the nine generations after Perez must have been born. A simple calculation reveals that if no generations were skipped in the genealogy of Ruth 4, the average age of a father when his son was born would have been 93 years old. That is an average, and one would expect some fathers to be younger than the average and some to be older than the average at the birth of their sons. Therefore, it is unreasonable to conclude that no generations have been skipped. It is more likely that the average age of a father when his son was born was 25, implying that there were about thirty-three or thirty-four generations from Perez to David, and that fewer than one-third of the generations are listed in Ruth 4.

And there is more proof that Ruth 4 presents a select genealogy for David rather than a complete genealogy. Matthew 1:5 states that Salmon fathered Boaz by Rahab. Since Jericho fell to Israel in 1406 BC, forty years after the Exodus from Egypt, this would place Salmon's fatherhood sometime around 1400 BC. There are four generations after Salmon. This means that without skipping generations from Salmon to David, the average age for a father when his son was born would have been 90 years old. Instead, given that the sequence from Boaz to David is probably without gaps, it is likely that twelve or thirteen generations are skipped from Salmon to Boaz.

Working in the opposite direction, five generations after Perez culminates in Salmon, who had to have been born during the wilderness wanderings and could not have been more than 40 years old in 1406 BC (Numbers 14:35; 32:13). The period between Perez's birth and Salmon's birth spanned at least 431 years and at most 451 years, producing an average age at fatherhood of 86 to 90 years, if no generations were skipped. This implies that there are missing generations—again, probably twelve or thirteen generations—somewhere between Ram and Salmon.

THE LEVITES' GENEALOGY IN 1 CHRONICLES

A genealogy in 1 Chronicles bears out that there are missing generations in David's genealogy. Unlike the other tribes, the Levites would have had reason to keep track of every generation. One had to be certain of direct descent from Aaron in order to serve as a priest. Similarly, other Levites had to be able to prove descent from Levi to serve in the tabernacle or temple. In 1 Chronicles 6:33–37, there is a genealogy of eighteen generations from Korah, who was an adult at the time of the Exodus (Exodus 6:21, 24; Numbers 16:1–49; 26:9–11), to Heman, who was a temple musician in David's day (1 Chronicles 6:33), making the average age of a father when his son was born about 25 years old.

Is it reasonable, then, to assume that during the same period, there were only five generations from Salmon to David? Moreover, the author of Ruth may have had a reason to skip some generations. He wished to place Boaz—the main male character in Ruth—in the honored seventh position in the list and David, Israel's great king, in the tenth, in imitation of the genealogies in Genesis.

RUTH 4:18–22
1. Perez
2. Hezron
3. Ram
4. Amminadab
5. Nahshon
6. Salmon
7. Boaz
8. Obed
9. Jesse
10. David

As we have seen, the Genesis genealogies also place prominent people in positions associated with the numbers seven and ten. In this way, the author of Ruth may have recognized that the Genesis 5 and 11 genealogies did not present every generation and omitted some in order to place certain names in particular positions.

For other examples of biblical genealogies that skip some generations, see Ezra's genealogy (Ezra 7:1–6). Six generations are missing between Azariah and Meraioth (compare 1 Chronicles 6:7–10), making Azariah Meraioth's fifth great-grandfather. Also note Jesus' genealogy in Matthew 1. Matthew 1:17 notes fourteen generations from David to the Babylonian captivity. However, 1 Chronicles 3:10–15 lists seventeen generations. Matthew has omitted three names following Joram (Ahaziah, Joash, and Amaziah; 1 Chronicles 3:11–12). It is clear why Matthew omitted these three names: He wanted to present three lists of fourteen generations, perhaps for easy memorization (Matthew 1:17).

So if these generations do not allow us to calculate the dates of early events in Genesis, what is their purpose? Why do they give the age when a man caused the eventual birth of one of his descendants? Since the very beginning of the church, Christians have seen a golden thread that runs through the book of Genesis: the messianic promise that God will—through a coming Savior—reverse the fall and its effects. This promise begins at Genesis 3:15, which speaks of a seed of the woman who will crush the serpent's head (cf. Romans 16:20), thereby bringing salvation to all nations and peoples. The messianic promise was repeated in various forms to Abraham (Genesis 12:3; 17:16; 18:18; 22:18), Isaac (Genesis 26:4), and Jacob (Genesis 26:4; 27:29; 28:14). In his last recorded words, Jacob passed this promise on to Judah (Genesis 49:8–12).

MESSIANIC CONNECTIONS

An unbroken chain of recipients of the messianic promise reaches from Abraham to Judah. However, where is the chain from Adam to Abraham? It is found in the genealogies of Genesis 5 and 11, where each man was blessed with an especially long life. Note that Abraham thought he was old at 100 years of age (Genesis 17:17), yet God blessed him with an even longer life of 175 years. Esau thought Isaac was near death at 136 years old (Genesis 27:2, 41), but God blessed Isaac so that he lived to be 180 years old. Jacob was blessed with 147 years. In each case, these men lived much longer than normal for their era (i.e., the twenty-second through nineteenth centuries BC). This may also be true for the men in the Genesis genealogies.

This may imply that in Genesis 5 and 11, the age of each patriarch when he caused the birth of his eventual successor is counted from the time that God blessed that man with the promise that he would be an ancestor of the Messiah. The patriarch receiving that blessing by faith became the cause of the birth of a descendant who would sometime later also receive this blessing. Indeed, there are three lines of evidence that point to this as the reason each patriarch could cause his eventual successor to be born. The first was discussed above: the genealogy of David in the book of Ruth.

Second, there is the disappointment over Cain. When Cain was born, Eve stated the reason for giving him his name: "I have obtained a man with Yahweh" (Genesis 4:1; the name Cain sounds like the Hebrew word for "obtained"). This clearly points back to God's promise that the woman was to bear a seed (Genesis 3:15). It implies that Eve assumed (incorrectly) that Cain was at least the first step in bringing forth God's promise. Of course, that hope was dashed with the events of the rest of Genesis 4: the murder of Abel and Cain's banishment. So Genesis 5:3 indicates that when Adam was 130 years old, God graciously renewed His promise of a deliverer to crush the serpent's head, this time promising Adam that he would indeed have a son who would fulfill the pledge of Genesis 3:15.

Third, consider Noah's words following his drunkenness and the subsequent actions of Ham, Shem, and Japheth. For Ham's son Canaan, there is a triple prediction of what would happen to him and his descendants (Genesis 9:25–27). There is also a prediction of what would happen to Japheth's descendants (Genesis 9:27a).

However, there is no prediction about Shem. Instead, there is a blessing from Yahweh, the God of Shem. This presumes that Yahweh and Shem had a prior close relationship. Genesis may be implying that this relationship was initiated by Yahweh when Shem was 100 years old, and Yahweh revealed that Shem would be the bearer of the messianic promise (Genesis 11:10). This is why there is a time lag between Shem's age of 100 and his implied age of 102 when Arpachshad was born. This would also explain the time lag between Terah's age of 70 years (Genesis 11:26) and the birth of Abram sixty years later. In both cases, the ancestor caused the eventual birth of a son through his trust in God's promise.

CONCLUSIONS

We ought to conclude that the genealogies of Genesis 5 and 11 are not in the Bible to help us calculate the age of the earth or the date of the flood. Instead, they are signposts, pointing forward to God's Messiah, who was promised to come to crush Satan's head. However, we should not conclude that the earth is billions of years old, as if hundreds of millions of generations are missing from the Genesis genealogies. That is a misreading of what Genesis is telling us. While we cannot date the age of the universe from information in Genesis, we can affirm that the men mentioned in the early chapters of Genesis were real, historical persons whom God used to bless all humankind.

Our curiosity about the genealogies in Genesis leads us to ask interesting questions about the events before the time of Abraham. Yet the information contained in the genealogies of the earliest chapters of the Bible was not designed to answer every question we might have. We cannot know the typical lifespan of people before the flood or how quickly it might have become reduced after Noah and his sons left the ark. Nor can we use the genealogies to construct a chronology of the early history of the earth and its human inhabitants. But we have something more important than this knowledge—the assurance that God has always been committed to saving humans from the curse of sin and death, as He worked through many generations to bring our Lord Jesus into the world at the perfect time in history (Galatians 4:4–5). "All mankind fell in Adam's fall; one common sin infects us all. . . . But Christ, the second Adam, came . . . to be our life, our light, our way" (*LSB* 562:1, 4).

DISCUSSION QUESTIONS

1. How does Galatians 4:4 summarize this chapter?
2. Why did some men in Genesis live so long?
3. How does the genealogy in Ruth 4 shed light on the genealogies in Genesis 5 and 10?
4. Why doesn't it work to calculate the age of the world using the genealogies in Genesis 5 and 11?

CHAPTER 5

WHAT ABOUT ALL THE VIOLENCE IN THE OLD TESTAMENT?

"Yahweh is a man of war."
(Exodus 15:3)

Horror and heartbreak were two of the most visceral reactions to the events of September 11, 2001. Radicalized Muslims declared war on America and killed almost three thousand that day. Yet bloodshed and barbarity in the name of religion isn't anything new. There were Muslim conquests in the seventh century, Christian crusades from the eleventh through twelfth centuries, as well as the Thirty Years' War across Europe in the seventeenth century. In fact, the idea of religious warfare goes as far back as the OT.

Israelites were involved in sixty battles, beginning with their exodus from Egypt (1,441 BC) and concluding with the Babylonian exile (587 BC). Little wonder that the verb meaning "make war" is used 164 times in the OT and the noun "war" 320 times. Moses even says, "Yahweh is a man of war" (Exodus 15:3). About one-fourth of Israel's military engagements contain the Hebrew word *herem*.

The verb *herem* denotes "to devote to destruction." Deuteronomy 7:2 is typical: "When Yahweh your God has delivered them [Israel's enemies] over to you and you have defeated them, then you must destroy them totally [*herem*]. Make no treaty with them. Show them no mercy."

Show them no mercy? God's *herem* mandate is strikingly different from admonitions in the NT: "Love your enemies" (Matthew 5:44); "Turn the other cheek" (Luke 6:29); "Walk the extra mile" (Matthew 5:41); "Bless and do not curse" (Romans 12:14).

How can people who follow a crucified Lord—a Savior who bled and died for His enemies—embrace parts of the OT that describe God as ordering *herem*, vengeance and judgment upon Israel's adversaries?

Divinely sanctioned violence is one of the most emotionally charged issues people have with Israel's sacred texts. It's not surprising that some reject the OT because of God's commands for the Israelites to wipe out their enemies.

Divine fury appears in a number of places in the OT. Only eight people—Noah and his family—survived the worldwide flood. God's ten plagues against Egypt decimated the land of the Nile and killed thousands; then every Egyptian soldier who chased the Israelites into the Red Sea drowned. And the book of Judges is about as gruesome and gory as it gets in the OT—especially when we take a look at Samson. He once killed thirty men in Ashkelon (Judges 14:19). Empowered by God's Spirit, Samson struck down a thousand Philistines with a donkey's jawbone (Judges 15:9–20). Most horrifying is when Samson finally took his own life, along with those of three thousand people (Judges 16:23–30). Of the thirty-nine books in the OT, only three don't describe divine violence—Ruth, Ecclesiastes, and the Song of Songs.

While we could look at a number of the thirty-six books that do depict God's fierce judgment, we've decided to take a deep dive into the book of Joshua. Why? Joshua's conquest of Canaan is ground zero for *herem*. The term comes thirty-seven times in the biblical author's descriptions of Israel's defeat of the Canaanites. The second most frequent use of *herem* in the OT—ten times—appears in 1 Samuel 15. That's why we compare the book of Joshua with this story of Saul's warfare against the Amalekites.

The OT describes two kinds of warfare: battles fought against cities *outside* the Promised Land (Deuteronomy 20:10–15) and battles fought against cities *within* Canaan (Deuteronomy 20:16–18).

The first category commanded Israel to spare their enemies. For example, God directed His people not to attack neighbors like Moab and Ammon (Deuteronomy 2:9, 19), or Edom (Deuteronomy 2:4–5; 23:7). The second type of warfare mandated *herem*—a key motif in the book of Joshua.

THE GENESIS BACKGROUND

Our discussion about divine violence in Joshua begins with two verses in the book of Genesis. In Genesis 12:3, Yahweh pledges to Abraham, "The one who treats you with contempt, I will curse." When the same verbal root "to curse" appears in Israel's malediction texts (e.g., Deuteronomy 27), it appears in a *passive* form (e.g., "Cursed *be* the man who makes a carved or cast metal image" [Deuteronomy 27:15]). Israel curses its enemies in the *passive* voice—"cursed be." God, on the other hand, curses in the *active* voice—"I will curse." This grammar and theology are summed up when Yahweh says in Deuteronomy 32:35, "Vengeance is mine, I will repay" (cf. Romans 12:19). God does the cursing. Israel is His instrument.

Israelites, therefore, were never to take the role of avenger. They were to leave that up to God. Far from being vindictive, therefore, *herem* texts in the OT describe what Israelites did in response to divine commands. They didn't have free rein to attack anyone and everyone. Moreover, Yahweh was never automatically on Israel's side—a truth that His Messenger conveys to Joshua (Joshua 5:13–15).

At one point, the Israelites go into battle against the Philistines with the ark of the covenant. And they do this without God's approval. The result? Total disaster (1 Samuel 4). Both Joshua 7 and Numbers

14:41–45 record similar Israelite military defeats. And just as God expelled Canaanites from the land (Joshua 6–12), His threat to do the same to Israel (Leviticus 18:24–30) came to pass, as narrated in 2 Kings 17 and 25. The upshot? Yahweh never gave Israel a "most favored nation" status. All the nations stood equally before Him.

Did God unfairly pick on the Canaanites? Hardly. That's why Amos 1–2 announces judgment on *eight* nations for their barbaric treatment of other people. Yahweh doesn't show partiality. In every OT battle, divine indignation comes not because of people's race, culture, language, ethnicity, skin color, or nationality. God judges unrepentant sinners. Divine condemnation was equally applied to Canaanites and Israelites (Deuteronomy 13:12–18).

The second text in Genesis that helps us understand Joshua's military campaigns are God's words to Abraham in a dream: "The iniquity of the Amorites is not yet complete" (Genesis 15:16). Here, the term *Amorites* is synonymous with *Canaanites*. God has great patience. His decision to enact judgment upon the Amorites/Canaanites wasn't a spur-of-the-moment decision or a knee-jerk reaction. God gives them four hundred years to repent. To repent of what? Let us count the ways.

CANAANITE CULTURE

Extrabiblical texts, unearthed in Syria in 1929, describe Canaanite atrocities—incest, child sacrifice, violence, bestiality, and homosexuality. These same sins are cataloged in Leviticus 18 and 20. How did the Canaanites become so perverse? They imitated the gods that they worshiped.

Baal and Asherah—two of the most prominent Canaanite deities—were part of a highly developed religious system. By engaging in sex at a high place (a hill, a mountain, or a raised altar), Canaanites believed they could entice Baal and Asherah into having sexual relations in heaven. They believed this brought rain that would water their crops. What were the Canaanites doing? They were deifying sex and money.

Canaanites also deified violence. In another one of their mythical dramas, Mot (the god of the underworld) swallows Baal (the fertility god). One of Baal's sisters, named Anat, then unleashes her violent power, defeats Mot, and brings Baal back to life.

Yahweh gave the inhabitants of Canaan four hundred years to turn from this wickedness. God promised Abraham that in him all the people of the earth would be blessed (Genesis 12:3), and Canaanites are the first people group mentioned (Genesis 12:6). Little wonder, then, that Abraham interceded for Sodom and Gomorrah, and God was willing to hear his prayer (Genesis 18–19). Canaanites subsequently considered Abraham to be a prophet (Genesis 20:7). Up next? God showed mercy and grace to Abimelech and the people of Gerar (Genesis 20:17–18). Abraham's renown continued to spread—so much so that some Hittites called him "God's prince" (Genesis 23:6).

Abraham wasn't alone in demonstrating kindness to Canaanites. Isaac resolved a conflict with some inhabitants in the land (Genesis 26), while Jacob sought to live peaceably with the inhabitants of Shechem. All in all, Israel's patriarchs sought to live in peace with the residents of Canaan, demonstrating justice and righteousness—attributes God expected from Abraham and his offspring (Genesis 18:19).

Instead, however, the Canaanites refused and doubled down on their sin. God therefore mandated severe action against the Canaanites—both as judgment for their sin and to keep Israelites from being led astray by their perverse practices (e.g., Numbers 7:2–6; 20:16–18).

It's therefore a misreading of the OT to think that God ordered the Israelites to remove innocent people. Canaanite idolatry wasn't an alternate lifestyle. Instead, their worship connected them to demons (Deuteronomy 32:17; cf. Psalm 106:37), whose agenda was to kill and destroy. This is why God commanded Joshua to bulldoze the Canaanites and their idol shrines (e.g., Numbers 33:52; Deuteronomy 7:5; 12:2–3). And any remaining inhabitants would become "barbs," "thorns," and "trouble" for Israel (Numbers 33:55).

The book of Joshua, therefore, describes an encounter between two different worldviews: one that honors and upholds love, respect, and dignity and another that fosters brutality and an "anything goes" sexual morality.

Accordingly, God's mandate for Israel to wipe out Canaanite shrines and immoral practices demonstrates that Joshua was engaged in spiritual war. It wasn't political or national, and it was hardly ethnic cleansing. Israel's defeat of the Canaanites wasn't because of Israel's righteousness (Deuteronomy 9:5). Instead, it was on account of Canaanite unrighteousness. Moreover, God expressly warned Israelites that if they turned to idols, He would judge them in the same way He judged the Canaanites—God's people would be thrown out of the land (e.g., Leviticus 18:28; Deuteronomy 28:25–68). This pledge to remove Israelites from Canaan demonstrates God's fairness and commitment to justice—regardless of race or nationality.

With Genesis 12:2–3; 15:16 in hand, and the theological implications of these verses serving as our foundation, we now look at divine violence in the OT as portrayed in the book of Joshua.

THE BOOK OF JOSHUA

It's natural to read about Joshua's military victories and assume his army killed every last Canaanite. Evidence for this position comes in Joshua 10:40:

> Joshua struck the whole land, the hill country and the Negeb and the lowland and the slopes, and all their kings. None were left; he devoted to destruction [*herem*] all that breathed, just as Yahweh the God of Israel commanded.

This all-inclusive description of total destruction is hyperbole. We shouldn't understand it literally. It's how Israelites, in their historical context, described a definitive victory. It's like saying, "The Minnesota Vikings *killed* the Green Bay Packers!" Well, not really.

Biblical hyperbole isn't confined to Joshua. Take a look at what Mark writes in his Gospel:

- John came, baptizing in the wilderness and proclaiming a baptism of repentance for the forgiveness of sins. *All* the country of Judea and *all* Jerusalem were going out to him. (Mark 1:4–5)
- Simon and those with him searched for Jesus. When they found Him, they said, "*Everyone* is looking for You." (Mark 1:36–37)

Note also what Paul writes: "One of the Cretans, their own prophet said, 'Cretans are *always* liars, evil beasts, lazy gluttons.' This testimony is true" (Titus 1:12–13).

These statements in Mark and Titus aren't intended to be understood strictly to the letter. Neither should we literally interpret Joshua 10:40.

There's more evidence that the Israelites didn't literally devote "to destruction all that breathed." First, Joshua and company only burned three Canaanite cities—Jericho, Ai, and Hazor (Joshua 6:24; 8:28; 11:13). Second, Deuteronomy 6:10–11 confirms that the Israelites left most of the land intact: "Great and flourishing cities that you did not build; houses filled with every good thing that you did not provide; wells that you did not dig; and vineyards and olive trees that you did not plant."

Another reason we believe Joshua's invasion wasn't wholesale destruction is that Canaanite cities were armed fortresses. In addition, in this agricultural society, most people lived in the countryside. Joshua's targets weren't civilians but instead military strongholds. It's erroneous, therefore, to argue that Canaan's cities were teeming with thousands of people. Most were military outposts with only a handful of noncombatants. Thus, God's mandate for the Israelites to utterly defeat their enemies was aimed at military installations, officers, and leaders. The goal wasn't genocide or ethnic cleansing. Women and children were killed in these battles, but they weren't the targets.

Massive extermination was Israel's last resort. Note, for instance, that some enemies surrendered and were spared: Rahab and her family in Jericho (Joshua 6:25; cf. Hebrews 11:21; James 2:25), the

Gibeonites (Joshua 9:16–27), as well as some men from Bethel (Judges 1:22–26). Also of import is that for six days, Jericho's inhabitants could have joined Israel, but most didn't (Joshua 6).

Further evidence that Israel's conquest of Canaan wasn't a complete slaughter comes in Joshua 13:1: "Now Joshua was old and advanced in years, and Yahweh said to him, 'You are old and advanced in years, and there remains yet very *much land to possess*.'" This is why Judges 1:27–36 catalogs a number of Canaanites who were still alive after Joshua's death. In his farewell speech, Joshua warned the Israelites that enemies were still in the land (Joshua 23:7, 12–13; cf. Joshua 15:63; 16:10; 17:13; Judges 2:20–23).

Deuteronomy 7 likewise teaches that a number of Canaanites survived Israel's blitzkrieg. Deuteronomy 7:2 commands Israel to completely destroy the Canaanites, while Deuteronomy 7:3–5 warns the people not to intermarry with them. Which is it? Obliterate or not engage in intermarriage? Deuteronomy 7:5 gets at the heart of the issue—destroy pagan images, altars, and sacred sites. Exodus 34:10–13 is similar. The point? Eradicating Canaanite religion was more important than eradicating the Canaanites themselves.

The same features appear in 1 Samuel 15, where, on the surface, it appears that Saul completely annihilated the Amalekites. Note, however, that the Amalekites appear later in the biblical record (e.g., 1 Samuel 27:8; 30:1, 17, 18; 1 Chronicles 4:43). Moreover, the wicked Haman in the book of Esther is an Agagite, which connects him with the Amalekites (Esther 3:10; 1 Samuel 15:8). How did Haman appear in Esther if all his ancestors were wiped out? Just like Joshua, Saul convincingly defeated his enemies. He didn't kill every man, woman, and child.

Here's what happened in the book of Joshua: The Israelites scored a number of convincing defeats over their armed enemies. Israel's main objective, though, was to uproot and tear down Canaanite worship sites and their paraphernalia. Unlike other ancient Middle Eastern nations that went to war to secure possessions and slaves, Israel rejected the violence-for-riches model. Instead, when attacking Jericho, they were to give everything to Yahweh (Joshua 7:1). Only later were they allowed by Yahweh to take some plunder.

These were, at their core, spiritual battles. The strategy wasn't to hunt down and kill every last Canaanite. God primarily directed Israel to "drive out" Canaanites—to rid the land of idolaters and their idols (Exodus 23:27–30). Territorial gain was never Israel's chief motivation to go to war.

Furthermore, Joshua's battles against the Canaanites were divine mandates for specific times and specific places. They were unrepeatable. None of them were intended to be universalized, much less normalized. God never gave the Israelites a blank check to kill wantonly.

The book of Joshua is a pivotal moment in history when judgment was being brought on the land and God's plans to save the whole world were being enacted. This required *herem* warfare (e.g., Judges 1:17). If Israel was to be contaminated by false worship and idolatry, they would be unable to fulfill their calling as God's missionaries to the world.

God's judgment of the Canaanites is thus one part of His plan to redeem people from the horror of human history. It's not indiscriminate violence. Yahweh doesn't delight in the death of the wicked

(Ezekiel 18:23), but He's not above getting His hands dirty to win back the world. Yahweh is anti-violence, but He's not *non*violent.

Cruelty isn't part of Yahweh's character; He's not like the Canaanite gods, who delight in human sacrifice. Instead, Yahweh is just, and He confronts evil with righteous judgment and sometimes overwhelming power. Yahweh won't allow rampant moral perversion to go unchecked.

It's not in God's nature to destroy but to redeem. He's not bloodthirsty, but neither will He sit by passively while evil destroys people. When God uses force, it's His last resort. He judges only with tears in His eyes, and it's always with a view toward future salvation.

SPIRITUAL BATTLES

Divine warfare (*herem*) in the OT was a spiritual undertaking. This is what Exodus 12:12 teaches, when God says, "I will strike all the firstborn in the land of Egypt, both man and beast; and on *all the gods of Egypt I* will execute judgments" (ESV). Accordingly, Moses' Song of the Sea (Exodus 15:1–18) not only celebrates Yahweh's triumph over Pharaoh and his armies but also has clear overtones of an even more profound and significant victory—the defeat of Egypt's gods and goddesses: "Who among the gods is like You, O Yahweh? Who is like You, majestic in holiness, awesome in glory, working wonders?" (Exodus 15:11). Deborah's song in the book of Judges likewise indicates that God's battles take place on two levels: one on earth (Judges 5:19) and the other in heaven (Judges 5:20)—with the spiritual dimension being the most important.

There are a number of additional passages that accentuate this spiritual feature of divine warfare. For instance, the Israelites ask God if they are to engage in war or not (2 Samuel 23:1–6); they spiritually prepare for battle (2 Samuel 11:13); leaders offer sacrifices before engaging in a military campaign (1 Samuel 13); people rely on God for the victory (e.g., Judges 6:16; 7:2; 1 Samuel 17:47); and after they defeat their enemies, the Israelites give thanks to God (Psalm 124). Additionally, while Isaiah teaches that God enacts vengeance—"His sword is all blood, it is gorged with fat" (Isaiah 34:6)—it's because He is "contending for Zion" (Isaiah 34:8). Without vengeance upon Israel's enemies, there can be no salvation for Israel. "Behold, your God will come with vengeance, with the retribution of God. He will come and save you" (Isaiah 35:4). What comes as Law for God's adversaries comes as Gospel for God's people.

We must note, however, that while the OT doesn't back down from God's wrath and judgment, its major accent is on His steadfast love and covenant faithfulness—for Israel and through Israel to the nations. Twenty-six times, Psalm 136 announces that divine mercy endures forever, while Psalm 30:5 celebrates that though Yahweh's judgment is for a moment, His favor lasts for a lifetime.

GOD'S JUSTICE

It's natural to ask if it was fair for God to execute divine judgment (*herem*) in the OT. But think about it. Who are we to judge the Judge? Who are we to put God on trial? God doesn't need to conform to our sense of justice. Instead, we need to conform to His. "All His ways are just" (Deuteronomy 32:4). To argue otherwise is to put ourselves above God—to insist that He must accommodate to our standards. It boils down to this question: Is God allowed to judge the world and determine the course of history? The answer, of course, is yes. Yahweh gives, and He takes away (Job 1:21).

When Adoni-bezek, who had cut off the thumbs and big toes of those captured in war, had the same done to him, he confessed, "God has repaid me for what I have done" (Judges 1:7). Though harsh in our eyes, divine vengeance is always right. "Yahweh is a God of justice" (Isaiah 30:18). Thus, God at times punished sin to avenge the victims who had been cruelly mistreated.

DIVINE WARFARE IN THE NEW TESTAMENT

Some teach that in the OT, God *allows* violence, but He doesn't command it. Until the coming of Christ, this argument goes as such: God puts up with Israel; He accommodates His people's ancient Middle Eastern context of bloodshed and battles; then, with the advent of Christ, God demonstrates His real nature—love, mercy, and kindness. Those advocating this interpretation point to this NT verse: "Where sin abounds, grace abounds all the more." (Romans 5:20). OT accommodation gives way to the NT's revelation. And what is that? "God is love" (1 John 4:8 ESV).

This approach fails to account for the fact that God pledges to judge the world through Christ (e.g., John 5:27; Acts 17:31). The "accommodation revelation" model also misses the point that Paul makes in Galatians 3:29—namely, that the baptized "belong to Abraham's seed, and are thus heirs according to the promise." As heirs of Abraham, Christians are heirs of Yahweh's promises of blessing *and* cursing. Recall these words: "I will bless those who bless you, and the one who treats you with contempt, I will curse" (Genesis 12:3).

It should not surprise us, therefore, that cursing enemies appears in many places in the NT (e.g., Acts 8:20, 13:10–11; 1 Corinthians 16:22; Galatians 5:12; 2 Timothy 4:14; Revelation 6:9–11; 14:19–20; 18:4–8, 20; 19:1–3, 15). The classic example comes in Galatians 1:8–9, where Paul invokes a curse (*anathema* in Greek) upon the enemies of the Gospel. (The term *anathema* is lexically and theologically equivalent to the Hebrew word *herem*). Paul, too, recognized God's fury in his day: "For God's wrath is revealed from heaven against all ungodliness and unrighteousness of people, who by their unrighteous behavior suppress the truth" (Romans 1:18). Standing in this same tradition, Jesus also uttered prayers of divine curses upon His enemies (e.g., Matthew 11:20–24; 23:13–39; Mark 11:14).

To be sure, Moses writes, "Yahweh is a man of war" (Exodus 15:3), but so is Jesus. On the Last Day, Christ "judges and makes war," is "dressed in a robe dipped in blood," and out of His mouth "comes a sharp sword with which to strike down the nations" (Revelation 19:11–15). In like manner, Paul, in 2 Thessalonians 1:6–9, describes Christ as dispensing vengeance when He returns.

None of these NT passages are anomalies. God's judgment appears throughout Paul's letters (e.g., Philippians 1:28; 1 Thessalonians 2:14–16). Luke, for his part, records God's act of killing Ananias and Sapphira (Acts 5:1–11). Jude, Christ's half brother, taught that Jesus destroyed unbelieving Israelites after the exodus (Jude 5). And Peter warns about God's coming judgment (2 Peter 2:4–22).

Clearly, there's continuity between warfare texts in the OT and NT. There's also discontinuity. The baptized are never called to resort to physical violence. *Never*. Jesus told Peter, "Put your sword back into its place. For all who take the sword will perish by the sword" (Matthew 26:52 ESV). Our spiritual battle isn't with "flesh and blood" (Ephesians 6:12). Rather, our fight is "against the rulers, against the authorities, against the cosmic powers over this present darkness" (Ephesians 6:12 ESV). These supernatural enemies are conquered with "the sword of the Spirit, which is the word of God" (Ephesians 6:17 ESV). Scripture is our weapon, prayer is our power, and love is our language. We defend biblical truth "with gentleness and respect" (1 Peter 3:15 ESV).

Christians aren't part of a theocracy—that is, we don't belong to a specific God-ordained nation. Instead, the church consists of people from every nation, language, tribe, and ethnicity. The baptized are "sojourners and exiles" (1 Peter 2:11) with no holy land to live or die for. God's final revelation is in Christ (Hebrews 1:1–2). God won't ever again commission His people to take up arms. *Ever*.

Why? Jesus defeated Satan and his minions not by killing but by being killed. Christ's losing was His winning. His defeat was His victory. Christ's resurrection on the third day announced His conquest over hell, sin, the devil, and the grave. "He [God] disarmed the rulers and authorities and put them to open shame, by triumphing over them in Him [Christ]" (Colossians 2:15 ESV). On the Last Day, Jesus will return to fully defeat all His foes. Then, He will be acclaimed "King of kings and Lord of lords" (Revelation 19:16 ESV).

CONCLUSIONS

Israel's battles with the Canaanites were one-time, divinely directed events. They didn't become the nation's paradigm for subsequent treatment of other countries. The book of Joshua never became the model for warfare. Note, for instance, what Leviticus 19:34 teaches about non-Israelites living among God's people: "You must treat the stranger who sojourns with you as the native among you, and you must love him as yourself, for you were strangers in the land of Egypt: I am Yahweh your God."

This verse doesn't come out of the blue. Abraham's offspring were commissioned to bring divine blessings to all the families of the earth (Genesis 12:3). That's why a "mixed multitude" came out of Egypt (Exodus 12:38) and why Moses wasn't afraid to marry a Cushite (Numbers 12:1). God frequently commanded His people to have compassion on non-Israelites (e.g., Deuteronomy 10:18–19). "You shall have the same rule for the sojourner and for the native, for I am Yahweh your God" (Leviticus 24:22). Foreigners could even participate in Israel's worship life (Numbers 9:14). Non-Israelites—Jethro, Ruth, Naaman, and all of the Ninevites in the book of Jonah—became believers in the one true God. Prophetic texts are replete with God's plan to save all the nations (e.g., Isaiah 2:1–4; 65:17–25; Micah 4:1–4).

The book of Job provides a helpful way to conclude this chapter. As the book begins, God lifts the curtains and we see the invisible spirit world, where, behind the scenes, God and Satan are conversing about Job's faith. Satan wagers that if God removes His gifts from Job's life, Job will curse Him.

We're aware of this discussion in heaven between God and Satan. But Job? He has no clue. When all hell breaks loose, Job repeatedly and with increasing intensity cries out, "God, where are You?"

Like Job, there's a chasm between our knowledge of God and His decisions, especially in the sphere of OT *herem* warfare. And just as God appeals to Job to trust and believe, He likewise invites us to follow. Like Job, then, we put a hand over our mouth (Job 40:4) and instead marvel at the richness and mystery of God's inscrutable plans. "God moves in a mysterious way His wonders to perform; He plants His footsteps on the sea and rides upon the storm" (*LSB* 765:1).

DISCUSSION QUESTIONS

1. How does Exodus 15:3 summarize this chapter?
2. Why are Genesis 12:3 and 15:16 so important in the discussion about divine violence in the OT?
3. What are the continuities between divine warfare in the OT and the NT? What are the discontinuities?
4. How does the Bible portray the spiritual component of both OT and NT warfare?

CHAPTER 6

HOW SHOULD WE UNDERSTAND FIGURATIVE NUMBERS IN THE OLD TESTAMENT?

"A thousand years in
Your sight are like a day that
has just passed."
(Psalm 90:4)

Numbers are used in daily life for many purposes. Often, they are meant to denote actual quantities and precise measurements. The number of dollars in your bank account is not an estimate or a rough indication of your money on deposit; it is exact. The numbers of days in a month, months in a year, years in a century are precise. At other times, numbers are not meant to be exact but are approximations. We often use such estimates when speaking about the population of a city or country or about someone's annual income. However, sometimes numbers are used for rhetorical effect and are not intended as either exact or approximate figures. We have a variety of such uses in common English parlance, as in these idioms:

- *In one piece*—whole and unharmed
- *Go back to square one*—at the beginning again
- *Once in a blue moon*—infrequently
- *Three sheets to the wind*—intoxicated
- *Six ways to Sunday*—in every possible way or every direction (an Americanism)
- *Dressed to the nines*—dressed very smartly, flamboyantly, or fashionably
- *Nine times out of ten*—something very likely or commonly occurring
- *At the eleventh hour*—almost too late
- *Feel like a million dollars*—feeling very good
- *One in a million*—something exceedingly rare

However, it is more difficult to recognize such expressions in languages other than our native tongue since they are not using the words literally.

Numbers can also have an important symbolic or emblematic significance. The number seven serves this way for us. We speak of seven continents, though the seven is arbitrary. Europe and Asia are clearly part of the same land mass. Greenland is a large land mass, but it is considered part of North America. We also speak of seven colors of the rainbow, though this, too, is rather arbitrary since the several colors blend into one another and are not strictly different (e.g., indigo and violet). Throughout history, various cultures have spoken of "the seven seas." This is usually taken to mean the Arctic, North Atlantic, South Atlantic, North Pacific, South Pacific, Indian, and Southern oceans. However, this requires splitting both the Atlantic and Pacific oceans into two sections. Moreover, it appears more than a little arbitrary to delineate the Atlantic and Pacific oceans from the Arctic and Southern oceans. This points to the emblematic power of seven in our thought.

Other numbers can also be used this way. It is not unusual to hear or read the expression "the four winds" based on the idea of the four cardinal directions. Yet winds rarely come out of the direct north, south, east, or west. Moreover, it is arbitrary to assign four cardinal directions. Why not six or eight? We also speak of four seasons, though the changes in weather, animal behavior, and plant life are often not so stark as to clearly delineate one season from the other. For instance, we think of bird migration as happening in the spring and fall, although some birds, such as many shorebirds, begin their southern migration in midsummer.

It should not surprise us that numbers were used rhetorically and symbolically among the ancient Israelites as well. Let us examine some of these rhetorical and symbolic uses of numbers in the OT.

NUMBERS AS RHETORIC AND SYMBOL

SEVEN

In the OT, seven has significance primarily because of the seven days of the creation week (Genesis 1:1–2:3). Thus, seven and its multiples, especially fourteen, are often used for rhetorical and symbolic purposes and are especially connected with OT worship.

Perhaps the Bible's first rhetorical use of *seven* occurs already in Genesis 4 when God places a mark on Cain and vows, "Anyone who kills Cain will suffer vengeance seven times over" (Genesis 4:14). Seven here is a rhetorical device signifying the ultimate vengeance, since it is obvious that Cain could not be avenged by killing his murderer seven times.

At Ruth 4:15, the women of Bethlehem tell Naomi that her daughter-in-law Ruth is worth more to her than seven sons. As Ruth had only two sons, both of whom had passed away, this is clearly a rhetorical use to imply that Ruth is worth more than any number of sons. Similarly, in her song of praise, Hannah declares that the barren woman has borne seven sons, even though she had borne only one (Samuel) at that time (1 Samuel 2:5).

The book of Proverbs uses the number seven rhetorically several times to signal completeness or comprehensiveness. The first is Proverbs 9:1: "Wisdom has built her house; she has carved out her seven pillars." Here, wisdom's house is the earth, and the seven pillars rhetorically signal that wisdom's domain is throughout the world.

Later, at Proverbs 24:16, we read: "Though a righteous person may fall seven times, he will get up, while wicked people will stumble in misfortune." Seven is used here to signal that the righteous person will always get up, in contrast to wicked people who will not.

Another proverb employs seven in a similar way: "A lazy person considers himself wiser than seven people who answer sensibly" (Proverbs 26:16). Thus, the lazy person thinks he is wiser than everyone who "answers sensibly."

All of these are rhetorical uses of the number seven. This can be seen in the fact that none of them can be easily explained by positing seven literal items or occurrences for each. Wisdom's house could just as easily be said to have a different number of columns, but the author chose seven. If a righteous person stumbles for the eighth time, will he get up? Seven is not the limit but a rhetorical use. Does the lazy person think he is wiser than seven people but not eight? Obviously, that is not what the proverb implies.

The prophets also use the number seven rhetorically. Isaiah prophesied:

> Moonlight will be as bright as sunlight, and the sunlight will be seven times brighter—like the light of seven days—on the day that Yahweh bandages His people's injuries and heals the wounds He inflicted. (Isaiah 30:26)

This rhetorical use not only uses seven to signal the meaning "as bright as possible," but it also reminds readers of the seven-day creation period.

Jeremiah prophesied: “The mother of seven has become exhausted. She breathed her last breath. Her sun set while it was still day. She was ashamed and humiliated” (Jeremiah 15:9). His prophecy says that even the strongest of women would falter when Jerusalem fell to the Babylonians.

Important symbolic uses of seven include Abraham’s giving seven ewe lambs to Abimelech to confirm his treaty with him (Genesis 21:28–30); Jacob bowing to Esau seven times (Genesis 33:3); the seven years of plenty and seven years of famine in Egypt, which demonstrate God’s control over His creation (Genesis 41); Joseph mourning the death of Jacob for seven days (Genesis 50:10); each new high priest wearing Aaron’s robes for seven days (Exodus 29:30–35); and seven priests with seven trumpets marching around Jericho (Joshua 6). Samson used seven in a symbolic way twice to deceive Delilah, with the seven denoting a complete loss of his superhuman strength (Judges 16:7, 8, 13, 14). When Delilah finally learned of the importance of Samson’s hair, she shaved off seven locks, perhaps superstitiously invoking the symbolism of the number seven (Judges 16:19).

Additionally, Elisha told Naaman to wash himself seven times in the Jordan River to be cleansed from his leprosy (2 Kings 5:10–14). God could have cured Naaman with only one washing, but seven was symbolically important in signaling God’s complete power over His creation. This contrasted to the powerlessness in all the false gods of the nations, a fact that Naaman acknowledged (2 Kings 5:15).

Zechariah saw a vision of a lampstand with seven lamps, with each lamp having seven spouts (Zechariah 4:2). These seven were explained to him as symbolizing the eyes of Yahweh that scan the entire earth, referencing God's complete knowledge of everything in the world.

Seven is used with symbolic import frequently in worship. This is seen already in Genesis 7, when Noah was told to take seven pairs of clean (i.e., sacrificial) animals onto the ark seven days before the flood began (Genesis 7:2–4, 10). In fact, the sacrifice of seven, or multiples of seven, animals for invoking God or celebrating special occasions is very common in the OT (e.g., Numbers 23:1, 4, 14, 29; 28:11, 19, 21, 27, 29; 29:2, 4, 8, 10, 13, 15, 17, 20, 23, 26, 29, 32, 36; 2 Chronicles 13:9; 15:11; 29:21; 30:24; Job 42:8). Special religious feasts lasted seven days (1 Kings 8:65; 2 Chronicles 7:8), including the Feast of Unleavened Bread (Exodus 12:15, 19; 13:6, 7; 23:15; 34:18; Numbers 28:17; Deuteronomy 16:3) and the Feast of Booths (Leviticus 23:34; Deuteronomy 16:13). Cleansing from sin with the blood of a sacrifice was accomplished by the high priests sprinkling it seven times (Leviticus 4:6, 17; 14:7, 27; 16:14, 19; Numbers 19:4).

Seven is also connected with the dates for Israelite festivals. Passover was celebrated on the fourteenth day of the first month (Exodus 12:6, 18; Leviticus 23:5; Numbers 9:2–3; 28:16). The Day of Atonement was celebrated in the seventh month (Leviticus 16:29; 23:24, 27, 34, 39, 41).

Finally, the Israelites were to celebrate special years in multiples of seven (Leviticus 25). The sabbatical years, when the land would be left fallow, occurred every seven years. The Jubilee years, when slaves were freed and land was returned to its original families, occurred every seventh sabbatical year.

While not every occurrence of the number seven in the OT is rhetorical or symbolic, there are quite a few instances of such uses. Although not always immediately obvious to casual readers of the Bible, being aware of the symbolic importance of the number seven allows us to understand the message of God's Word more clearly.

TEN

While not as prominent as the number seven, ten is also an important number used rhetorically and symbolically in the OT. Unlike seven, which is clearly associated with creation, the origin of the emblematic use of the number ten is less obvious. Perhaps it also stems from Genesis 1, where "God said" is used ten times (Genesis 1:3, 6, 9, 11, 14, 20, 24, 26, 28, 29), while at other times, it seems as if it might originate from a full complement of ten digits on human hands.

There are several rhetorical uses of the number ten and its multiples in the OT. In Genesis 31:7, 41, Jacob complained that Laban changed his wages ten times. However, there is no record of ten such adjustments to Jacob's earnings. Instead, this is a rhetorical use meaning "many times." Similarly, in Numbers 14:22, God denied entry into the Promised Land to those who had tested Him ten times by not obeying. Other uses of ten or multiples of ten used for rhetorical purposes include the following:

- They blessed Rebekah, saying to her, "Our sister, may you become thousands upon ten thousands. May your offspring possess the city gates of his enemies." (Genesis 24:60)
- Five of you will pursue a hundred, and a hundred of you will pursue ten thousand. Your enemies will fall before you in combat. (Leviticus 26:8)

- When I cut off your supply of bread, ten women will bake your bread in a single oven. They will ration your bread by weight, so that you will eat but not be satisfied. (Leviticus 26:26)
- How could one pursue a thousand, or two put ten thousand to flight, unless their Rock had sold them, unless Yahweh had given them up? (Deuteronomy 32:30)
- He said, "From Sinai Yahweh came and dawned on them from Seir. He shone on them from Mount Paran and came with ten thousand holy ones, with lightning from His right hand for them." (Deuteronomy 33:2)
- "Hannah, why are you crying?" her husband Elkanah would ask. "Why won't you eat? Why are you troubled? Am I not better to you than ten sons?" (1 Samuel 1:8)
- The troops said [to David], "You must not go! If we have to flee, they will not pay any attention to us. Even if half of us die, they will not pay any attention to us because you are worth ten thousand of us. Therefore, it is better if you support us from the city." (2 Samuel 18:3)
- Though a thousand may fall at your side and ten thousand at your right hand, the pestilence will not reach you. (Psalm 91:7)
- Wisdom makes the wise person stronger than a city's ten rulers. (Ecclesiastes 7:19)
- My love is dazzling and ruddy, notable among ten thousand. (Song of Songs 5:10)

- A river of fire was flowing, coming out from His presence. Thousands upon thousands served Him; ten thousand times ten thousand stood in front of Him. (Daniel 7:10)

- Even if I were to write out for him ten thousand aspects of My teachings, they would be regarded as something strange. (Hosea 8:12)

- For the Lord God says: The city [whose troops] march out a thousand strong will have only a hundred left, and the one [whose troops] march out a hundred strong will have only ten left in the house of Israel. (Amos 5:3)

- Would Yahweh be pleased with thousands of rams or with ten thousand streams of oil? Should I give my firstborn for my transgression, the offspring of my body for my own sin? (Micah 6:7)

- Yahweh of armies says this: "In those days, ten men from nations of every language will grab the robe of a Jewish man tightly, begging, 'Let us go with you, because we have heard that God is with you.'" (Zechariah 8:23)

Ten is less common as a symbolic number in the OT, but there are a few instances of its symbolic use. Most notable are the Ten Commandments (Exodus 20; Deuteronomy 5). Interestingly, when God gave this all-inclusive compendium of His Law from Mount Sinai, He did not list it as ten sayings. However, later references to them in the OT count them as ten (Exodus 34:28; Deuteronomy 4:13; 10:4). This signals that they are a comprehensive summary of God's code for Israelite conduct.

Like seven, the number ten is occasionally used with symbolic importance when connected with Israelite worship. The Passover lamb was to be set aside on the tenth day of the first month (Exodus 12:3). The Day of Atonement was the tenth day of the seventh month (Leviticus 16:29; 23:27). The tabernacle was made with ten curtains, ten posts, and ten bases (Exodus 26:1; 27:12; 36:8, 12). And, of course, Israelite offerings were tithes—one tenth of their income (Genesis 11:35; 14:17–20; 28:22; Leviticus 27:30–33; Numbers 18:21–32; Deuteronomy 12:5–18).

OTHER NUMBERS

Seven and ten are the most prominent numbers used rhetorically or symbolically in the OT. Other numbers can occasionally occur in these senses. Like our four cardinal directions, the prophets occasionally refer to four corners of the earth or four winds rhetorically (Isaiah 11:12; Jeremiah 49:36; Ezekiel 7:2; 37:9; Zechariah 2:6). This may underlie the symbolism of the four living creatures with four faces and four wings in Ezekiel's visions (Ezekiel 1:4–28, 10:1–21). The number twelve often is a symbolic reference to Israel's twelve tribes, and this symbolism is frequently explained (e.g., Exodus 24:4; 28:21; 39:14; Joshua 4:8; 1 Kings 18:31). However, there are a few cases where the symbolism is implied only: twelve lions on the steps leading to Solomon's throne, symbolizing his authority over all Israel (1 Kings 10:20; 2 Chronicles 9:19), and twelve oxen supporting the basin in the courtyard of the temple in Jerusalem (1 Kings 7:25, 44; 2 Chronicles 4:4, 15; Jeremiah 52:20).

PILED-UP NUMBERS

There is another use of numbers for rhetorical purposes: the piling up of numbers in sequence, in parallel phrases, or in lines of poetry. There are two types of this use of numbers: sequential and parallel.

SEQUENTIAL

In sequential use of numbers, two numbers are simply placed in sequence, perhaps connected by the conjunction *or* or *and*. (In many cases, the numbers are simply juxtaposed without any linking conjunction in Hebrew. However, English versions add a conjunction as required by English usage.) This type of expression is common in English when we wish to give a rough estimate. For instance, when asked how long ago an event happened, if we cannot remember exactly, we might reply, "About two or three years ago."

Most commonly, the second number is one greater than the first number. The most common of these is found in the Ten Commandments section of Exodus and Deuteronomy:

> I, Yahweh your God, am a jealous God, dealing with the children for the fathers' iniquity to the third and fourth generations of those who hate Me. (Exodus 20:5; Deuteronomy 5:9; see also Exodus 34:7; Numbers 14:18)

Here, the use of "third and fourth generations" depicts a family living together that includes three generations (children, parents, grandparents) or, in the case of unusual longevity, four generations (including a great-grandparent). If the children follow the example of their ancestors' rejection of God, they, too, will be punished.

However, God, in His grace, promises otherwise for those who turn to Him and love Him: "But showing faithful love to thousands, to those who love Me and keep My commands" (Exodus 20:6).

Here are two more well-known examples:

- The one condemned to die is to be executed on the testimony of two or three witnesses. No one is to be executed on the testimony of a single witness. (Deuteronomy 17:6)
- One witness cannot establish any iniquity or sin against a person, whatever that person has done. A fact must be established by the testimony of two or three witnesses. (Deuteronomy 19:15; see also Matthew 18:16; 2 Corinthians 13:1; 1 Timothy 5:19; Hebrews 10:28)

Clearly, "two or three" indicates an indefinite, small number but emphasizes that a single witness is not sufficient evidence to convict someone of a crime.

As in English, this type of expression can be used to express an approximate number:

- He looked up at the window and said, "Who is on my side? Who?" Two or three eunuchs looked down at him. (2 Kings 9:32)
- But there are many people, and it is the rainy season. We don't have the stamina to stay out in the open. This isn't something that can be done in a day or two, for we have sinned greatly in this matter. (Ezra 10:13)

- Once or twice the merchants and those who sell all kinds of goods spent the night outside Jerusalem. (Nehemiah 13:20)
- As Jehudi would read three or four columns, Jehoiakim would cut the scroll with a scribe's knife and throw the columns into the fire in the hearth until the entire scroll was burned up in the hearth. (Jeremiah 36:23)
- See also Judges 5:30; 2 Kings 6:10; 13:19; Job 33:29; Ecclesiastes 11:2; Ezekiel 21:14; Amos 4:8.

PARALLEL

In parallel use of two numbers, one occurs in a phrase or in a line of poetry, and a larger one occurs in a parallel phrase or line of poetry. (Scholars often call this a "graded numerical saying.") Sometimes, the second number is ten times larger than the first:

> As they danced, the women sang to each other, "Saul has killed his thousands, but David his tens of thousands." Saul was furious and disliked this song. "They credited tens of thousands to David," he complained, "but they only credited me with thousands. What more can he have but the kingdom?" (1 Samuel 18:7–8; see also 1 Samuel 21:11; 29:5)

The pairing of thousands and ten thousands is common in this type of expression and is simply designed to convey large numbers. The numbers are meant to be rhetorical, not literal. (See Psalm 91:7; 144:13; Micah 6:7, where the sequence is clearly intended to mean "very many.") King Saul would have been offended, however, by being put on the same level as his subject David, a commander in his army. This led him to take the numbers as indicating David's victories were more celebrated than his own. Saul's reaction signals the beginning of his hostility toward David.

The pair is reversed in Deuteronomy 33:17, the only time a larger number precedes a smaller one:

> His firstborn bull has splendor, and horns like those of a wild ox; he gores all the peoples with them to the ends of the earth. Such are the ten thousands of Ephraim, and such are the thousands of Manasseh. (Deuteronomy 33:17)

The reversal is striking since no other use of dual numbers does this. It is an intentional inversion of the numbers so that the reader might recall Jacob's blessing on the two sons of Joseph, Manasseh and Ephraim (Genesis 48:13–20). Joseph wished the older son, Manasseh, to receive a greater blessing. However, Jacob pronounced the greater blessing on Ephraim. Both tribes would become very large and influential, but Ephraim would outstrip Manasseh.

Deuteronomy 32:30 also uses the thousands/ten thousands pattern but combines it with another pattern: a number followed by a number one greater. It does this in two pairs, with one and thousands followed by two and ten thousands:

> How could one pursue a thousand, or two put ten thousand to flight, unless their Rock had sold them, unless Yahweh had given them up? (Deuteronomy 32:30)

Here, Israel's overwhelming military victories are credited to God, who allows a few to rout many.

There is only one case where the second number is increased by ten over the first:

> Our lives span seventy years or, if we are strong, eighty years. Even the best of them are struggles and sorrows; indeed, they pass quickly, and we fly away. (Psalm 90:10)

This verse sets forth the seeming limits on longevity for the typical person: seventy or eighty years is what one can expect. However, as with other uses of rhetorical numbers, they are generalizations and not intended to be read as strict limits. Many die before reaching their seventieth birthday, and a few live past their eightieth birthday.

Also, there is one instance where the second number is eleven times the first:

> If Cain would have been avenged seven times, then Lamech [will be avenged] seventy-seven times. (Genesis 4:24)

Here, Lamech was bragging to his wives that he could get away with murder like his ancestor Cain, even increasing the number that God gave to Cain by a factor of eleven (see Genesis 4:15).

The most common form of parallel numbers is a saying that contains a number in one line and a number that is one greater in the next line:

- Return, faithless children—(this is) Yahweh's declaration—for I am your master, and I will take you, one from a city and two from a family, and I will bring you to Zion. (Jeremiah 3:14)

- He will revive us after two days, and on the third day He will raise us, so we can live in His presence. (Hosea 6:2)
- When Assyria invades our land, when it tramples our fortresses, we will raise against it seven shepherds, even eight leaders of men. (Micah 5:5)

Note the various uses of this rhetorical device. In Jeremiah, it signals "a few from here and a few from there." Hosea used it to speak of the same day twice. Two days after today is the third day, counting inclusively. Micah employs the seven-eight pair to say that God will raise up a number of leaders to rescue His people from the Assyrians.

Isaiah used pairs of consecutive numbers:

> Only gleanings will be left in it [Israel], like an olive tree that had been beaten—two or three olives at the very top of the tree, four or five on its fruitful branches. [This is] the declaration of Yahweh, the God of Israel. (Isaiah 17:6)

Isaiah's two-three and four-five parallels signal the devastation of Israel when God allows their enemies to invade and wreak havoc in their land. They will be like an already-harvested olive tree that has only a few olives remaining, hardly worth the effort to harvest.

Perhaps Amos, among all the prophets, makes the most dramatic use of this figure of speech. The first two chapters of his book contain eight oracles of judgment against various nations. Each oracle begins similarly, with a parallel number:

> Thus says Yahweh: "For three crimes of Damascus, and for four, I will not revoke punishment, because they have threshed Gilead with threshing sledges of iron." (Amos 1:3)

Similar opening statements are found at Amos 1:6 (Gaza); 1:9 (Tyre); 1:11 (Edom); 1:13 (Ammon); 2:1 (Moab); 2:4 (Judah); 2:6 (Israel). Interestingly, though Amos indicts each nation for three or four crimes, he does not go on to list that many accusations against each one. For Amos, this is a simple rhetorical device that emphasizes each nation's heinous crimes.

The phrase "for three . . . and for four" also indicates Yahweh's long-suffering; He seeks to postpone the judgment as long as possible. Yahweh is "slow to anger and abounding in steadfast love" (Exodus 34:6). His first priority is to forgive sins; He desires to put off the Judgment Day as long as possible. However, Genesis 15:16 indicates that—although Yahweh is very patient—He does have a limit. When a quota of sins is reached, Yahweh changes from forbearance to wrath.

While Amos does not list three or four crimes for each nation, some uses of numbers in parallel include a list, and it always contains as many items as the larger number. An example is Job 5:19–26:

> From six troubles He [God] will deliver you; in seven no evil shall touch you. During famine He will redeem you from death, and in war from the power of the sword. You shall be hidden from the spiteful gossip and will not fear destruction when it comes. You will laugh at destruction and hunger and will not fear wild animals. For you will

> have a covenant with the stones of the field, and the wild animals will be at peace with you. You will know that your tent is secure, and you will inspect your home, and nothing will be missing. You will also know that your offspring will be many, and your descendants like the earth's grass. You will come to your grave at a ripe old age, like a stack of sheaves harvested in season.

This saying lists seven ways God provides protection and security:

- Safety from misfortunes that affect entire populations—famine and war
- Safety from verbal attacks that turn into physical harm
- Safety from misfortunes that affect individuals—hunger and attack by wild animals
- Safety when away from home
- Safety when at home
- Many children
- Long life

A second numerical parallel in Job:

> For God speaks in one way, and in two, though man
> does not perceive it. (Job 33:14)

The two ways that God speaks are discussed in the following verses: dreams (Job 33:15–18) and sickness (Job 33:19–22).

The final parallel in Job:

> Then Job answered Yahweh: I'm so insignificant. How can I answer you? I've put my hand over my mouth. I have spoken once, and I will not reply; twice, but now I can add nothing. (Job 40:3–5)

What are the two times when Job spoke to God that he now realizes were inappropriate challenges to God? Job cursed the day of his birth (Job 3:1–26), challenging God's wisdom in even allowing him to be born. This challenge comes at the beginning of the poetical discourses in Job 3–39. Later, at Job 29:1–31:40, Job recalled his former way of life, compared it to his present state of suffering, and surveyed a catalog of sins he did not commit. He challenged God's wisdom in allowing him to suffer. After this, Job no longer spoke until Job 40:3–5. Thus, the two challenges to God come from Job's first and last words in the poetic section of the book.

One parallel numeric saying is found in Psalms:

> God has spoken once; twice I have heard this: strength belongs to God, and to You, my Lord, belongs faithful love, for You repay each according to his works. (Psalm 62:11–12)

The two items here are sayings: "strength belongs to God" and "to You, my Lord, belongs faithful love." David notes God's power to punish evildoers and His faithful love toward believers.

Proverbs contains a number of these sayings. The first is in Proverbs 6:16–19:

> The Lord hates six things; seven are detestable to Him: arrogant eyes, a lying tongue, hands that shed innocent

> blood, a heart that plots wicked schemes, feet eager to run into evil, a dishonest witness who gives false testimony, and someone who stirs up trouble among brothers.

Notice that the first five all involve body parts: eyes, tongue, hands, heart, feet. The last two reference persons who commit abhorrent acts. Thus, Solomon here plays on four numbers—two of them explicit, six and seven, and two implied, five and two.

Finally, in Proverbs 30, we find four of these sayings, all involving the three-four pair. The first instance is in Proverbs 30:

> Three things are never satisfied; four never say, "Enough!": Sheol; a childless womb; earth, which is never satisfied with water; and fire, which never says, "Enough!" (Proverbs 30:15–16)

The first three items are indeed distressing—Sheol is the place where the dead are, but it never fills. A childless woman who wishes to be a mother is frustrated (e.g., Sarah, Hannah). A parched, dry ground in an arid land never seems to get enough water. But the most devastating is the last—fire will never be quenched as long as it has fuel and oxygen. This last is so terrible because elsewhere in Proverbs, fire can signify a quarrel (Proverbs 26:20, 21). Some quarrels become grudges that feed on themselves like a fire feeding on fuel.

The next numerical parallel follows a few verses later:

> Three things are amazing to me; four I can't understand: the way of an eagle in the sky, the way of a snake on a rock, the way of a ship at sea, and the way of a man with a young woman. (Proverbs 30:18–19)

The first three "ways" are all locomotion without legs—something that, in many ways, causes wonder and amazement when observed. The final, however, is the most mysterious: the attraction and love between two young people that can be experienced but is impossible to fully explain.

The third saying continues in the next several verses:

> The earth trembles under three things; it cannot bear up under four: a servant when he becomes king, a fool when he is stuffed with food, an unloved woman when she marries, and a servant girl when she ousts her queen. (Proverbs 30:21–23)

The four people here can all be unbearable. A servant—perhaps a slave—who becomes king seems to be contrary to the established social order of the ancient Middle East. A fool whose appetite has been satisfied can freely spout his foolish thoughts and foist them on others without fear of being deprived. A third unbearable situation, filled with pathos, is a woman—a servant girl—who discovers she is in a loveless marriage and has been from the beginning. The final climactic unbearable situation is the servant (or slave) girl who ousts a queen. It upends the entire social order.

The final numerical parallel in Proverbs is as follows:

> Three things are stately in their stride, even four are stately in their walk: a lion, which is mightiest among beasts and doesn't retreat before anything, a strutting rooster or a goat, and a king at the head of his army. (Proverbs 30:29–31)

This is, perhaps, the most cleverly constructed of all the book's numerical sayings. The list is three-four: three animals followed by a person. However, it can also be seen as two-two, with the first and the last items containing an extended description and the middle two items being much shorter and connected by "or." Moreover, the first and last lines depict the most powerful, while the middle two lines present animals that can inflict damage if provoked but are far less dangerous. Once again, the final item in the list is the most important—just as one would not court danger from a lion or attack by a rooster or goat, one surely would not provoke a king presiding over his army.

Interestingly, among these four parallel numeric sayings, which each have a list of four items, there is another numeric saying with only the number four:

> Four things on earth are small, yet they are extremely wise: ants are not a strong community, yet they store their food in summer; hyraxes are not a mighty community, yet they make their homes in cliffs; locusts have no king, yet all of them march in ranks; you can catch a lizard in your hands, yet it lives in kings' palaces. (Proverbs 30:24–28)

Here, once again, the final item is the most important, and we have three animals followed by a person. The observations about ants, hyraxes, and locusts are interesting, but the lizard is the wisest: It can get into the palace to see the king, but most people cannot.

CONCLUSIONS

The OT contains many numbers that are to be understood literally. However, many other numbers are used rhetorically or symbolically and are not intended to be understood absolutely. The four items in the sayings of Proverbs 30 are not intended to be exhaustive lists but are simply three examples that lead up to a climactic fourth. The numbers seven and ten often have important symbolic significance, even when indicating a certain number of items, such as the seven times Naaman was to wash in the Jordan River. Understanding how Moses and the prophets use numbers can help us more fully understand the message and artistry found in their inspired writings. We find the same use by the hymnist: "A thousand ages in Thy sight are like an evening gone, short as the watch that ends the night before the rising sun." (*LSB* 733:4)

DISCUSSION QUESTIONS

1. How does Psalm 90:4 summarize this chapter?
2. What strikes you most about the number seven in general? The number seven in OT worship texts?
3. What do you think is the most significant symbolic use of the number ten in the OT?
4. How has this chapter sensitized you to the use of numbers in the OT?

CHAPTER 7

DOES GOD SUFFER IN THE OLD TESTAMENT?

"Yahweh regretted that He made human beings on the earth, and His heart felt deep, piercing sorrow."
(Genesis 6:6)

For many, the God of the OT is detached, removed, and above it all. And, if Yahweh does get involved, it appears that, more often than not, He comes with wrath and indignation. Therefore, the title of this chapter may intrigue you. Does Yahweh, the God of Abraham, Isaac, and Jacob, genuinely feel people's hurt and pain?

Indeed! God experiences great anguish when He looks at what happened to the world shortly after He created it (Genesis 6:6–7). Yahweh is sorry that He appointed Saul as Israel's king (1 Samuel 15:11, 35). At one point in the book of Zechariah, God says, "They will look upon Me, whom they have pierced" (Zechariah 12:10). God? Pierced with a spear? Note also Judges 10:11–13—a record of God's frustration with Israel, where He flatly states, "I will deliver them no more" (Judges 10:13). Yet Judges 10:16 goes on to record, "He became restless over the misery of Israel." Yahweh's heart is tender and compassionate. He becomes unsettled and anxious over the sin of His people. "How often they rebelled against Him in the wilderness and grieved Him in the wasteland!" (Psalm 78:40).

Divine pathos becomes even more vivid in Isaiah 63:9, "In all their distress He was distressed." In the next verse, we read of how Israel's rebellion "grieved His Holy Spirit" (Isaiah 63:10). The term for "grieved" is the same word that appears in Genesis 6:6, when God laments over humankind's waywardness. "Grief" likewise describes Eve's curse of pain during childbirth (Genesis 3:16), as well as Adam's curse of work by the sweat of his brow (Genesis 3:17). Do you see the connections? Humanity's suffering—ever since the fall in the Garden of Eden—falls upon God. Our pain is His pain.

It's hardly surprising that Israel's authors employ images like husbands and wives, as well as parents and children, to describe God's pain, loss, and grief. To further our case in this chapter—that we are to take divine pathos seriously—we begin with some comments about emotions as they are understood in Israel's sacred texts.

EMOTIONS IN THE OLD TESTAMENT

Is it wise to investigate how God's feelings are expressed in the OT? After all, there are no Hebrew terms that are exact equivalents to the English words *feelings* or *emotions*. Consider, for instance, the Hebrew word for love. Unlike English definitions for love, the Hebrew verb *ahav* doesn't normally refer to having a visceral feeling; instead, it most often means making a commitment to a covenant (e.g., Deuteronomy 6:5–8). "Love" in the OT, then, describes actions more than it does emotions, although it can at times have an emotional component (Exodus 21:5; 1 Samuel 18:1, 20, 28).

Here's another example. The Hebrew word for "heart" usually emphasizes a person's mental and rational capacities, but often with an underlying emotional factor. Most of the time, we employ "heart" especially to describe our feelings. "She broke my heart." Hebrew, however, emphasizes rational thought, as when David told Solomon, "For Yahweh searches all hearts and understands every plan and thought" (1 Chronicles 28:9; see also Genesis 6:5).

It follows that, on the one hand, transposing our emotional categories upon Hebrew words runs the risk of cultural transfer. On the other hand, it's equally inaccurate to argue that because our culture and language are different from Israel's, there are no connections whatsoever between the words we use to describe feelings and the words ancient Hebrew authors employed. A middle ground is the best approach—an acknowledgment of both our emotional dissimilarities and similarities with the OT.

Certainly, Hebrews could talk about emotions. *Kidneys* is one of their most frequently used words—what we might call our gut. The Hebrew term *kilyah* is the seat of emotions and is often translated in the ESV as "heart" (e.g., Psalms 16:7; 73:21; Job 19:27) or "inmost being" (Proverbs 23:16). In other texts, *kilyah* is rendered "stomach"—that is, where feelings reside.

It's incorrect, therefore, to say that the OT is nonemotional—or, still less, anti-emotional. Any connections we make, of course, will contain a certain amount of slippage between the original texts and our words—as does every translational and interpretive endeavor.

THE ANTHROPOMORPHIC INTERPRETATION

Having dispelled the idea that it's improper to investigate what the OT says about feelings, let's now dive into the heart of the issue. Does Yahweh really suffer and feel heartache? We're confronted with two interpretive options.

The first is to maintain that, because Yahweh is absolutely transcendent, He stands outside the world. Therefore, passages describing God as grieving, suffering, or in pain must be considered metaphorical and symbolic. In these passages, God inspires OT authors to describe Him employing human categories. These parts of the OT use vivid language to depict Yahweh's emotions, but they don't describe what's really going on with God—only how He appears.

The verse might say that God is weeping, hurting, and aching, but He's really not. God condescends to the human level so as to communicate with us. This divine accommodation is often called anthropomorphism. God just *looks* like He feels pain.

Advocates for this approach quickly point out that, in most cases, God communicates using words literally. He loves Israel (Jeremiah 31:3). He is Spirit (Psalm 51:11). He is eternal (Psalm 90:2). God is holy (Isaiah 6:3). God literally created the heavens and the earth, spoke to Moses from a burning bush, parted the Red Sea, and inspired prophets to write His Word. Yet when the OT speaks of God suffering, anthropomorphic proponents argue that it doesn't depict reality.

How did this reading of divine pathos come to dominate the church's understanding of Yahweh? We can blame the Greeks.

THE INFLUENCE OF GREEK THOUGHT

Plato (ca. 427–348 BC) put forth the idea that the deity is static, unchanging, and unable to suffer. Early Christian leaders, wanting to distinguish the God of Abraham, Isaac, and Jacob from the irrational behavior of the gods and goddesses of paganism, embraced Plato's argument. By the fourth century AD, the church began to deny that the God of the OT has emotions. After all, feelings would interrupt God's eternal tranquility and perfect serenity. Further, empathy would incapacitate God; He wouldn't be able to pursue His plan to redeem the world through His Son, Jesus. Suffering would cripple God as God. It must be, the argument concludes, that since God is a perfect being and suffering is a sign of imperfection, God cannot and will not ever suffer. God is impassible. He is unable to experience angst and agony.

More and more, official church teaching—influenced by Platonism—insisted that God's perfection entails perfect reason devoid of feelings. The mind became everything. The heart and its emotions counted for little or nothing.

This doctrine went hand in glove with the church's growing tendency to teach that feelings are compulsive and uncontrollable forces, that they have a negative impact on reason, that they're blind, irrational forces. Emotions are wild animals that must be domesticated and controlled. It's best to keep them in check. The virtuous Christian life was defined by an emotionless life, just as Plato and the Greek Stoics insisted. Feelings? They inhibit right thinking, right action, and right living. The conclusion? If the OT depicts God as experiencing pain, it can't be literal.

This interpretation believes that God is loving and compassionate and that He actively intervenes to relieve suffering throughout the OT—but He Himself doesn't feel pain or any sorrow. After all, as adherents of this position point out, Israel's Scriptures teach that God doesn't change (Psalm 102:27; cf. Hebrews 13:8; James 1:17). It's therefore impossible to think that Yahweh has emotions that come and go in response to situations. "I Yahweh do not change" (Malachi 3:6).

OUR INTERPRETATION

There's another way to interpret OT texts that exhibit divine pain and suffering. This approach also believes Yahweh is completely transcendent—over, above, and apart from creation. The seraphim in Isaiah's vision call Him "holy, holy, holy" (Isaiah 6:3). But Yahweh is also immanent—present in creation and intimately involved with it. He walks in the Garden of Eden looking for Adam (Genesis 3:8). When the tower of Babel was complete, "Yahweh descended to see the city and the tower" (Genesis 11:5). He also comes down to Jacob at Bethel (Genesis 28:10–18), then again at Peniel (Genesis 32:22–30). Yahweh meets Moses in the burning bush (Exodus 3:1–14) and on Mount Sinai "in fire" (Exodus 19:18). Exodus 24:17 is even more explicit: "The appearance of Yahweh's glory was like a devouring fire on the top of the mountain in the sight of the people of Israel." Divine glory descends into the tabernacle (Exodus 40:34) as well as Solomon's temple (1 Kings 8:10–11). Yahweh is involved in the world that He made.

And when God comes down, people aren't only impacted by Him. God is also impacted by people. To be sure, Yahweh's characteristics are unchangeable. He is forever eternal, holy, loving, all-powerful, and the like. Yet Yahweh also feels pain, rejection, and heartache.

We appreciate the early church fathers who, when making their case against pagan myths, argued for the complete otherness of the triune God. However, in order to accentuate God's sovereign majesty and holiness, these teachers of the faith went too far when they argued that, unlike the pagan gods who acted like people, the true God doesn't possess feelings like affliction and misery.

There's a better explanation. Instead of embracing the idea that emotional descriptions of God are anthropomorphic—human ideas projected onto God—the reverse is true. Emotions and feelings of suffering begin with God, not people. We have emotions because God created us in His image and likeness (Genesis 1:26–27). Emotions are God's idea, not ours. Feelings start with God, not us.

We have no need to force Greek philosophical constructs upon the OT by invoking terms like *metamorphic* or *anthropomorphic*. Yahweh exhibits a vast array of emotions in the Hebrew Scriptures, including feeling the pain of His people.

DIVINE PATHOS IN EXODUS

Exodus 2 concludes with these words: "God heard their groaning, and God remembered His covenant with Abraham, Isaac, and Jacob. God looked upon the Israelites, and God took notice of them" (Exodus 2:24–25a). Then, these words: "And God knew" (Exodus 2:25b). God knew what? Among other things, God *knew* the pain of His people (Exodus 3:7). In the context of Exodus 3:7, the verb *knew* denotes more than "to be aware of." Instead, it means Yahweh was involved in, engaged in, and experienced Israel's sufferings. How can we be so sure? "God called to him *from the bush* saying, 'Moses! Moses!'" (Exodus 3:4).

Yahweh doesn't deal with Israel's suffering from a distance. He doesn't bark out orders like "My people will talk with your people." Yahweh doesn't issue an edict from on high. No. Yahweh sees and experiences suffering from the inside—the inside of a burning bush. He's the God of sorrows and is acquainted with grief. Yahweh demonstrates solidarity with the Israelites in their slavery. "I have come down to deliver them [the Israelites] out of the power of the Egyptians and to bring them up out of that land to a good and spacious land, a land flowing with milk and honey" (Exodus 3:8).

Although Yahweh is the Holy One of Israel and therefore transcendent, He's not so otherworldly that He is unmoved by human suffering. God chooses to become engaged in Israel's brokenness under Egyptian servitude. This doesn't render Him powerless. Far from it! It prompts Yahweh into action. Following His appearance to Moses in the burning bush, God unleashed ten plagues against Egypt, bringing the empire to its knees.

DIVINE PATHOS IN ISAIAH

Isaiah records Yahweh's suffering in several passages. The prophet's initial oracle sets the stage for divine pathos. "I have raised and reared sons, but they rebelled against Me" (Isaiah 1:2). Isaiah doesn't begin his book by depicting God's anger but instead by depicting God's sorrow—the sorrow of a Father whose children have forsaken and rejected Him. Yahweh isn't a general who has a difficult time with insubordination or a professor frustrated with unresponsive students. He's a long-suffering Father in great anguish over His wayward sons and daughters. "Israel does not know, My people do not understand" (Isaiah 1:3; cf. 30:1–14). This description of a Father and His rebellious children comes again toward the end of the book, when the prophet calls Yahweh "Father" (Isaiah 63:16; 64:8)—a title for God that appears only eight times in the OT.

Isaiah climactically describes God's grief in his Fourth Servant Song (Isaiah 52:13–53:12). Yahweh is the only person in Isaiah's book who is "high and lifted up" (Isaiah 6:1; 33:10; 57:15). It's therefore a stunning claim that the prophet depicts the Servant with the same words, "high and lifted up" (Isaiah 52:13). Yahweh and the Servant are united. What happens to one happens to the other.

Another stunning assertion is that God places humanity's sin and rebellion upon the Servant. "But in fact, He was pierced because of our rebellions, crushed because of our iniquities" (Isaiah 53:5).

Do you see the picture Isaiah is painting? The Servant, who is one with Yahweh—for both are high and lifted up—was fixed to a cross and pierced with a spear. A sponge was thrust into the Most High's face. Dice were tossed at His feet. The Most High bled. He sweat. He took the nails. This is what Paul teaches: "God was in Christ reconciling the world to Himself" (2 Corinthians 5:19). This is divine pathos at its pinnacle. "Well might the sun in darkness hide and shut His glories in when God, the mighty maker, died for His own creatures' sin" (*LSB* 437:3).

DIVINE PATHOS IN JEREMIAH

The motif of divine suffering appears even more frequently in Jeremiah. For instance, just as the lamenting Israelites asked questions like "How long?" "Why?" "How could you?" a similar divine lament appears when Yahweh asks, "What injustice did your fathers find in Me?" (Jeremiah 2:5). This is followed by a long list of accusations (Jeremiah 2:6–37). In other places, God asks, "How long will it be before you become clean?" (Jeremiah 13:27). Yahweh mourns, just like people do, when a relationship is broken.

In Jeremiah 2, we also learn that God suffers like a scorned husband as He watches His bride, Israel, chase after pseudolovers. Yahweh, like a jilted lover, states His case with the logic of a lawyer and with the longing of a broken heart:

- Has a nation changed its gods, even though they are not gods? (Jeremiah 2:11)
- Did you not bring this upon yourself by forsaking Yahweh your God, when He led you in the way? (Jeremiah 2:17)

- My people have forgotten Me for days without number. (Jeremiah 2:32)

Israel is indifferent, callous, apathetic, totally detached. God's people don't care that they don't care. Israel became like a stubborn animal, a wild vine, a rebellious camel, a thief caught in the act—even a nymphomaniac (Jeremiah 2:20–28). Yahweh is crushed.

Divine emotions are also on display in Jeremiah 31:20: "Is Ephraim My dear son? Is he My child in whom I delight?" Yahweh then shows His deep emotions for His people: "My *insides* are turbulent for him. I have great compassion for him." The term *insides* literally denotes the stomach, belly, or inner organs. Yahweh's emotions are off the charts. But they don't incapacitate Him. Instead, Yahweh's pain moves Him to turn His people's mourning into joy; He replaces their overwhelming sorrow with deep gladness (Jeremiah 31:13, 25).

Just like Yahweh, Jeremiah faced opposition from every quarter—family and friends (Jeremiah 11:18–23; 12:1–6), kings and their officials (Jeremiah 20:1–6; 26:1–24; 36:1–31), and even Judah's remnant (Jeremiah 42–44). The prophet felt like a lamb led to the slaughter (Jeremiah 11:19). Israel's rejection of Jeremiah mirrors their rejection of Yahweh. The two are one.

Take, for instance, this lament: "For the shattering of the daughter of my people I am shattered. I mourn, and dismay has seized me" (Jeremiah 8:21). Again, "Who will make my head water and my eyes a fountain of tears, that I might weep day and night for the slain of the daughter of my people" (Jeremiah 9:1). Who is weeping in these verses? Who is lamenting and wailing? The portrayal is intentionally ambiguous. Both Jeremiah and Yahweh cry. Both shed tears. Both suffer. Why the close connection? The prophet ate God's words (Jeremiah 15:16) and so incarnated the divine life.

When Israelites heard and saw Jeremiah, they heard and saw Yahweh. When the prophet was moved with the feelings of abandonment and rejection, he was reflecting God's emotions. Jeremiah revealed divine *pathos*.

Jeremiah and Yahweh are far from stoic. Rather, both are torn apart by human pain, and both burn with a loving desire to be reconciled with people. Both set aside detached, cerebral responses and are instead moved by tragedy and hardship. Yahweh doesn't only give Jeremiah words to speak. He also decrees that His prophet embody divine suffering.

DIVINE PATHOS IN HOSEA

This comingling between Yahweh and Jeremiah becomes most clear in the case of Hosea—a prophet who embodies God's marriage with Israel through his own tortuous relationship with his wife, Gomer. Yahweh commands Hosea to take "a woman of prostitution" because Israel, in like manner, was committing spiritual prostitution (Hosea 1:2). The nation had abandoned Yahweh, her Husband. Both God and Hosea are married to faithless partners. To hear and see one was to hear and see the other:

- She will chase her lovers but not catch them, and she will seek them but not find them. Then she will say, "I will return to my first husband. For it was better for me then than it is now." (Hosea 2:7)

- I will marry you forever. I will marry you in righteousness and in justice, in steadfast love and in mercy. (Hosea 2:19)

In Hosea 11:1–9, we again read about God grieving over Israel's disloyalty. This isn't the voice of a judge calling the court to order; it's the wail of a Father over His lost son:

> When Israel was a child, I loved him, and out of Egypt I called My son. … I taught Ephraim to walk; I took them up by their arms. … I led them with cords of kindness, with the bands of love. … They refused to return to Me. (Hosea 11:1–5)

Yahweh is deeply hurt. "How can I give you up, O Ephraim? How can I hand you over, O Israel? How can I make you like Admah? How can I treat you like Zeboiim?" Then these words: "My heart changes within Me; My compassions grow warm" (Hosea 11:8). Yahweh's heart is aroused. His insides grow tender. Compare God's heart with that of Joseph's: "His compassion grew warm for his brother, and he sought a place to weep" (Genesis 43:30). Also note the woman of the living son, early in Solomon's reign: "Her compassion grew warm for her son" (1 Kings 3:26).

In Hosea, Yahweh is resolved not to execute judgment against His wayward people. Divine love prevails over divine wrath. God's pain leads Him to forgive the Israelites and grant them a new standing in grace.

In the second half of Hosea 11:9, Yahweh says He's "God and not a man, the Holy One in your midst." As the Holy One of Israel, Yahweh is categorically transcendent. Yet He's not so far removed that He's indifferent to sin and suffering. On the contrary, Yahweh chooses to become involved in Israel's mess—so much so that, even if He must suffer, He won't pull back. His emotions boil to the point where they redirect His course of action.

When we speak of being moved by our feelings, we sometimes use language like "I'm *falling* in love," which gives the impression that we can't help ourselves. We're swept along by an ocean of emotion: a surge of jealousy, a fit of rage. Such language suggests that emotions dictate our conduct, behavior, and responses—we have no choice but to follow our feelings.

While this may be true of people, it's not true of Yahweh. Emotions never take over His plans or priorities. Yahweh is the Holy One of Israel. When He dishes out wrath, He doesn't lose control. When His heart breaks, He still keeps His wits about Him. Since Yahweh is holy, His emotions are always pure, perfect, timely, righteous, correct, and morally upright. Yahweh isn't a force, an idea, an ideology, a doctrine, or a theological proposition. Yahweh is a person, who genuinely responds with grief and sadness—always within the framework of His faithfulness and reliability, expressed fully in Christ Jesus.

DIVINE PATHOS IN THE NEW TESTAMENT

Divine pathos with Israel is writ large in Jesus. The Greek verb *splanknizomai* best captures the connection. Often translated "to have compassion," *splanknizomai* denotes a churning stomach, overwhelming feelings, or a warm and tender heart. The English word *spleen* derives from *splanknizomai*—colloquially, it means our gut. Jesus has a heart of deep emotion (*splanknizomai*) for the crowds who are like sheep without a shepherd (Matthew 9:36). With great pity (*splanknizomai*), He heals a leper (Mark 1:41). Jesus tells a parable about a father who is overtaken with emotion (*splanknizomai*) as he runs toward his prodigal son (Luke 15:20).

Moreover, in, with, and under the prophetic suffering of Jeremiah and Hosea, we see Christ, *the* Prophet. As men of sorrows familiar with suffering, these prophets foreshadow *the* Man of the greatest sorrows, who is most familiar with pain and intense suffering. Jesus weeps over Lazarus (John 11:35) and Jerusalem (Luke 19:41). He feels great dread in Gethsemane (e.g., Luke 22:44). Finally, and most fully, Yahweh's pain and angst in the OT point to Christ's suffering on the cross. We therefore read passages about God's suffering in the OT in light of Good Friday and Good Friday in light of divine anguish in the OT.

CONCLUSIONS

The God of the OT isn't an Aristotelian "unmoved mover," an impassive God who moves the world but is unmoved by it. Yahweh is instead personal, active, loving, and capable of suffering. He chooses to identify with His people in their pain and agony. Yahweh hears the cry of His people in Egypt and comes down to rescue them. He reveals Himself in the prophets as a God deeply saddened by Israel's sin.

It's incorrect to teach that Yahweh doesn't have feelings—an assumption driven by ancient Greek thought. Yahweh does more than respond to Israel's sorrow with rational reflection and critical analysis. It pains Him to see people suffer.

Yahweh isn't an emotionless poker player who never shows his hand. Neither is He a detached scientist watching an experiment unfold. Yahweh is a frustrated Father, a jilted lover, a covenant partner whose heart breaks over His wayward people. Yet in every case, when we read about God's emotions of pity and pain, He never loses control or becomes overwhelmed by His feelings. Divine grief doesn't entail becoming emotionally unstable. Through it all, God's faithfulness and gracious purposes remain constant and undiminished.

Thus, God in His essence—not symbolically or figuratively—feels affliction and distress. This is one of His most important characteristics. Yes, Yahweh is exalted and infinite in power and wisdom. But it's His loving compassion that distinguishes Him from other gods and goddesses—both ancient and modern.

Yahweh, therefore, isn't immutable in an absolute sense. Neither is He idle, nor an indifferent bystander in the midst of unspeakable human suffering. Yahweh isn't only aware of our tears but shows solidarity with our pain while climactically, in Christ, bearing the sin of the world on Calvary's cross. Yahweh is holy, sovereign, and utterly removed from sin. Yet, at the same time, He's imminent, personal, and relational. Divine suffering in the OT is finally beyond our understanding. It's a mystery in the same way that God's thoughts and ways are mysterious (Isaiah 55:8–9).

The questions, therefore, aren't, Is God emotional or rational? Is He all heart or all head? It's not either-or; it's both-and. For in Christ, God not only suffered with people, but He also suffered for all people of all time.

DISCUSSION QUESTIONS

1. How does Genesis 6:6 summarize this chapter?
2. Why is divine pathos in the OT often misunderstood? What brought this about?
3. What are the top three OT passages that teach us about Yahweh's suffering?
4. How does God's pain and distress in the OT open up new understandings of Christ in the NT?

CHAPTER 8

ARE OLD TESTAMENT SEXUAL LAWS STILL BINDING?

"A man will leave his father and his mother and be united to his wife, and they will become one flesh."
(Genesis 2:24)

One of the greatest crises facing the church today is how it defines human sexuality. Dominant cultural shapers—Hollywood, higher education, and the media—continue to push Christians into accepting gay, trans, bi, and homosexual lifestyles. Societal indoctrination continues to attack biblical sexual ethics.

The movement redefining traditional sexual standards goes by many names, but most frequently it's called LGBTQIA+—an acronym that stands for lesbian, gay, bisexual, transgender, queer, intersex, and asexual people. The plus sign denotes those not listed but who identify as part of the movement. These include non-binary, pansexual, and demisexual people.

Until the last fifty years or so, almost every church and denomination accepted the Bible's teaching about sexual expression—a marriage of one man and one woman for life. While most of the global church still stands upon this biblical norm, a number of Christians in America and Europe have departed from God's teaching about sexuality. What started as a small trickle during the turbulent decade of the sixties has now become a tsunami.

The argument goes like this. During the American Civil War, Southern churches argued that they had the Bible on their side, contending that God's Word is proslavery. That's why they drew their swords, shot their guns, and fired their cannons. But times have changed. Now, very few Christians hold to the view that slavery is divinely sanctioned. The same could be said about birth control, in vitro fertilization, and women's roles in society. History has moved past all of this.

Just so, many argue that it's time to put the church's prohibition against same-sex relations in the theological dustbin of history, which is full of teachings once embraced that are no longer relevant. And for those Christians who don't endorse the LGBTQIA+ agenda? The least they can do is affirm those who do. It's time to "agree to disagree."

Those who hold this position maintain that when biblical writers denounce homosexuality, they aren't forbidding same-sex intimacy. Instead, such passages only forbid relationships that take advantage of others—pederasty, prostitution, and rape. Advocates for this interpretation believe that God lovingly affirms mutual and committed same-sex relationships. The bottom line? They believe the Bible only addresses exploitative homosexual practices, not mutual, loving same-sex relationships.

The OT has a lot to say about this. Although Israel's Scriptures don't directly address LGBTQIA+, they do warn about same-sex relationships—often called homosexuality. In this chapter, we intentionally avoid the word *homosexuality* in favor of the term *homosexual intimacy* and related phrases. Why the distinction? Homosexuality often denotes both having a same-sex orientation and engaging in same-sex intimacy. The OT clearly condemns same-sex lustful desires and acts, but it doesn't probe into someone's underlying orientation. It's important, therefore, that we differentiate between the two.

The church welcomes people who struggle with their orientation but who choose to live chaste and decent lives—in the same way it welcomes people who fight to avoid heterosexual sins that include premarital sex, extramarital affairs, and pornography.

The issue, then, is succumbing to the temptation and engaging in same-sex intimacy. To feel an attraction is different from yielding to it. A variety of OT texts address same-sex intercourse. They include stories about Ham and Sodom and Gomorrah, as well as laws in Leviticus 18 and 20. However, Yahweh's foundation for proper and godly sexual expression first comes in Genesis 1–2.

LAYING THE FOUNDATION

The foundation for the OT's teaching about sexuality comes in Genesis 1:27: "So God created man in His own image, in the image of God He created him; male and female He created them" (ESV). Males and females are different. There are obvious anatomical differences between the two. God made men and women to sexually complement each other in order to procreate: "Be fruitful and multiply and fill the earth" (Genesis 1:28 ESV).

This God-created complementarity between male and female is part of His bigger design in Genesis 1. Throughout the chapter, we read about reciprocal pairs working in harmony with one another: heaven and earth, sea and land, the Creator and His creation. Though God made a diversified universe, it's not random and aimless. He created individual elements to unite. It's through these unions that different parts join together to make a harmonious and beautiful world. Where would the sun be without the moon? And the day without the night? And the fish without water? Just so, males and females are different, yet God created them to mutually complement one another. Men and women are each unique and noninterchangeable—they each do things the other cannot. God created them different *from* each other, yet also *for* each other.

Genesis 2:18 accents this idea: "It is not good for man to be alone." Adam needs a helpmeet, a partner, another person who enables him to be complete. Genesis 2 concludes with the statement that a man and his wife are to become one flesh (Genesis 2:24). This one-flesh union includes our emotional as well as our sexual lives.

God created sex not only to populate the world but to complete and complement both genders. Divinely ordained sexual expression requires not just two people but two sexually differentiated people who are suitable for an anatomic, physiologic, and procreative relationship. Every type of writing in the OT—narratives, poetry, proverbs, and laws—presupposes this teaching in Genesis 1–2. Our response? "Gracious Savior, grant Your blessing to this husband and this wife, that in peace they live together in Your love throughout their life" (*LSB* 860:1).

SAME-SEX RELATIONSHIPS IN GENESIS AND JUDGES

The ideal portrayed in Genesis 1–2 goes downhill—fast. Genesis 9:20–27 describes the first occasion of same-sex intimacy. After God rescued Noah and his family from the worldwide flood, Ham "saw the nakedness of his father" (Genesis 9:22). This sounds innocuous enough. Ham gazed upon Noah before his father was able to get dressed. But then Noah curses Ham's son Canaan. The punishment hardly seems to fit the crime.

Noah isn't upset because of what Ham saw. Noah is beside himself because of what Ham did (Genesis 9:24). Ham committed incestuous, homosexual rape—an unspeakable act. Confirming this interpretation is that the phrase "uncover the nakedness of" in Leviticus describes incest (cf. Leviticus 18:6–18; 20:11, 17–21).

What did Ham have to gain by raping his father Noah and telling his two older brothers about it? The best guess is that Ham was trying to usurp the authority not only of Noah but also of Shem and Japheth. Ham wanted to become the family's patriarch and then hand the position down to his son Canaan.

The apple doesn't fall far from the tree. Ham and Canaan's descendants followed suit. Sodom and Gomorrah—notorious for defying and rebelling against God's moral mandates—were cities populated by Canaanites (Genesis 10:18–19). And, among other sins, the men of these cities sought out sex with other men (Genesis 19:4–5). Unnatural sexual relations brought about the demise and destruction of Sodom and Gomorrah (Genesis 19:24–28; cf. 2 Peter 2:6–9; Jude 7).

Just as God responds to the unseemly sexual relations between the sons of God and the daughters of man in Genesis 6:4–7 with a worldwide flood, in like manner, the unnatural relations depicted in Genesis 19 are followed by a parallel judgment—a downpour of fire and brimstone. The men of Sodom were "wicked, great sinners before Yahweh" (Genesis 13:13) and thus deserving of divine judgment.

A similar scene appears in Judges 19:22–25. An old man implores the men of Gibeah not to do a wicked and vile thing—have sex with another man (Judges 19:23–24). Male penetration of another male was considered outrageous and unheard of. What led to such abominable acts? Israelites at the time of Judges rejected the clear teachings in Genesis 1–2. Instead, "everyone did what was right in his own eyes" (Judges 21:25).

These narratives in the books of Genesis and Judges describe God's judgment against same-sex intimacy. Leviticus codifies Israel's sexual standards, which are binding for all people. Before we study these texts, it will be helpful to step back and engage a broader discussion on how to interpret OT laws.

INTERPRETING OLD TESTAMENT LAWS

Those who maintain that God forbids same-sex relationships—especially in Israel's legal statutes—may encounter someone who responds along these lines. "Well, then, you must also believe that selling your daughter into slavery is God's will." Then he might point to Exodus 21:7, "If a man sells his daughter as a slave, she is not to go out in the same way that male slaves do." He may continue challenging your position by citing Exodus 35:2, where God commands that those who break the Sabbath should be killed. "In addition to selling your daughter as a slave, you're also going to kill everyone who breaks the Sabbath?" Confident that he has you cornered, he reads Leviticus 11:7 to you, where God declares that pigs are unclean, so people can't eat them. This advocate of same-sex intimacy then taunts you by saying, "But you love hot dogs and pork chops, and you can't live without bacon!" He then marshals additional passages to argue his point:

- Do not let your cattle breed with a different kind. Do not sow your field with two kinds of seed. Do not wear a garment of cloth made of two kinds of material. (Leviticus 19:19)
- Do not round off the hair on your temples or clip the edges of your beard. (Leviticus 19:27)

What's his point? If we're going to apply OT laws correctly, then we must apply all of them equally. We can't pick and choose those that suit us. It's faulty biblical interpretation to obsess about prohibitions regarding same-sex relationships and ignore the rest. This seems like an insurmountable argument. But is it?

Not really. This position assumes that we must take the same approach to all the laws in the OT. However, for millennia, Christian interpreters of Israel's Scriptures have maintained that not every part of Israel's legal code is equally binding. This methodology differentiates between four categories of regulations in the OT. They're frequently called the ceremonial, civil, clean and unclean, and moral mandates, as prescribed in the Ten Commandments.

OT ceremonial laws are fulfilled in Christ's death on the cross, when He paid for all sin for all people of all time. Jesus thus teaches that His body is the ultimate temple, and His death is the ultimate sacrifice for sin (e.g., John 2:19–21; Matthew 20:28; Mark 14:36). Christians, therefore, are no longer bound to the temple or obedience to its sacrificial system. These laws are obsolete (Hebrews 10:11–14). In fact, none of Israel's liturgical regulations apply to Christians because these regulations ended on Good Friday and Easter.

In like manner, OT civil laws are no longer applicable to the baptized because Jesus established a church, not a government. "On this rock I will build My church" (Matthew 16:18 ESV). In the OT, Israel was a nation-state consisting mostly of Hebrews. In the NT, believers come from every tribe, language, people, and nation (Revelation 5:9). Therefore, we aren't subject to Israelite legal regulations (e.g., Exodus 20:22–23:33; Deuteronomy 17:1–20). Instead, God calls Christians to submit to the laws of the country they live in

(Romans 13:1–7; 1 Peter 2:13–14), because OT laws relating to the civic life of God's people are no longer pertinent for believers today. They were intended only for the people of Israel living in the land of Palestine as they awaited the coming of the Messiah.

OT laws regarding what is clean and unclean have also been annulled (Mark 7:18–23; Acts 10:9–33). Jesus touched lepers and dead people—actions that were taboo in the OT. Moreover, Christ teaches that spiritual cleanness is no longer a matter of what we come in contact with. The evil isn't out there. Evil is in our hearts. Christians are cleansed, therefore, by Christ's shed blood on the cross and then renewed through the Holy Spirit. Jesus purified what was previously unclean (Acts 10:15).

What law is left? The moral law—the Ten Commandments and their ancillary applications. Hebrews 10:16 states that the Holy Spirit writes these laws on our hearts. They are therefore mandatory. A good example comes in Leviticus 19:18: "Love your neighbor as yourself" (ESV). The NT summarizes the moral law with the word *love*—love toward God and our neighbor (Matthew 22:34–40; Romans 13:8–10).

Here's our point: Leviticus has parts that apply to Christians and parts that don't. It's incorrect, therefore, to insist that Christians must either obey all of God's commands in Leviticus or none of them. A nuanced approach is better because it employs the methodology we see in the NT.

THE BOOK OF LEVITICUS

The book of Leviticus has two parts: chapters 1–16 (mostly connected with worship) and chapters 17–27 (mostly connected with living the life of faith). The two passages that address same-sex relationships, Leviticus 18:23 and 20:13, appear in the second half of the book.

Leviticus 18 begins and ends with the same motif—God warning Israel about the transgressions of their neighbors (Leviticus 18:1–5; 18:24–30). These sins would lead to the expulsion of most non-Hebrew people from Canaan. The message in Leviticus 18 is clear. If the Israelites live like Canaanites, they, too, will be thrust out: "If you defile the land, it will vomit you out just as it vomited out the nations who were before you" (Leviticus 18:28).

Leviticus 18:6–23 describes the sins of the nations and mandates that Israelites avoid them. Yahweh forbids incest in Leviticus 18:6–18 to safeguard women and girls from male predators within their family. It also ensures healthy children by forbidding inbreeding. The law against adultery (Leviticus 18:20) protects marriages and makes them more stable. By forbidding bestiality (Leviticus 18:23), God hinders the revolting mixture of two kinds of species—one created in the image and likeness of God and the other that was not. Homosexual activity (Leviticus 18:23) is rejected because it flouts the most basic feature of human sexuality: gender and sex.

God calls His people to be holy (Leviticus 19:2). In this context, *holy* denotes separation and distance—from the abominations of Israel's neighbors. Yahweh, the Holy One of Israel, mandates that His people reject the practices of their pagan surroundings.

Unlike Yahweh, Canaanite gods and goddesses were hardly holy. They weren't separate from but instead were viewed as part of creation. Canaanites worshiped thunder, rain, water, sex, death, and the like. The world and the Canaanite deities were part of one universal reality. It was life with no boundaries.

Such a worldview held that there were no barriers prohibiting incest, same-sex intimacy, or bestiality. In contrast, Yahweh's transcendence implies a worldview that distinguishes between father and daughter, male and female, people and animals. Within this context comes these two key passages:

- A man should not lie with a man as he does with a woman; this is an abomination. (Leviticus 18:22)

- If a man lies with a man as he does with a woman, both of them have committed an abomination; they are surely to be put to death; their blood will be on their own heads. (Leviticus 20:13)

Why such harsh words? Because same-sex intimacy denies God's gift of male and female complementarity, as taught in Genesis 1–2. And note, neither Leviticus 18:23 nor 20:13 provides any loopholes. Yahweh created male and female for lifelong sexual pairing—no ifs, ands, or buts. Additionally, Levitical mandates apply equally to both Israelites and non-Israelites (Leviticus 18:26) because God created every male and female "to be fruitful and multiply, to fill the earth and subdue it" (Genesis 1:28).

The prohibitions in both Leviticus 18:23 and 20:13 employ the term *male* (in Hebrew, *zakar*). Had the word been *youth* (in Hebrew, *na'ar*), only pederasty would be condemned. There are also no exemptions for same-sex partners who engage consensually or are in a committed relationship. God stands against every form of sexual distortion.

Three additional features in these verses make it clear that mutual consent between two males is also condemned: (1) Both parties are punished; (2) the verb used is *lie*, as opposed to *seize and lie*, which would imply rape; and (3) the comment that "their blood will be on their own heads" (Leviticus 20:13) implies an awareness of the action and its consequences. Unlike in Egypt, where only pederasty was condemned, or in Mesopotamia, where apparently only forcible homosexual relations were forbidden, the OT forbids every form of same-sex intimacy. The complete prohibitions in Leviticus 18:22 and 20:13 are thus unique in ancient literature.

Further, Leviticus 18:22 comes in the context of other sexual acts that are prohibited today, such as incest (Leviticus 18:6–18), adultery (Leviticus 18:20), and bestiality (Leviticus 18:23). The same is true for the context of Leviticus 20:13, where other sexual offenses include adultery, sex with one's stepmother or daughter-in-law, marriage to a mother and daughter at the same time, and human-animal sex (Leviticus 20:10–16). The church doesn't follow the civil penalty for these sins—death—but it has historically embraced their categorical repudiation because they fail to align with the creational mandates in Genesis 1–2.

While Leviticus 18 labels the sins catalogued as abominations, it reserves the singular term *an abomination* for homosexual intercourse (Leviticus 18:22). The word implies something disgusting, detestable, abhorrent, and utterly vile. In fact, same-sex lovemaking is the only sin in all of Leviticus 17–26 that is called an abomination. Why? Male-to-male sexual relations put men in the position of women, which blurs the distinctions between the two genders, breaking boundaries that are explicit in human anatomy and physiology.

We don't want to overstate what Leviticus 18 teaches about illicit sex by claiming that everything in the chapter is applicable today. Note the command prohibiting sexual intercourse with a woman "while she is in her menstrual uncleanness" (Leviticus 18:19 ESV). This mandate is no longer in force, as we saw earlier in this chapter that the NT does away with the categories of clean and unclean.

THE NEW TESTAMENT PERSPECTIVE

It's become fashionable for people to argue that anything the OT teaches about same-sex intimacy is passé and therefore irrelevant. After all, these adherents say, love is the only ethic taught in the NT—love toward God and our neighbor (Matthew 22:34–40; Romans 13:8–10). Case closed.

Is this the only command the NT gives regarding sexual morals? Live and let live? Love and affirm? It's your life, do with it as you please?

Romans 1:26–27 is one of the most important passages in the NT regarding gay and lesbian intimacy. Within the context of these verses (Romans 1:18–32), Paul's list of sins are *manifestations* (not provocations) of divine wrath. They are God's punishments upon rebellious people—much like the divine judgment upon Egypt by means of ten plagues (Exodus 7–12). The depravities in Romans 1:18–32 make this point: The refusal to acknowledge the Creator (Romans 1:20) distorts creation—including human sexuality.

Perverse sexual orientations are God's judgment. Three times in the second half of Romans 1 Paul employs the phrase "He gave them over" (Romans 1:24, 26, 28; perhaps as a reference to Psalm

81:12). Thus, same-sex relationships are the result of people's blatant rebellion against God, who created the heavens and the earth.

In Romans 1:27, Paul describes same-sex relationships as men "burning with passion for one another." Ruled out, then, is the argument that the apostle only condemns rape, prostitution, and pederasty (man-boy relationships) but that Paul affirms consensual same-sex intimacy. Instead, he condemns all sexual relations between people of the same sex—both man-to-man and woman-to-woman.

Key here is Paul's expression "contrary to nature" (Romans 1:26). Same-sex intimacy defies the Creator and His creation. Men and women are biologically designed to sexually complement one another. Therefore, just like Leviticus 18 and 20, the apostle takes us back to Genesis 1–2, where we learn that God ordained human sexuality to take place between a husband and wife. This union ensures procreation and the formation of nuclear families.

Paul's overall point is important. In Romans 1–3, the apostle teaches that all people stand guilty before God. It's inappropriate, therefore, to condemn homosexual acts and ignore heterosexual sins such as prostitution, premarital sex, rape, out-of-wedlock births, cohabitation, pornography, adultery, and extramarital affairs.

- The wrath of God is revealed from heaven against *all* ungodliness and unrighteousness. (Romans 1:18 ESV)
- There will be tribulation and distress for *everyone* who does evil, the Jew first and also the Greek. . . . For God does not show partiality. (Romans 2:9, 11)
- *All* have sinned and fallen short of God's glory. (Romans 3:23)

Paul furthers his instruction from Romans 1:26–27 in 1 Corinthians 6:9, where he employs the Greek word *malakos*, which literally denotes "soft." In this context, however, the term refers to a man taking the female role in same-sex intimacy. Paul also uses the word *arsenokeites*, "homosexual activity"—a term that recurs in 1 Timothy 1:10. *Arsenokeites* is a compound word that derives from two words in the ancient Greek version of Leviticus 18:22; 20:13—*arsen*, "male," and *koite*, "lying." The apostle thus aligns his teaching with the OT. Why is that? "For whatever was written in former days was written for our instruction" (Romans 15:4). To argue that OT texts only reflect Israel's history and therefore don't apply to people today is to ignore this edict. In both the OT and NT, same-sex intercourse crosses divinely set boundaries, rebelling against God's creation of complementary-gendered people.

CONCLUSIONS

People tolerate homosexual relationships more today than in previous eras because they're inundated by our culture that increasingly tries to redefine sexuality and gender. Add this to the mantra "you have to be you" and Pandora's box continues to unleash a harmful and destructive view of human sexuality. Any curbing of sexual desire—the argument goes—leads to psychological damage. Everyone should be free to express their sexuality as they see fit. "What I do with my life is none of your business!"

How individual Christians and denominations handle this full-court press to affirm same-sex relationships reveals what they think of the Bible. For at the heart of the issue is how to properly understand the Bible. Is it God's Word—perfect and without error, inspired by the Holy Spirit? Or is the Bible a collection of culture-bound documents—wrong on some things, right on others?

We believe that the texts considered in this chapter—from Genesis to 1 Timothy—are sexual mandates in all times and for every person. Those who argue from the Bible that mutually consenting LGBTQIA+ people are exempt from God's directives are twisting texts so they align with their position.

The Bible condemns every act of homosexual intercourse because, according to Genesis 1–2, marriage is the union between two complementary people—a man and a woman. Same-sex intimacy doesn't provide this. It also doesn't provide children with a deep connection to each half of humanity through a parent of each gender. Jesus (Mark 10:6–7) affirms the "one flesh" of Genesis 2:24.

Jesus, however, never held sexual sinners in disdain or looked upon them with contempt. Instead, as with other fallen people, He tried to claim them for membership in the reign of God. This is our posture as well—to condemn all action that is contrary to the Bible while also readily forgiving the brokenhearted and repentant.

We therefore reject every self-righteous attitude that discriminates or isolates people on the basis of their homosexual orientation. Orientation need not lead to same-sex intimacy or God-forbidden lust. That's because, contrary to society's thinking, sexual expression isn't essential for human fulfillment and flourishing. Note the examples of Jesus, Paul, and countless other single Christians through the ages. Accordingly, we invite sexually involved homosexuals who seek fellowship in the church to join with us in turning away from sin to the life of faith. "If we confess our sins, He is faithful and just and will forgive our sins and cleanse us from all unrighteousness" (1 John 1:9).

DISCUSSION QUESTIONS

1. How does Genesis 2:24 serve as the theme of this chapter?
2. Why is Genesis 1–2 the foundation for the Bible's teaching about sexuality?
3. What are the four categories of laws in the OT? What category does same-sex intimacy come under?
4. How does the NT agree with what the OT teaches about homosexual activity?

CHAPTER 9

WHAT ABOUT DIVINE ANGER AND VENGEANCE IN THE OLD TESTAMENT?

"Vengeance is Mine, I will repay."
(Deuteronomy 32:35)

There's much to love about the OT. God provides a son for Abraham and Sarah (Genesis 21). He sends food and water for Elijah (1 Kings 19). And God announces double comfort for all our sin (Isaiah 40:1). But God also sends a flood in Noah's days that wipes out almost everything. Yahweh rains down fire and brimstone on Sodom and Gomorrah. Samson, empowered by God's Spirit, kills thousands of Philistines. Divine wrath also wipes out the capital cities of Samaria and Jerusalem. Then there's the last verse in Isaiah: "They shall go out and look on the dead bodies of the men who have rebelled against Me. For their worm shall not die, their fire shall not be quenched, and they shall be an abhorrence to all flesh" (Isaiah 66:24). Is that any way to end a book—especially a book in the Bible?

Divine anger and vengeance are so strange because we live in a society whose watchwords are tolerance and acceptance. The goal in life is to get along and go along. Always be calm and collected. And, if you feel a rush of rage, it's best to put a lid on it. But then, suddenly, there appears a tidal wave of OT passages in which Yahweh unleashes indignation and judgment.

Jeremiah 31:3 is an important promise. Yahweh loves us with an everlasting love. This is the main message of the OT. However, God's affection isn't the only message of the OT. There is also divine fury.

How should we interpret God's anger exhibited in Israel's Scriptures? The first approach holds that God doesn't get angry—not really. When people experience setbacks and disasters, they wrongly interpret them as divine judgments. From the human perspective, God unleashes rage and wrath. However, these scriptural descriptions are anthropomorphic. It only appears that God acts this way. Truth be told, God is beyond anger and fury. He dwells serenely in the heavens—detached and removed. God doesn't have any emotions, ever.

Another approach, the position we argue for in this chapter, takes the OT's descriptions of divine ire seriously—that is, God actually gets angry. In doing so, though, He doesn't sin. It's incorrect to think that divine anger can be completely likened to our anger. While both God and people get angry, God's anger is a perfect expression of His justice and holiness. His rage is never irrational or unreasonable—though it may appear that way. Yahweh's indignation isn't a vice; it's a virtue.

A virtue? Yes. God doesn't remain neutral in the face of evil. Yahweh's rage arises because of His deep love for the world. Yahweh can't love life without detesting death. He can't be devoted to light without abhorring the darkness. Because of His goodness, God hates every form of wickedness.

It's tempting to think an angry God is an imperfect God. Upon reflection, however, not to express rage and indignation at abject evil would show that Yahweh is deficient. Not to be angered by injustice, disease, racism, and all sorts of depravity is to be morally lacking. Divine fury wells up from God's heart of love—precisely because of His great compassion for the world.

Think about the alternative—Yahweh never gets upset about evil. What would it be like if He never lifted a hand against atrocities and looked the other way when people are raped and tortured, bombed and brutalized?

This isn't the God of the OT. Yahweh doesn't tell the pharaoh of the exodus, "No big deal." Instead, He sternly orders, "Let My people go!" (Exodus 8:1 ESV). Yahweh doesn't tell Babylon, "I'll overlook it this time." No, He announces the empire's doom in a number of texts (e.g., Isaiah 13, 47; Jeremiah 50–51). God puts it this way: "For wicked men are found among My people; they lurk like fowlers lying in wait. They set a trap; they catch men. . . . Shall I not punish them for these things?" (Jeremiah 5:26, 29 ESV).

YAHWEH'S ANGER

The OT has a lot to say about divine anger—in fact, 72.5 percent of the 714 references to anger in the OT apply to Yahweh. What ignites His rage? Man's inhumanity to man. Note, for example, in Amos:

- Amos 1:3–5—Arameans used animals pulling flint-studded pieces of wood back and forth across the prostrate bodies of Gileadites to impale and skin them alive.
- Amos 1:6–10—People in Gaza and Tyre were guilty of slave trade.
- Amos 1:13–15—Ammonites ripped open pregnant women. With one slash of the sword, they killed two people.
- Amos 2:1–3—Moabites, adding insult to injury, burned a dead king's bones.

These oracles have a common theme—the strong taking diabolical advantage of the weak, from the fetus in utero to the corpse in the grave.

Yahweh isn't only concerned about His temple and its maintenance. He also watches over people to see whether justice is exercised among them. And when it isn't? God's judgment isn't a soft scolding. Divine ire is like fire (e.g., Lamentations 2:4; Jeremiah

4:4), rushing water (e.g., Isaiah 30:27; Jeremiah 7:20), and a blazing oven (e.g., Psalm 21:9). In order to judge people, Yahweh employs thunder (e.g., 1 Samuel 7:10), hail (e.g., Joshua 10:11), darkness (e.g., Exodus 14:20), water and earthquakes (e.g., Judges 5:4–5). This anger evokes terror and panic in the hearts and lives of His enemies (e.g., Exodus 14:24–25; Joshua 2:9, 24; 5:1).

It takes Yahweh a long time to get angry. In fact, His long-suffering appears a number of times in the OT (e.g., Exodus 34:6; Numbers 14:16; Psalms 86:15; 103:8; 145:8; Joel 2:13; Jonah 4:2). For instance, in the Amos 1–2 texts considered above, eight times the prophet highlights divine forbearance ("for three transgressions and for four"). Yahweh bends over backward before He executes judgment. Amos also documents five plagues, each ending with the refrain "'But you did not return to Me,' declares Yahweh" (Amos 4:6, 8, 9, 10, 11). It's only after He tried everything else that Yahweh announced Israel's final doom: "Prepare to meet your God" (Amos 4:12 ESV).

Divine forbearance is further demonstrated when Yahweh continues to send prophets to the Northern and Southern Kingdoms to warn people of coming judgment—waiting centuries before driving people out of the Promised Land (2 Kings 17:13). He also gives Nineveh forty days to repent (Jonah 3:4). Yahweh is willing to relent if anyone turns from their wickedness (Jeremiah 18:7–8).

God doesn't judge out of the blue or suddenly fly off the handle. Divine anger is always measured, appropriate, perfect, and Yahweh's last resort. Why? It grieves Yahweh to become angry (Lamentations 3:33).

The verses before Yahweh calls forth a worldwide flood depict His great remorse and anguish:

> Yahweh regretted that He had made people on the earth, and it brought Him heart-piercing sorrow. So Yahweh said, "I will blot out people whom I created from the face of the earth." (Genesis 6:6–7)

Divine wrath comes in the context of divine grief. Yahweh would much rather be kind and compassionate (Hosea 11:9).

God isn't naturally angry. People provoke Him to wrath (e.g., Deuteronomy 9:18; 1 Kings 14:9; Jeremiah 11:17). Divine animosity must be triggered for Yahweh to unleash condemnation and judgment (cf. Deuteronomy 32:21; Psalm 106:29; Isaiah 65:3). His wrath thus begins in time and will end in time. Rage is not His permanent—let alone eternal—characteristic. God doesn't stay angry forever (Psalm 103:9; Isaiah 57:16; Jeremiah 3:12; Micah 7:18).

The OT accents an imbalance between Yahweh's judgment and grace. The Gospel outlasts the Law one thousand to one (Deuteronomy 7:9–10). His anger lasts for a moment; His favor lasts a lifetime (Psalm 30:5). The day of vengeance pales in comparison to the year of God's favor (Isaiah 61:2). Yahweh quickly gets over His wrath. It's intense, but temporary. His mercy endures forever (Psalm 107:1).

DIVINE VENGEANCE

The Hebrew words translated as "anger," "rage," "wrath," and "indignation" are interchangeable. Vengeance, on the other hand, is significantly different. While human vengeance is an expression of senseless rage and excessive retaliation—a bitter grudge that settles the score and enacts personal revenge—divine vengeance repays unrepentant sinners according to what they've done. It's a just retaliation for sin and transgression. This, in turn, brings restoration (Isaiah 1:25–27).

God's vengeance restores people, nations, and the world. Isaiah 34:8 neatly states the idea: "A day of vengeance for Yahweh" is followed by the expression "the year of restoration for the cause of Zion." Judgment against Israel's enemies brings renewal to Israel.

This Law and Gospel feature appears in other Isaian texts that employ the term "vengeance" (Isaiah 35:4; 59:17; 61:2; 63:4). Yahweh's vengeance puts down the proud and lifts up the humble (Isaiah 2:6–22). This understanding of divine retribution derives from Deuteronomy 32:43, which states that God "avenges the blood of His servants and takes vengeance on His foes. He atones for His land and His people." After judgment, there is salvation.

Nahum's prophecy of Nineveh's doom is similar. The book begins with a description of God, who, like a mighty warrior, is roused to anger: "Yahweh is a zealous and avenging God; Yahweh avenges and is filled with wrath; Yahweh enacts vengeance on His foes and vents wrath against His enemies" (Nahum 1:2). God commands the whirlwind and storm and rebukes waters and makes them dry (Nahum 1:3–4). "The mountains quake before Him; the hills melt; the earth shakes before Him, the world and all who dwell in it" (Nahum 1:5). The prophet says, "Yahweh is slow to anger and great in power but He will by no means clear the guilty" (Nahum 1:3). Yahweh forgives the sins of those who repent, but for proud Nineveh and everyone like her, He enacts judgment. This isn't a benign deity but a forceful God who defeats everyone organized against a right ordering of the world.

Yahweh's goal is always peace—in Hebrew, *shalom*—a term that doesn't denote the end of warfare. Instead, *shalom* is God's gift that puts a broken and shattered world back together again. Note, for example, Joel 1, when Yahweh sends locusts as His agents of judgment. God's people return to Him (Joel 2:12–17), then Yahweh gives this promise: "I will restore (*shalom*) the years that the locusts have eaten" (Joel 2:25). Vengeance is penultimate. *Shalom* is God's ultimate plan. Hannah puts it this way: "Yahweh kills and brings to life; He brings down to Sheol and raises up" (1 Samuel 2:6).

THE DAY OF THE LORD IN ISRAEL'S PROPHETS

While predicting divine wrath and rage against Nineveh, Nahum doesn't employ the term "the day of the Lord." The prophet Amos first coined this phrase. The day of Yahweh is a day of darkness, not light (Amos 5:18, 20). This motif is closely linked to divine anger and vengeance. Isaiah 13 provides the fullest definition of the theme.

Using the Hebrew word for "all" three times (Isaiah 13:5, 7, 15), Isaiah describes the day of universal judgment. On this day, Yahweh's enemies will lose heart, and their courage will fail (Isaiah 13:6–8). The cosmos will convulse. Stars will darken (Isaiah 13:10) and the earth will shake (Isaiah 13:13) when God judges His adversaries (Isaiah 13:14–22).

The term "day of the Lord" appears twenty-nine times in the OT. It only appears in prophetic texts (e.g., Jeremiah 46:10; Ezekiel 13:5; Joel 1:15; 2:1, 11; Obadiah 15; Zechariah 14:1; Malachi 4:5). Closely related expressions include "the day of vengeance" (Isaiah 61:2) and "the day of Yahweh's anger" (Isaiah 13:13). In some contexts, "in that day" refers to the day of Yahweh (e.g., Amos 2:16; 8:9, 13). "The day of Jezreel" (Hosea 1:11), "the day of Midian" (Isaiah 9:4), "the day of Egypt" (Ezekiel 30:9), and "the day of Jerusalem" (Psalm 137:7) all refer to military action. Thus, "the day of Yahweh" is another expression for the battle of Yahweh.

Since "the day" is synonymous with warfare, OT authors liken Yahweh to a warrior in these passages. A case in point comes in Isaiah 29:1–4, an oracle about God and attacking Jerusalem's towers and raising the city's siegeworks. In another Isaian text, God rescues His people from evil by donning the clothes of a mighty soldier: "He dresses in righteousness as a breastplate, and a helmet of salvation on His head. He puts on garments of vengeance for clothing and wraps Himself in zeal as a cloak" (Isaiah 59:17).

The book of Zephaniah opens with these stern words: "I [Yahweh] will utterly sweep away everything from the face of the earth" (Zephaniah 1:2). By employing an image of the Noahic flood, Yahweh announces His plan to rid the world of every form of wickedness and evil. The rest of Zephaniah 1 describes the day of Yahweh. Note, for example, these words:

> A day of wrath is that day, a day of distress and anguish, a day of ruin and devastation, a day of darkness and gloom, a day of clouds and thick darkness, a day of trumpet blast and battle cry. (Zephaniah 1:15–16 ESV)

The day of judgment is coming because of Judah's sin, which includes idolatry, syncretistic worship, and spiritual indifference (Zephaniah 1:4–6).

THE DAY OF THE LORD IN LAMENTATIONS

While prophets predict the day of God's fierce judgment, the book of Lamentations describes its aftermath. The day of Yahweh frames the second part of Lamentations 1 (Lamentations 1:12; 1:21). The theme also works as an inclusion for chapter 2: "in the day of His anger" (Lamentations 2:1) and "in the day of Your anger" (Lamentations 2:21), along with "in the day of Yahweh's anger" (Lamentations 2:22). In chapter 3, Jeremiah recounts his experience with the day (e.g., Lamentations 3:3), while chapters 4 and 5 depict the impact of divine judgment upon Judah and Jerusalem. "The day" thus looms large over the entire book, casting its ominous shadow at every turn.

Much of the book's vocabulary comes from earlier texts exhibiting "the day of Yahweh." Note, for example, these connections between Isaiah 13, Amos 5:18–20, and Lamentations:

- Isaiah 13:10; Amos 5:18, 20; Lamentations 2:1; 3:2, 6—Lack of light
- Isaiah 13:18; Lamentations 2:12; 4:2—Children's suffering
- Isaiah 13:16; Lamentations 1:10; 5:11—The abuse of women
- Isaiah 13:19; Lamentations 4:6—Sodom
- Isaiah 13:21–22; Amos 5:19; Lamentations 3:10; 5:18—Roaming wild animals

Lamentations interprets the day of Yahweh through the lens of God's covenant curses expressed in Leviticus 26 and Deuteronomy 28—that is, divine wrath came as a result of the vassal (Israel) rebelling against her suzerain (Yahweh). A number of sections in

Lamentations therefore depict Yahweh as being behind Zion's suffering (Lamentations 1:12–20; 2:1–8; 3:1–18, 42–47; 4:1–12).

Lamentations 2:1–9 is one of the most violent sections in the book. This section announces that divine indignation led to the demise of Jerusalem's temple, priests, and kings—even though God had earlier chosen all of them (Lamentations 2:6–7). Yahweh gives full vent to His anger and pours it out upon His people. He is even likened to an enemy (Lamentations 2:4, 5). There is no other book in the OT where God's wrath and violence are depicted with such gloomy colors.

DIVINE ANGER IN THE NEW TESTAMENT

When we turn the page from Malachi to Matthew, we might be tempted to think, "Finally, God's anger will decrease, and His love and mercy will finally increase—Christ Jesus has come!" It's not that simple. Divine wrath isn't just a feature in the OT. Jesus, just like fiery Israelite prophets, accuses and condemns with the best of them (e.g., Matthew 11:20–24; 23:13–29; 24:37–39; Luke 6:24–26; 10:13–15).

Some of Christ's parables include anger and violence (e.g., Matthew 18:34; 22:13; Mark 12:9; Luke 14:21; 19:27). And, just like OT spokesmen, Christ warns of God's coming wrath (e.g., Matthew 5:22; 18:8; Luke 21:23).

Paul likewise asserts that the Father of Jesus is a God of vengeance (1 Thessalonians 4:6). Both Romans 12:19 and Hebrews 10:30 favorably quote from Deuteronomy 32:35, where Yahweh says, "Vengeance is mine, I will repay." In his letters, the apostle features divine wrath (e.g., Romans 1:18; 2:5, 8; 3:5; 9:22; Ephesians 2:3; 5:6; Colossians 3:6; 1 Thessalonians 2:16). Additionally, Paul employs the day of the Lord motif to depict the end of this evil age and the beginning of paradise restored (e.g., Philippians 1:6; 1 Thessalonians 5:2).

More broadly, the NT asserts that God avenges through both the government (Romans 13:4; 1 Peter 2:14) and the church (2 Corinthians 7:11; 10:6). He may do it now (e.g., Luke 21:22), but He will certainly dispense it on the Last Day (e.g., 2 Thessalonians 1:5–12). Both Christians who are alive (Luke 18:1–8) and those who are asleep in Jesus (Revelation 6:10; cf. Revelation 19:2) cry out for vengeance—not to satisfy their lust for revenge but for God's kingdom to come, for His enemies to be judged, and for divine *shalom* to renew all things (cf. Revelation 21:5).

From another perspective, though, the day of the Lord is a past event. On Good Friday, God acted not only as the Judge but also as the one subjected to divine judgment. The sinless Son of God took upon Himself all our sin, and in doing so, suffered the full weight of divine wrath. "He who had no sin became sin for us, so that in Him we might become the righteousness of God" (2 Corinthians 5:21).

Isaiah is clear about all of this: "It was Yahweh's desire to crush Him [Jesus]" (Isaiah 53:10). Zechariah, for his part, teaches us that Yahweh commanded the sword to strike the Shepherd (Zechariah 13:7), with "sword" functioning as shorthand for a violent death (e.g., Jeremiah 14:15; Amos 7:9, 11). Christ gave His life as a ransom for many (Matthew 20:26; Mark 10:45) and became a curse for us (Galatians 3:13). God was behind it all (Acts 2:23).

To rescue a world opposed to Him, Jesus drank from the cup of divine fury (Matthew 26:39; Luke 22:42). This wasn't a cup of suffering or a cup of sorrow or martyrdom. Jesus drained the cup of God's wrath. Thus, He cries out to God, "Why have You forsaken Me?" (Matthew 27:46; Mark 15:34). The answer to this question is simple yet forever mysterious. Why did the Father turn His face away from Jesus? Because the Savior was bearing sin as well as the wrath of His Father—all out of His love for the world. "What wondrous love is this, that caused the Lord of bliss to bear the dreadful curse for my soul, for my soul. To bear the dreadful curse for my soul!" (*LSB* 543:1).

In Christ, God intensifies both divine love *and* divine judgment. His teachings about loving our enemies, turning the other cheek, and going the extra mile are absolutely important. But so are His words of retribution and condemnation. Jesus promises to drown evildoers in the depths of the sea (Matthew 18:6). He drives out money-changers from the temple (John 2:15), destroys unbelieving Israelites in the wilderness (Jude 5), and threatens to kill people in Thyatira if they persist in following a Jezebel-like prophetess (Revelation 2:23). At the end of time, John compares Christ's return to a rider on a white horse who judges and makes war (Revelation 19:11). On that day, He will also rule the nations with an iron scepter (Revelation 2:26–27; cf. Psalm 2:9).

This is the apostolic message. God curses all enemies of the cross (Philippians 3:18), for His wrath is against every form of evil and wickedness (Romans 1:18). While Paul pens 1 Corinthians 13, he later calls down a curse to all who do not love Jesus (1 Corinthians 16:22). The apostle's imprecations appear again in Galatians 1:8–9.

Paul believes that God will repay the coppersmith Alexander, who did him great harm (2 Timothy 4:14). Peter oversees the deaths of Ananias and Sapphira (Acts 5:1–11). He also tells Simon the magician, "May your silver perish with you" (Acts 8:20). And in vivid imagery, John envisions Babylon's judgment and doom (Revelation 18) so that creation may be restored to its pristine perfection (Revelation 21–22).

CONCLUSIONS

The triune God, who is righteous and holy and perfect, must actively judge and defeat evil. The Hitlers and Stalins and Maos of the world must be held accountable for their unspeakable acts of brutality and bloodshed. Someone must break the swords and turn spears into pruning hooks. By announcing that God is the Divine Warrior, the OT teaches that He has, does, and on the Last Day will eradicate all evil everywhere. Paul puts it this way: "Behold, then the kindness and severity of God" (Romans 11:22). Divine love and wrath are therefore compatible. It's in God's nature to become angry when He sees His beloved people abandoned, rejected, and left for dead.

It's not accurate, however, to think of God's anger as momentary insanity or a loss of self-control. While this may be true of human anger, it doesn't accurately describe God, whose rage is never unreasonable or unexplainable. Yahweh can be angry and not sin (cf. Ephesians 4:26).

We experience anger from sinful and imperfect people whose rage may be neurotic, uncontrollable, or without reason. Rarely do we encounter healthy, mature expressions of anger. But this is the triune God. He takes sin seriously because He takes people seriously.

When God sees atrocities, when He witnesses deception and deceit, when He watches the high and mighty snuff out the poor and lowly, if He doesn't respond with judgment, then He's not a loving God. But He who created the world and called it "very good" (Genesis 1:31) springs to action when people distort and destroy His creation. Yahweh isn't a benevolent deity who sees evil and shakes His fist. Instead, He actively judges and eradicates everything that is malevolent and vile.

We may conceive of a god who is soft on sin and goes easy on those who break his commandments. But this is not the God of the Bible. To soften the truth of God's wrath and vengeance is to acquiesce to the present corrupt state of the world. If we accept the status quo and put up with whatever happens, then we have no hope of evil's demise and the restoration of all things. But God won't let us do that. Jesus gives us the Lord's Prayer, where we say, in part, "Deliver us from evil." God most certainly does deliver us and will do so fully on the day of His *shalom*, the Last Day, when Christ returns.

DISCUSSION QUESTIONS

1. How does Deuteronomy 32:35 summarize this chapter?
2. Describe a time when you had justified anger. Does this experience shed any light on the nature of God's anger?
3. Discuss the two different ways of understanding divine anger and vengeance in the OT. Which one seems the most accurate?
4. What part of the chapter makes the most sense to you? What part of the chapter is the most challenging to you?
5. How does Good Friday help you better understand God's wrath?

CHAPTER 10

PREDICTING THE FUTURE: HOW MANY YEARS?

"Be alert, since you don't know what day your Lord is coming."
(Matthew 24:42)

If you watch television or check your mobile phone, you encounter predictions every day. Weather reports forecast temperatures and rain for the next week. The sports report on the evening news often includes prognostications on upcoming games. Financial news often gives projections about the future of the stock markets. Political pundits on talk shows will opine on what will happen in the next election.

The OT contains many prophetic utterances of Moses and the prophets. While these were not focused solely on predicting the future, that is often what people think of when they hear the word *prophecy*. There is a difference, however, between the projections into the future we hear every day and the predictions of the prophets: The prophets received their information about the future from God, so their prophecies were accurate. But what does "accurate" mean?

The OT contains many prophetic predictions. While some foretell the rise or fall of nations, others tell of the birth of a child or, in some cases, the death of a person. Many point forward to the Savior. Still others describe the final judgment of God and the coming of His eternal kingdom. Perhaps some of the hardest to understand are those that predict a future event in terms of how many years into the future it will happen. These are not common. In fact, more often, the prophets do not give a time when an event will take place. When they do reference a time, it is often simply a description of the future, perhaps a distant future. For instance, when Balaam foresaw the coming of the Messiah, he said, "I see Him, but [He is] not here; I behold Him, but not now" (Numbers 24:17). How are these time spans to be understood? Are they precise, down-to-the-minute calculations, or are they intended to be more general and approximate? For instance, in Genesis 17:21, God promised Abraham that Isaac would be born "at this time next year." Isaac was born a year later. However, what did "this time" mean? The same day? The same month? The same season? Genesis does not make this clear, although it does give enough information for us to know that God gave this promise to Abraham in 2067 BC and that Isaac was born in 2066 BC.

There are five prophetic predictions of a future time that speak of a span of years before fulfillment: four hundred years for Israel's time in Egypt, sixty-five years until the kingdom of Israel would cease to be a nation, seventy years when the Phoenician city of Tyre would be forgotten, seventy years for the desolation of the land of Israel and the judgment on Babylon, and seventy weeks for the future of Jerusalem. Let's look at each of these to see how predictions of future spans of time were intended to be understood.

THE FOUR HUNDRED YEARS OF ISRAEL'S TIME IN EGYPT

In Genesis 15, we read about God's reaffirmation of the promise He made with Abram when He called him to leave his homeland (Genesis 12). This reaffirmation includes the following promise:

> Then Yahweh said to Abram, "Know for certain that your offspring will be resident aliens in a land that does not belong to them. They will enslave them and oppress them for four hundred years. However, I will judge the nation they serve, and afterward they will go out with many possessions. But you will go to your fathers in peace and be buried at a ripe old age. In the fourth

> generation they will return here, for the iniquity of the Amorites has not yet reached its full measure." (Genesis 15:13–16)

This promise explicitly gives the period of the Israelite residency in Egypt as four hundred years. It also mentions that they will return to the land of Canaan in "the fourth generation." How are these prophecies to be understood? Amazingly, the book of Exodus records the exact time when Israel left Egypt:

> The time that the Israelites lived in Egypt was 430 years. At the end of 430 years, on that same day, all Yahweh's regiments went out from the land of Egypt. (Exodus 12:40–41)

It would appear that Moses, the author of both Genesis and Exodus, did not believe the predicted four hundred years to be an exact number of years, but under the inspiration of the Holy Spirit, he took them as an approximation. He made no attempt to explain the discrepancy between 400 and 430 years, nor was he embarrassed by it. He simply expected his readers to understand that God kept His promise to Abram.

There has been much discussion in commentaries about the meaning of the fourth generation returning to the land of Canaan. Clearly, there were more than four generations in the 430 years that Israel was in Egypt. Perhaps this is best understood as the fourth generation after the beginning of the enslavement and oppression of Israel by the new pharaoh, "who did not know Joseph" (Exodus 1:8). This would entail about eighty or ninety years from the generation that had reached adulthood when the oppression started to the adult generation that reentered the Promised Land. This was four generations in the case of Moses:

1. Exodus 1:1–22—The oppression of his parents began before he was born.
2. Exodus 2:1–25—It continued during Moses' early life and adulthood.
3. Exodus 2:22; 18:3–4—It lasted into the time of Moses' sons Gershom and Eliezer, who were members of the rebellious generation that died in the wilderness.
4. Numbers 14:35; 26:65; 32:13; Joshua 5:6—The next generation entered the land.

Since the time for a generation (from father to son) can vary in length, this is another indication that the four hundred years should be understood as approximate. When Jacob entered Egypt, he was not expected to mark that day on his calendar and then have his descendants count to the exact day the prophecy would be fulfilled. The prophecy was faithfully fulfilled by God, but Israel was expected to simply know and trust that as the four hundred years approached, God was working to deliver them from the Egyptian oppression. The approximate nature of the prophecy called for faith in God rather than exact chronological calculations.

Therefore, we can see that the prophecy that God delivered directly to Abram of a four-hundred-year residency in Egypt was fulfilled in approximate terms. God never forgot His promise. He had compassion on Israel since He knew their plight, and He fulfilled it in sending Moses to lead Israel out of Egypt at the proper time. (See Exodus 2:25: "God saw the Israelites, and God knew.")

THE SIXTY-FIVE YEARS UNTIL THE KINGDOM OF ISRAEL WOULD CEASE TO BE A NATION

At Isaiah 7:8, in the famous Immanuel prophecy, Isaiah made this announcement to King Ahaz of Judah:

> The chief of Aram is Damascus, the chief of Damascus is Rezin (within sixty-five years Ephraim will be too shattered to be a people). (Isaiah 7:8; parentheses in original)

Ahaz's first year on the throne began in the fall of 732 BC, and Israel was conquered by the Assyrians just nine years later in the middle of 723 BC. Isaiah's prophecy must have come sometime in those nine years, since at the time of his prophecy, Israel was still an independent nation.

Isaiah 7:8 is controversial because the period appears too long, with Israel ceasing to be a nation so soon after the prophecy and not sometime nearer to the sixty-five years Isaiah mentions. However, the prophecy does not speak of a kingdom but says, "Ephraim will be too shattered to be a *people*." The northern ten tribes of Israel are called Ephraim here after their most prominent tribe. The prophecy appears to predict the loss of the ethnic identity of the northern tribes of Israel, not their existence as an independent nation. When Israel was conquered, the Assyrians deported the ten tribes to some regions of upper Mesopotamia (2 Kings 17:6). There they intermarried with the resident peoples and gradually assimilated into the general population, losing their ethnic identity as Israelites. This prophecy predicts this process to be complete within sixty-five years. Once again, we see that the time span is an approximation, since some may have assimilated faster than others.

THE SEVENTY YEARS WHEN TYRE WOULD BE FORGOTTEN

At the end of Isaiah's prophecies about God's judgment on various nations in Isaiah 13–23, we find a prophecy against the Phoenician city of Tyre on the Mediterranean coast north of Israel (Isaiah 23:1–18). Its final verses say:

> On that day Tyre will be forgotten for seventy years—like the lifetime of one king. At the end of seventy years, what the song says about the prostitute will happen to Tyre: "Pick up your lyre, stroll through the city, you forgotten prostitute. Play skillfully, sing many songs so that you will be remembered."
>
> At the end of the seventy years, Yahweh will restore Tyre. She will go back into business, prostituting herself with all the kingdoms of the world throughout the earth. However, her profits and wages will be dedicated to Yahweh. They will not be stored or saved, for her profits will go to those who live in Yahweh's presence, to provide them with ample food and magnificent clothing. (Isaiah 23:15–18)

This condemnation, which compares Tyre's business practices to prostitution, probably refers to the waning of Tyre's economic influence with the rise of the Assyrian Empire under Sennacherib.

In 701 BC, Sennacherib campaigned along the Mediterranean coast southward through Phoenicia and as far south as Jerusalem (2 Kings 18:31–19:35; 2 Chronicles 32:1–22; Isaiah 36:1–37:36). While God miraculously delivered Jerusalem, Phoenicia came under Assyrian dominance for many years.

The prophecy defines the seventy-year period as being "like the lifetime of one king," probably a statement that is a bit sarcastic, since most kings did not live that long. This implies that the seventy years are a round number in the same way that a lifetime is estimated as seventy years at Psalm 90:10. This corresponds well with the time of the Assyrian dominance of Tyre from Sennacherib in 701 BC to at least the last Assyrian governor of Phoenicia mentioned in surviving Assyrian sources. His term ended in 637 BC—about sixty-four years after Sennacherib. Or, because we may not know about all of the Assyrian governors of Phoenicia, the period might extend to 627 BC with the death of the last great king of Assyria, Ashurbanipal—a span of seventy-four years. Assyria was ruled by three more kings until Nineveh was conquered by the Babylonian king Nabopolassar in 612 BC.

Between the death of Ashurbanipal and the conquest of Nineveh, there was a collapse of Assyrian power. Most likely around 630 BC, Tyre began to emerge not only as a free city but also as the leading city of the Phoenician coastal states. Tyre was not alone in this—Assyria was in decline, and the peoples in the various regions of the empire began to shake free of its influence. It is probably sometime during this period that Tyre went back into business, as Isaiah prophesied. Therefore, the era of Tyre's eclipse was prophesied to be approximately seventy years, most likely beginning in 701 BC.

THE SEVENTY YEARS OF DESOLATION FOR THE LAND OF ISRAEL

Tyre was not the only place that fell under God's condemnation for seventy years, according to the prophets. Famously, in late 606 or early 605 BC, Jeremiah prophesied:

> This entire land [of Judah] will become a desolate ruin, and these nations [surrounding Israel] will serve the king of Babylon for seventy years. When the seventy years are complete, I will punish the king of Babylon and that nation—this is Yahweh's declaration—for their iniquity: the land of the Chaldeans, and I will make it a ruin forever. (Jeremiah 25:11–12)

Eleven years later, in late 595 or early 594 BC, he pronounced:

> For this is what Yahweh says: "When seventy years for Babylon are complete, I will attend to you [Israel] and will confirm My promise concerning you to bring you back to this place." (Jeremiah 29:10)

According to Jeremiah 25:12, the end of the seventy years appears to be when God would "punish the king of Babylon." This would imply Babylon's conquest by the Persian King Cyrus the Great in October 539 BC. Note that this was only sixty-seven years after Jeremiah's prophecy. However, Jeremiah was prophesying a future event, not something that would happen immediately.

The fall of Judah and the surrounding nations to the Babylonians took place between 605 and 587 BC. In the summer of 605 BC, the Babylonian King Nabopolassar captured Jerusalem and took some of its residents into captivity, including the prophet Daniel. He placed Zedekiah on the throne of Judah in 597 BC. This would calculate to sixty-six years until the fall of Babylon—approximately seventy years.

After Zedekiah rebelled, the Babylonians again conquered Jerusalem and left it a ruin in August 587 BC. Babylon itself would be conquered only forty-eight years later. Thus, it would appear that Jeremiah's words did not refer to this event.

There are three other references to the seventy years of the land's desolation. The first is 2 Chronicles 36:21, which references the first year of Cyrus the Great (beginning in the spring of 538 BC):

> He [Nebuchadnezzar] deported those who escaped from the sword to Babylon. They became servants to him and his successors until the rise of the Persian kingdom. This fulfilled the word of the LORD through Jeremiah, and the land enjoyed its Sabbath rest all the days of the desolation until seventy years were fulfilled.
>
> In the first year of King Cyrus of Persia, in order to complete the word of Yahweh spoken through Jeremiah, Yahweh roused the spirit of King Cyrus of Persia to issue a proclamation throughout his entire kingdom and also to put it in writing: This is what King Cyrus of Persia says: "Yahweh, the God of the heavens, has given me all the kingdoms of the earth and has appointed me to build Him a temple at Jerusalem in Judah. Any of His people among you may go and may Yahweh his God be with him. They may go up." (2 Chronicles 36:20–23; cf. Ezra 1:1–4)

This explicitly states that God roused Cyrus to issue the proclamation "to complete the word of Yahweh spoken through Jeremiah." This would calculate the fulfillment of Jeremiah's prophecy as sixty-seven years, once again making the seventy years an approximate span, not an exact one.

Daniel also referenced the seventy years prophesied by Jeremiah when he prayed about the desolation of Jerusalem and pleaded for its restoration:

> In the first year of Darius, son of Ahasuerus, a Mede by birth, who was made king over the Chaldean kingdom—in the first year of his reign, I, Daniel, understood from the books according to the word of Yahweh to the prophet Jeremiah that the number of years for the desolation of Jerusalem would be seventy. (Daniel 9:1–2)

While there is some dispute on the identity of Darius the Mede—whether this was another name for Cyrus or one of his subordinates (Daniel 5:31; 6:28)—it is clear that his first official year would have begun in the spring of 538 BC. Once again, it appears that the actual span since the beginning of the fulfillment of Jeremiah's prophecy was sixty-seven years.

However, it appears that the decree of Cyrus in 538 BC did not immediately bring the desolation of the land to an end, since Judeans from the Babylonian captivity did not return to the land and begin to rebuild the temple in Jerusalem until 533 BC (Ezra 2:68), some seventy-two years after Jerusalem was first captured by the Babylonians and Daniel was taken into captivity.

There are yet two more references to the seventy years of Judah's desolation:

> Then the angel of Yahweh responded, "LORD of armies, how long will You withhold mercy from Jerusalem and the cities of Judah that You have been angry with these seventy years?" (Zechariah 1:12)
>
> [Yahweh said:] "Ask all the people of the land and the priests: When you fasted and lamented in the fifth and in the seventh months for these seventy years, did you actually fast for Me?" (Zechariah 7:5)

Zechariah's vision in Zechariah 1 took place in February 519 BC, and God's reply recorded in Zechariah 7 was given in December 518 BC. These two dates seem to point to Jerusalem's final fall to the Babylonians in 587—some sixty-eight or sixty-nine years earlier—as the starting point for the fulfillment of Jeremiah's seventy-year prophecy. However, the earlier prophecies appear to point to Jerusalem's first fall to Babylon in 605 BC as the starting point.

So, what do all these references to the desolation of Judah for seventy years tell us about Jeremiah's prophecies? We can draw a number of conclusions:

- The seventy years were never understood to be exact. They were always interpreted as approximations.
- The beginning and ending dates of the seventy years were not understood uniformly by the prophets and writers of the OT, reinforcing the view that the seventy years were never to be taken as an exact time span.

- All of the OT writers understood the beginning of Jeremiah's prophecy to have taken place around the time of the Babylonian assaults on Judah and Jerusalem. All of them considered the seventy-year period to have ended sometime during the early decades of the Persian Empire founded by Cyrus the Great. However, none of them were at pains to calculate the seventy years exactly, nor were they uncomfortable with defining the beginning and ending points of the seventy years differently.

Once again, we see that a prophecy concerning a span of years stretching into the future was considered to be approximate, not exact. They were intended to reinforce the belief that God was in control of the unfolding of history, but they were never designed for OT believers to simply mark their calendars and passively wait for the fulfillment on an exactly anticipated date.

DANIEL'S SEVENTY WEEKS FOR THE FUTURE OF JERUSALEM

When Daniel prayed for Jerusalem's restoration at the end of Jeremiah's prophesied seventy-year period, the angel Gabriel came to him with a prediction about the future of Jerusalem:

> Seventy weeks are determined concerning your people and your holy city to end transgression, to finish sin, and to atone for iniquity; to bring everlasting righteousness, to seal up vision and prophet, and to anoint a Most Holy One. You should know and have insight: from the going forth of a word to restore and rebuild Jerusalem until Messiah, a Leader: seven weeks and sixty-two

> weeks when it again will have been built [with] plaza and moat, but during troubled times. Then after the sixty-two weeks, Messiah will be cut off and have nothing. Both the city and the holy place will be destroyed with a Leader who is coming, and its end will be with a flood. Until the end will be war, and desolations have been determined. He will confirm a covenant for the many [during] one week. In the middle of the week, He will cause sacrifice and offering to cease. On the wing of detested things [is] a desolator, until the decreed end is poured out on the desolator. (Daniel 9:24–27)

This is not only a prophecy about Jerusalem but also a prophecy about the promised Messiah, who would "be cut off and have nothing"—a clear reference to Jesus' crucifixion, which would "atone for iniquity" and "bring everlasting righteousness." Moreover, Jesus referred to Daniel's prophecy when teaching His disciples on the Mount of Olives (Matthew 24:15; Mark 13:14).

But how are we to understand the seventy weeks that Gabriel predicted? They were not to be taken literally, as if all the events spoken about—from the decree to rebuild Jerusalem through the coming of the Messiah and ending with another desolation of Jerusalem—would happen in 490 days. Since antiquity, the seventy weeks have been understood in a symbolic manner. Often, it is suggested that the seventy weeks represent 490 years, each week making up a heptad of years. However, there are several problems with this interpretation.

Let us consider the possible starting point of the seventy weeks, "the going forth of a word to restore and rebuild Jerusalem," and how this might be calculated if we assume that the seventy weeks are 490 years.

- Some have proposed it was 538 BC when Gabriel was sent to Daniel to reveal Jerusalem's future. However, this would place the end at 48 BC, too early for the final events of the prophecy.
- The decree of Cyrus in 538 BC allowed Judeans to return to Jerusalem and rebuild the temple. Isaiah prophesied that Cyrus would allow the rebuilding of Jerusalem and its temple (Isaiah 44:28; 45:13). However, this also would place the end at 48 BC.
- The prophecies of Haggai (Haggai 1:1–15) and Zechariah (Zechariah 1:1–17) with the subsequent decree of Darius I Longimanus in 520 BC (Ezra 6:6–12) could be the starting point. However, this would place the end in 30 BC—once again, too early for the final events of the prophecy.
- Maybe it is the letter of Artaxerxes to Ezra in 458 BC, which sent him to Jerusalem (Ezra 7:12–26). Four hundred ninety years later would be AD 33, the year of Jesus' crucifixion. However, the prophecy suggests the Messiah's being "cut off" would happen after the sixty-two weeks that follow the first seven weeks, or after 483 years (i.e., [7 + 62] x 7 = 483), not after 490 years. Moreover, Artaxerxes's letter nowhere urges the rebuilding of Jerusalem, which had already begun some seventy years earlier.

- It could be when Artaxerxes gave permission to Nehemiah in 445 BC (Nehemiah 2:1–9). Yet the permission given to Nehemiah was not about rebuilding Jerusalem and was confined to rebuilding its defensive wall. Much of Jerusalem had already been rebuilt—including the temple—starting some eighty years earlier. This would place the end of the seventy weeks in AD 46, too early for the desolation of Jerusalem—a probable reference to the Roman conquest of the city in AD 70. It would also place the crucifixion at the end of 483 years in AD 39, six years too late. To overcome this difficulty, some have proposed that Gabriel was speaking about "prophetic years" that were 360 days long. They find support for this in Revelation, where 1,260 days appear to correspond to 42 months, yielding 30 days for each month (Revelation 11:2–3; 12:6; 13:5). This allows the years to be reduced in length so that the crucifixion could be placed in AD 32. However, Jesus was crucified on a Friday that was also a Passover. In AD 32, Passover was on Sunday, April 13. In addition, Daniel was told to "know and have insight" about the seventy weeks. Daniel had no access to Revelation, and there is no indication that the OT ever equates one year to 360 days. How could he "know and have insight" about something yet to be revealed long after his day?

Instead of futilely attempting to calculate the seventy weeks, it is better simply to understand the seventy weeks as strictly symbolic and the periods within them to be symbolic without any direct correspondence to the length of time for the seventy weeks or subdivisions within them calculated as years. This would then simply indicate significantly longer or shorter periods of time. They would then represent the following events:

- Seven weeks: Jerusalem is rebuilt—from Cyrus's decree (538 BC) to the work of Nehemiah to rebuild the city wall (445 BC).
- Sixty-two weeks: Jerusalem has been rebuilt, but in "troubled times" stretching from Nehemiah to Jesus' birth in 2 BC. Included in these troubled times would be the persecution by the Syrian king Antiochus Epiphanes of the Jews, who were faithful to God, and Antiochus's desecration of the temple in 167 BC.
- One week: This represents the period from Jesus' birth to the destruction and conquest of Jerusalem by Roman Emperor Hadrian in AD 135, when Jews were banned from entering the city. The middle of this week, when "sacrifice and offering" would cease, would be the conquest of Jerusalem in AD 70 by the Roman general and future emperor Titus, when the temple was destroyed.

Therefore, we can see that it is doubtful that the seventy weeks revealed by Gabriel to Daniel are to be a way to account for an exact period of time. This is in keeping with what we have seen with other prophecies that speak of periods of time: They are not to be understood as exactly calculable periods but are approximations, or in the case of the seventy weeks in Daniel 9, completely symbolic.

CONCLUSIONS

When God revealed the future to the prophets, He did so to give His people hope that would strengthen and sustain their faith as they awaited the coming of the Messiah. However, that hope was never tied to a strict calculation of years, as if OT believers could set an alarm clock that would wake them up to see a prophecy's fulfillment on a particular day. Instead, the prophecies called for patient faith that trusted God and saw His plans for Israel and for all nations unfold as history moved inexorably toward the Messiah's coming. In the same way, Christians today have the promise of Jesus' return to take His resurrected saints into His eternal kingdom at a time that has not been revealed to us. Yet the promise is just as certain as the prophecies of the OT. This is why Jesus urges us, "Be alert, since you don't know what day your Lord is coming" (Matthew 24:42; cf. Luke 12:40). A well-known hymn puts it this way: "The Bridegroom comes, awake! Your lamps with gladness take! Alleluia! With bridal care yourselves prepare to meet the Bridegroom, who is near" (*LSB* 516:1).

DISCUSSION QUESTIONS

1. How does Matthew 24:42 summarize this chapter?
2. What do you learn about Israel's time in Egypt from this chapter?
3. What new insights have you gained regarding messianic prophecies?
4. Discuss Jeremiah's seventy years as well as Daniel's seventy weeks.

CHAPTER 11

IS THERE ANY VALUE IN OLD TESTAMENT LAMENTS?

"Pour out your heart before Him,
for God is our refuge."
(Psalm 62:8)

The last sixty years have given us the Vietnam War, the legalization of abortion, the killing fields of the Khmer Rouge, the Rwandan genocide in 1994, the 9/11 terrorist attacks, mass murders, and countless government atrocities. We see barbarity on our TVs, read about it in our news feeds, and listen to talking heads debate about it endlessly on social media.

Men shove women and children into trucks, drive them outside a village, then riddle their bodies with bullets. Political leaders live the high life while they trap their citizens in abject poverty. Children are trafficked as sex slaves, countries are on the brink of economic collapse, and drug cartels continue to destroy lives—both with narcotics and their guns.

When we consider all this evil, it's tempting to shrug our shoulders, take a deep sigh, and trudge on with life as best we can. Is there a better way? Yes. OT laments.

OLD TESTAMENT LAMENTS

When offered an opportunity to study OT laments, most people respond with "Thanks, but no thanks." Or, if they do read a lament, it's because they're in a Bible-reading program—Genesis to Revelation—so they plod their way through Israel's protests, complaints, and flowing tears.

It's easy to dismiss these prayers. After all, Jesus came to die and rise again to forgive sin and give us the free gift of eternal life. It's time to rejoice, be glad, and celebrate. An angel announced to the shepherds, "I bring you good news of great joy" (Luke 2:10 ESV). The Magi saw the star leading them to the Savior, and "they rejoiced with great joy" (Matthew 2:10). Zacchaeus received Jesus with gladness (Luke 19:6), and Paul prayed with abounding joy (Philippians 1:4).

Why shed a tear? Why get lost in sadness and sorrow? It's best to push down loss and grief, to get on with life, to forget the past and make plans for the future. "Batten down the hatches. Full speed ahead!" Christ will be with us always. He has conquered every enemy. How could we even think about protesting and pouting? We've been baptized!

Besides, when tempted to complain, Paul sternly reminds us, "Who are you to answer back to God?" (Romans 9:20). Be tough. Pull yourself up by your bootstraps. God is the potter; we are the clay. But how long can we go on stuffing sadness down before it begins to adversely impact us mentally, physically, relationally, and spiritually?

The goal of the Christian life isn't to put our feelings under lock and key. Yes, Paul says that we're more than conquerors through Christ who loves us (Romans 8:37). But in the prior verse, the apostle quotes from an OT lament: "For Your sake we die every day; we are considered sheep to be slaughtered" (cf. Psalm 44:22). If Paul embraced OT laments—even in Romans 8, the most upbeat chapter in the Bible—we should as well.

Israel's protest prayers are more than grieving, grousing, grumbling, or emotional venting. They invite us to come honestly into God's presence and pour out our hearts to Him. Jesus says as much: "Blessed are those who mourn, for they will be comforted" (Matthew 5:4). Both testaments reject plastic prayers that sugarcoat life's darkest moments.

While the OT has a number of prayers that praise God, celebrate His goodness, and call upon Him with joy and thanksgiving, it also includes supplications that are filled with despair. These petitions describe intense despondency and desperation. There are a number of prayers uttered by traumatized people. Need a few examples?

- My sighing comes instead of my bread, and my groanings are poured out like water. (Job 3:24 ESV)
- Every night I flood my bed with tears; I drench my couch with my weeping. (Psalm 6:6 ESV)
- For these things I weep; my eyes flow with tears; for a comforter is far from me. (Lamentations 1:16 ESV)

Yes, God's people in the OT loved Psalm 23, but take a look at Psalm 22, with its cries of abandonment, rejection, and utter unrest. It begins with these haunting words: "My God, my God, why have You forsaken me?" (Psalm 22:1 ESV). This is a far cry from "God is good—all the time. All the time—God is good!"

What would we do if someone addressed God with these words in church? "Wake up! Why are You sleeping, O Lord? Arouse Yourself! Do not reject us forever! Why do You hide Your face? Why do You forget our pain and affliction?" (Psalm 44:23–24).

Protest prayers begin early in the OT. Cain offers the Bible's first lament in Genesis 4:13–14: (1) God's punishment is greater than Cain can handle; (2) Cain fears people will kill him; and (3) God has hidden His face. Rebekah, for her part, sobs, "If it is this way, why should I live?" (Genesis 25:22). Gideon similarly complains, "If Yahweh is with us, why has all of this happened to us?" (Judges 6:13).

When Saul and Jonathan die on Mount Gilboa, David wails over this unbearable loss (2 Samuel 1:23–27). Then, when his son Absalom is struck down, David laments again (2 Samuel 18:33). And even after Joab reprimands him, the king keeps on weeping (2 Samuel 19:4). Add to the list Elijah (1 Kings 17:20), Jeremiah (e.g., Jeremiah 12:1; 15:18), Jonah (Jonah 4:2), and Habakkuk (Habakkuk 1:2–3; 2:14). What do we learn from these people? They look reality square in the eye, shudder over what they see, address God in faith, and tell Him exactly how they feel. They dismiss theological jargon and shop-worn clichés.

OT laments refuse a stoic, passive acceptance of life's chaos. God never demanded that His people fall in line and blindly go along with the program—always saluting with a robust "Yes, sir!" Yahweh instead invites deep sadness before His throne. At the heart of OT laments are these questions: Can God still be trusted? Can we still believe in Him?

To lament is also a statement of faith. There was a time when Yahweh delivered state slaves, provided water and manna, overthrew kings and their armies, and gave Israel a land flowing with milk and honey. Instead of trying to explain loss, God's people reveal their innermost thoughts and long for God to renew His story of exodus and conquest in their day. "Yahweh, I heard Your report. I stand in awe of Your works, Yahweh. Repeat them in our day. In our time reveal them" (Habakkuk 3:2).

PSALMS OF LAMENT

The book of Psalms is chock-full of laments. At least thirty-five of the one hundred and fifty psalms are called psalms of lament. Standard lists include Psalms 3, 5–7, 13, 17, 22, 25–28, 32, 38, 39, 42, 43, 51, 54–57, 59, 61, 63, 64, 69–71, 86, 88, 102, 109, 120, 130, and 140–143.

Psalm 13 unfolds as follows: invocation (Psalm 13:1a), complaint (Psalm 13:1b–2), request (Psalm 13:3–5), and divine affirmation (Psalm 13:6). Most lament psalms, however, lack this tight structure. Why? Sorrow is rarely neat and organized. Much more often, lament psalms take two steps forward and four steps back. When we read these psalms, we might conclude that they were edited by a committee that couldn't make up its mind. Much appears to be random. They complain, protest, lament, trust—then protest, trust, lament, and complain some more. The psalms are often fragmented and lack coherence because that's what life looks like during deep sorrow.

Yet lament psalms aren't completely helter-skelter. They always incorporate these two features: (1) the situation is intolerable, and (2) it's up to Yahweh to make right what has gone so wrong.

Psalmists used metaphors to describe their despair. They feel like a broken piece of pottery (e.g., Psalm 22:15), like they're stuck in a deep pit (e.g., Psalm 30:9), like their bones burn like a furnace (Psalm 102:3). Israelites grieve the loss of God's presence (e.g., Psalm 38:21) and often describe themselves as poor and needy (e.g., Psalm 34:6). Weeping plays a big part in these petitions (e.g., Psalm 31:9)—as do emotions like fear, anger, confusion, and anxiety (e.g., Psalm 88).

These psalms acknowledge life's raw experiences. They cry out to Yahweh, "How long?" (e.g., Psalm 13:1–3), "Where is God?" (e.g., Psalm 79:10), "Why?" (e.g., Psalm 74:1), "Listen!" (e.g.,

Psalm 17:1). By rejecting fake and pretentious faith, these prayers affirm life's traumatic moments and place them all before Yahweh's throne of grace.

THE BOOK OF JOB

Job is the most well-known lamenter and protester in the OT. Although he's described as "blameless and upright," a man who "fears God and shuns evil" (Job 1:1, 8; 2:3), behind the scenes, we read about a conversation between God and Satan. Satan believes Job is only good because of God's gifts. He therefore wagers that if God removes His hand of blessing, Job will turn on God, and that will be that.

One day, Job looks out the window and sees the sky becoming darker by the minute. He thinks things can't get any worse, but that's exactly what happens. While reeling from the shock waves of his economic catastrophes—three calamities that took all of his livestock—news of an even greater tragedy comes: A storm takes the lives of his children, all ten of them.

After his numbed shock for seven silent days and nights (Job 2:13), Job breaks his silence in chapter 3 with a massive scream. He describes his life in terms of darkness, night, blackness, the grave, and death:

- Why did I not perish at birth? (Job 3:11)
- Why were there knees to receive me? (Job 3:12)
- Why was I not hidden in the ground like a stillborn child? (Job 3:16)

- Why is light given to those in misery? (Job 3:20)
- Why is life given to a man? (Job 3:23)

Job ends the chapter with these words: "What I feared has come upon me; what I dreaded has happened to me. I have no peace, no quietness; I have no rest, only turmoil" (Job 3:25–26).

Job goes on to complain that God has assailed him, shattered him, seized him by the neck and crushed him—even used Job as an archery target (Job 16:7–14). In these dark moments, Job dares to also appeal to God's love: "Even now I know that my witness is in heaven; my testifier is on high; my mediator is my friend, while my eye weeps to God" (Job 16:19–20).

Like every lamenter in the OT, Job clings fervently to God. "Though He slay me, I will hope in Him" (Job 13:15). He then makes one of the greatest confessions of faith in all of Scripture: "I know my Redeemer lives, and in the end He will stand on the earth. Even after my skin has been destroyed, yet in my flesh I shall see God" (Job 19:25–26). When Yahweh is involved, life's breakdowns lead to life's greatest breakthroughs.

THE BOOK OF HABAKKUK

Like Job, Habakkuk doesn't mince words. When faced with the colossal collapse of his world, the prophet cries out, "How long, Yahweh, must I call for help, but You do not listen? Or cry out to You, 'Violence!' but You do not save?" (Habakkuk 1:2). Denial was impossible. Past glories would not return. Habakkuk couldn't hope for a quick fix.

The prophet faced two disasters. The first was the loss of fair play and righteousness in his country. Habakkuk laments, "The wicked surround the righteous; so justice goes forth perverted" (Habakkuk 1:4 ESV). Ironically, Yahweh's response brings with it the prophet's second catastrophe. Instead of providing comfort, God promises to destroy Judah through an enemy nation. Yahweh asserts, "I am raising up the Chaldeans [that is, the Babylonians], that ruthless and impetuous nation who sweep through the breadth of the earth seizing dwellings not their own" (Habakkuk 1:6). This prompts Habakkuk to complain, "Why do You tolerate the treacherous? Why are You silent while the wicked swallow up those who are more righteous than themselves?" (Habakkuk 1:13).

Habakkuk is witnessing a horrific reversal. In Exodus 15:12, Yahweh swallows up the Egyptians in the Red Sea. Later, the sons of Korah, those who rebelled against Moses, are swallowed up by the earth (Numbers 16:30). However, in Habakkuk's time, instead of enemies being swallowed, God is sending Babylonians to swallow His people! Between 614 and 605 BC, Babylon conquered Assyria, Judah, and Egypt. Are Babylonians going to continue "destroying nations without mercy?" (Habakkuk 1:17). The prophet brings his suffering before Yahweh, who welcomes frustrations and heart-wrenching cries. "How long?" "Why?" These are the words of lament.

Habakkuk's protests demonstrate that he rejected a fake and pretentious faith. The prophet affirmed that suffering was real and significant. His language of lament pulsates with authenticity and transparency. Habakkuk provided the Judeans with a way to grieve their losses. As a consequence, the nation was empowered to face the Babylonian onslaught and eventually survive. They walked through (not over, under, or around) the valley of the shadow of death (cf. Psalm 23:4). Laments help us do that.

At the end of his book, Habakkuk's painful questions fade, and the sounds of battle are gone. No further anguish disturbs his heart. His outward circumstances are no different. What has changed? His perspective. Just like Job, having poured out his pain to Yahweh, Habakkuk becomes confident that God loves him and is working out His divine purposes (cf. Genesis 50:20; Romans 8:28). The prophet confesses his faith in Yahweh:

> Though the fig tree does not blossom, and there is no fruit on the vine; though the produce of the olive fails and the fields yield no food; though the flock is cut off from the fold and there are no cattle in the stalls, yet I will rejoice in Yahweh; I will take joy in the God of my salvation. (Habakkuk 3:17–18)

Weeping may endure for the long nights of life, but by expressing his sorrow and clinging fiercely to Yahweh's promises, Habakkuk could see joy rising in the eastern sky.

THE BOOK OF LAMENTATIONS

The book of Lamentations is the OT's quintessential lament. What Habakkuk witnessed on the horizon—Babylonian hordes razing and ransacking Jerusalem—Jeremiah, the author of Lamentations, lived through. He responded with anger and despair, yet there were glimmers of hope. The book's primary expression, though, is unspeakable suffering.

Most Christians are aware of Lamentations 3:22–23: "Indeed, Yahweh's steadfast covenant loving actions do not cease; indeed, His compassion does not come to an end. They are new morning by morning; great is Your faithfulness." Reading other parts of the book, though, might prompt the question "Why is *this* in the Bible?" The book replays memories of cannibalism (Lamentations 2:20; 4:10), famine (e.g., Lamentations 1:11; 2:12; 4:4–8), rape (Lamentations 1:10; 5:11), the complete dismantling of a city (Lamentations 2:1–10), as well as her people (e.g., Lamentations 4:1–10).

Israel's long history—from Genesis to 2 Kings—culminated in total disaster. It all appeared to be a complete and irrevocable end. Survivors were shocked (Lamentations 1:1; 2:1; 4:1, 2), were isolated (Lamentations 1:2), had memories of better days (Lamentations 1:7), and felt deep shame (Lamentations 1:8). They were at a loss for words (Lamentations 2:10). Judeans are depicted as bargaining with Yahweh (Lamentations 2:18–19; 3:40–42) and being full of anger (Lamentations 2:20), denial (Lamentations 3:39), tears (Lamentations 3:48–51), and blame (Lamentations 4:12–13; 5:7).

When we compare the book of Lamentations with Jeremiah's protests (Jeremiah 11:18–12:6; 15:10–21; 17:14–18; 18:18–23; 20:7–13), the latter appear mild. While Jeremiah complains that Yahweh has led him "like a lamb to the slaughter" (Jeremiah 11:19) or is "a deceitful brook" (Jeremiah 15:18), he doesn't accuse God of directly attacking him. However, in Lamentations, both daughter Zion (e.g., Lamentations 1:11–16; 2:4, 5) and Jeremiah (e.g., Lamentations 3:1–18) blame Yahweh for becoming their enemy.

Jeremiah brings it all before Yahweh: misery, sadness, anguish, heartache, darkness, hurt, affliction, tribulation, calamity, torment, isolation, wretchedness, misfortune, and unmitigated pain.

We may liken the book to a mournful violin exploring every note of inconceivable grief and sorrow. Its prayers arise from profound loss as well as from God's excruciating silence—the twin sisters of OT laments. Lamentations does more than chronicle Judah's economic, political, environmental, and architectural disasters. The book is a visceral cry; the first word in Lamentations 1:1 is frequently translated with the bland interrogative *how*. The Hebrew *eykah*, however, entails much more.

Forms of *eykah* often appear in OT funeral dirges (e.g., 2 Samuel 1:19, 24, 27), meaning "How could this be? I can't believe what just happened!" *Eykah* is a scream because there aren't any words that adequately express what's being felt. *Eykah* throbs with shock and despair. "Oh! Alas! Woe! Ah!"

Babylon ripped apart Jerusalem's walls, gates, citadels and—most importantly—the city's temple (Lamentations 2:1–9). Enemy soldiers decimated Judah's army (Lamentations 1:15), who ran for their lives (Lamentations 1:6). Political and religious leaders were either dead (Lamentations 1:15), exiled (Lamentations 1:3), starving to death (Lamentations 1:11), or drowning in sorrow (Lamentations 2:10). Survivors huddled together—broken and hopeless. Others, not so fortunate, were executed (Lamentations 5:12). Normal life, including judicial and economic processes, ceased, ushering in suffering and starvation (Lamentations 2:12, 20; 4:2–10; 5:2, 4–6). Access to life's basic needs evaporated (Lamentations 5:2, 4). The empire's military force reduced everything to dust.

And yet! In spite of everything, the book of Lamentations hangs on—sometimes by a thread—to God's faithfulness. The small trickle of prayers (e.g., Lamentations 1:9; 1:11; 2:20–22) becomes a steady stream (Lamentations 3:40–47). It then turns into a rushing river in chapter 5, where the community's cries and protests, laments and longings, are brought to Yahweh, whose steadfast love endures forever. This prayer places the book's tears and heavy sighs into God's hands. It is within the context of unspeakable despair that Lamentations 3:23 dares to assert "Great is Your faithfulness" (ESV).

What do we learn from Lamentations? The book invites us to place our shattered hearts into God's loving hands, to honestly face life's setbacks and their ensuing emotional fallout. Lamentations offers spiritual and theological categories to help us make sense of what happens in our world, as well as how to survive it. Its poems give us words and images that help us speak the unspeakable.

When we pray the book of Lamentations, we pray with the faithful who have been victims of violence, rape, murder, and every sort of mayhem. We plead with God to turn from judgment to mercy and to heal this broken world. The book corrects euphoric and celebratory notions of faith that romantically portray the Christian life as consisting of only sweetness and light. The cries of anguish in Lamentations help us avoid a one-sided, happiness-only mindset that fails to deal forthrightly with life's tragedies.

To survive, we need language. When survivors retell their trauma, they are able to integrate it, process it, and move on from it. And if we don't talk about our feelings? The traumatic event becomes toxic. It doesn't become a memory; it remains an ongoing nightmare. To reclaim the future, we need to verbalize our past. Lamentations is all of this—and so much more.

NEW TESTAMENT LAMENTS

It looks like laments play only a small part in the NT. After all, there's nothing equivalent to lament psalms or the books of Job, Habakkuk, or Lamentations. The typical OT cry "How long?" occurs only once, in Revelation 6:10, while "Why?" appears a handful of times, famously in Matthew 27:46 and Mark 15:34. And even this, Christ's crucifixion—the most tragic event—becomes God's means to defeat sin, death, evil, and Satan. The darkness of Good Friday gives way to the eternal light in resurrection victory. What is there to lament?

The early church raises a lament in Acts 4:23–30, as believers cry out using Psalm 2:1 as their prayer: "Why do the nations rage and the peoples meditate on nothing?" When Stephen was stoned to death, reverent men buried him and "made great lament" (Acts 8:2). Then, when Dorcas died, "the widows wept" and displayed the tunics and clothing she had made (Acts 9:39). And Jesus? He shows solidarity with those saddened at Lazarus's death (John 11:33, 35), as well as at Jerusalem's imminent destruction (Luke 19:41–44).

Matthew includes laments both early in his Gospel, in the middle, and toward the end. The first one describes Bethlehem's mothers agonizing over King Herod's ruthless decree to slaughter their sons. Matthew uses the words of inconsolable Rachel to express this sorrow: "A voice is heard in Ramah, weeping and great wailing; Rachel weeping for her children. She refuses to be comforted because they are no more" (Matthew 2:18; cf. Jeremiah 31:15). Rachel—a literary figure here—refuses to theologize, spiritualize, or explain her horror away. She rejects the notion of putting the past behind her and getting on with life. Instead, Rachel looks death straight in the eye and lets it shake her to the core. Her honest brokenness reflects those who grieve over Herod's senseless slayings in Bethlehem.

Contrast Rachel with Mary's song in Luke 1:46–55, where joy and gladness permeate the virgin's celebration. We tend to remember Mary but forget Rachel at Christmas. Yet the two belong together. Praise without lament runs the risk of creating a shallow, superficial faith. Lament without praise fosters hopelessness and despair.

The Canaanite woman is much like Rachel (Matthew 15:21–28). Her prayer includes these common features in OT laments: (1) an address, (2) a complaint, (3) a plea, (4) a confession of faith, and (5) divine silence. The woman's resilience and persistence comport with several of Israel's protest and lament prayers—especially Zion's in Lamentations 1–2.

Rachel and the Canaanite woman prepare us for the greatest lament in Matthew's Gospel—the Savior's cry of dereliction on Good Friday, when the Father casts Him into the utmost cauldron of distress: "My God, My God, why have You forsaken Me?" (Matthew 27:46 ESV).

Matthew also pens these words of Jesus: "Blessed are those who mourn, for they shall be comforted" (Matthew 5:4 ESV). Jesus doesn't eliminate laments from our lives; instead, He invites us to join Him in crying over a lost and dying world.

While tears are welcome in the kingdom of God, weeping and wailing are not Matthew's first or last words. His Gospel begins with the Son of David, the Son of God, coming into the world. It ends with this same Son bursting the bonds of death and rising from the dead. Christ's incarnation and resurrection provide buoyant hope for all who lament.

Is there a place for laments in Paul's theology? Yes, especially in Romans. Shame is a prominent theme in OT laments—a motif that comes up in Lamentations a number of times (e.g., Lamentations 1:21; 2:16; 3:46, 61–63; 5:1). Shame also appears in Romans's programmatic statement "For I am not ashamed of the gospel" (Romans 1:16 ESV). Shame rears its ugly head when Christian hope runs into the wall of experience—the life of the cross.

Shame is one reason Paul cites Habakkuk 2:4 in Romans 1:17: "The righteous shall live by faith" (ESV). As we saw earlier, Habakkuk writes within the context of Babylonian invasions in the late seventh and early sixth centuries BC and employs distinctive lament questions like "How long?" (Habakkuk 1:2) and "Why?" (Habakkuk 1:3). Building upon Habakkuk, Romans 8 connects creation, the elect, and the Spirit through the terms "I groan" and "groaning." The apostle discusses creation's suffering and its hopeful lament (Romans 8:22). Believers who have the firstfruits of the Spirit join in lamenting and groaning (Romans 8:23). The Holy Spirit prays for us with "groanings too deep for words" (Romans 8:26).

The new world has arrived in Christ and the Spirit, but this doesn't remove the sadness and sorrow of the old world. Just like Jesus in Gethsemane, we wait for our resurrection (Romans 8:23). Paul's adversative in Romans 8:37 ("No" in the ESV translation) announces that God doesn't reject the elect like sheep to the slaughter (Romans 8:36)—a statement that comes from Psalm 44:22, the only OT lament from an innocent suffering community. What is Paul doing? He is employing a lament to affirm the connection between the church—persecuted and even facing death—with innocent Israelites.

CONCLUSIONS

What do we lose when we overlook OT laments? Much, very much. In the face of injustice and pain, we can only utter weak and anemic prayers. Without these texts, we may end up thinking that God only cares about our praises. Then we might hesitate to tell Him about our angst and sorrow. If God's throne is only a place where we shower Him with esteem and acclaim, we not only ignore our own brokenness but also the brokenness of others. We dismiss people who are struggling and depressed, who are slogging through difficulties like sickness, disease, loneliness, divorce, and bankruptcy.

OT laments encourage us not to deny the past—nor to get stuck in it—instead, they invite us to work through our past. When engulfed in darkness, when its bitterness feels almost tangible, God doesn't command us to simply pray "Yes, Lord. Whatever You say." No. He wants us to speak our minds. Pour out our hearts. Faithfulness doesn't always imply the passive acceptance of trial and torment. The deep longing to reconnect with Yahweh lies at the heart of OT laments.

Unearthing painful memories and facing the angst buried within isn't easy. But when we become aware of an ugly emotion, God invites us to acknowledge it, repent of it, grieve it, mourn it, process it—whatever it takes to get it out in the open. We shouldn't allow negative feelings any overtime parking. One of the best things we can do with them is express them. Talk about them. Tell our story. Censoring, sidelining, and silencing the inner life never works.

There is something very godly about acknowledging our deep distress. In Genesis 6:6, God the Father looks at the sin of the world in Noah's day and His heart is grieved. In Luke 19:41, Jesus approaches Jerusalem and weeps over the city. In Ephesians 4:30, Paul writes that sin grieves the Holy Spirit.

When we are tempted to appear super-Christian—a facade that will surely fail us—OT laments summon us to be honest, to be human. The hymn writer puts it this way: "'Come unto Me, ye weary, and I will give you rest.' O blessed voice of Jesus, which comes to hearts oppressed!" (*LSB* 684:1).

DISCUSSION QUESTIONS

1. How does Psalm 62:8 summarize this chapter?
2. How do you pray when under stress?
   Short pleas: "God help me!"
   Bargaining: "God, if you get me out of this, I promise I'll . . ."
   Liturgical prayers: "Our Father, who art in heaven . . ."
   Uplifting prayers: "You are my refuge, my stronghold."
   Prayers of lament: "How long, O Lord?"
3. Why do you think Christians frequently neglect OT laments?
4. What does God promise those who lament?
5. What OT book of protests do you resonate with the most—Job, Habakkuk, or Lamentations?

CHAPTER 12

DO OLD TESTAMENT PROPHETS PREDICT CURRENT EVENTS?

"I will put My Spirit within you,
and you shall live, and I will
place you in your own land."
(Ezekiel 37:14 ESV)

Ongoing terror and warfare haunt the Middle East. Nuclear saber-rattling continues apace. Financial experts regularly predict economic collapse. Environmental catastrophes are increasing. Fires, hurricanes, heat waves, and droughts are wreaking havoc and destroying countless lives.

Did OT prophets predict these current events? Many say yes. What makes them so sure? They argue that a number of passages—especially from Ezekiel, Daniel, Amos, and Zechariah—predict these crises. Adherents of this worldview believe that the founding of the modern state of Israel in 1948 is the key to biblical prophecy. When the Jewish people returned to their ancestral homeland, these Bible teachers and pastors saw it as fulfilling what a number of OT prophets predicted—that Israel would once again live in the land of Abraham, Isaac, and Jacob. We now live in the last days, marked by cataclysmic warfare and unprecedented natural disasters. Who came up with these ways of reading Israel's prophets?

DARBY, SCOFIELD, LAHAYE, AND JENKINS: DISPENSATIONALISM

From the fall of Jerusalem in AD 70 until the 1840s, the question of who owned Palestine was answered politically. Whoever had the military might and diplomatic ability owned the land. In the 1840s, however, a Plymouth Brethren minister from England named John Nelson Darby began teaching that the question of Palestine's ownership needed to be answered theologically. By introducing the method of biblical interpretation known as premillennial dispensationalism, Darby divided biblical history into seven dispensations, or periods of time. The end of the sixth dispensation will be triggered by Israel's return to the land—often called the "super sign" of biblical prophecy.

Picking up where Darby left off, C. I. Scofield propagated these views in his influential Scofield Reference Bible, first published in 1909. The Scofield Reference Bible is the single most important document that promotes the teaching that the last days will arrive when the Jews return to their land. This will be followed by the seventh dispensation—Christ's one-thousand-year reign on earth.

While Scofield popularized the teachings of Darby, Tim LaHaye and Jerry Jenkins took Scofield's ideas and disseminated them a hundredfold. LaHaye and Jenkins, authors of the Left Behind series of novels, also believe the fuse that ignited the last days was ethnic Israel's return to the land of Palestine in 1948. Wars, earthquakes, famines, tribulations, and natural disasters have since escalated and will continue until Christ raptures the church out of the world.

Question: What's driving this premillennial dispensational viewpoint of OT prophets? Answer: An argument that claims to be a literal interpretation of these texts but skirts how the NT interprets them.

AMILLENNIALISM

On the other hand, there are Christians who read OT prophetic texts symbolically—that is, in keeping with the way that the books in the NT interpret them. This approach is called amillennialism. Its advocates believe Jesus is the interpretive key to Israel's prophetic corpus, not the modern state of Israel. Current events don't explain OT prophecies; instead, Jesus does.

Before we look at specific passages, let's further compare premillennial dispensationalism with amillennialism.

AMILLENNIALISM	PREMILLENNIAL DISPENSATIONALISM
God's promises to Israel are fulfilled in Christ.	God's promises to Israel are fulfilled in the 1948 country of Israel.
All earthly promises to Israel have been either fulfilled or invalidated through Israel's disobedience and unbelief.	God's promises concerning Israel's return to the land and rebuilding of the temple are yet to be fulfilled.
Israel was God's OT people, a foreshadowing of the church, and the church is the universal people of God.	Israel and the church will always remain separate.
The church was prophesied in the OT in OT language.	Christ instituted the church as plan B; plan A is with the Jews.
Christ came to die for the sin of the world.	Christ came to establish an earthly kingdom for Israel.
All promises to Israel are fulfilled through Christ for the church.	All promises to Israel are fulfilled exclusively through the Jews.

EZEKIEL

Let's now look at some prophetic passages, beginning with Ezekiel. Premillennial dispensationalists argue that OT prophecies regarding not only the land but also such promises as the rebuilding of the temple and the reinstitution of its sacrifices must be literally fulfilled. Their interpretation of Ezekiel 37–48 is a crucial part of this position.

Ezekiel 37 begins with a gruesome scene—a valley full of dry bones. It looks like a Civil War battlefield or Hiroshima after the atomic bomb blast. God tells Ezekiel to stand in the middle of the bones and start preaching. Through the prophet, God says, "I will open your graves and I will raise you from your graves. I will bring you into the land of Israel" (Ezekiel 37:12).

Does this predict World War II, when Nazi Germany decimated Europe's Jewish population? Do these verses say that, following Auschwitz-Birkenau, God would give the Jews their own country in 1948? This is how premillennial dispensationalists explain Ezekiel. It is difficult, however, to conceive how such an entirely futuristic interpretation would have brought comfort to Judean exiles in Babylon, to whom Ezekiel was sent to minister in the sixth century BC.

Conversely, amillennialists understand that Ezekiel's vision of the dry bones has multiple fulfillments—the first being Cyrus's decree that allowed Judahite exiles in Babylon to return to their land (Ezra 1). This resurrection from political death points to Christ's resurrection from the dead as well as to our baptismal life. "We were buried therefore with Him by baptism into death, in order that, just as Christ was raised from the dead by the glory of the Father, we too might walk in newness of life" (Romans 6:4 ESV).

Christ's return will set in motion the final plan to destroy death. Bones—all dry and dead bones—will get a fully functioning body. Why? Because Jesus is the death of death. When He comes again, death will be swallowed up in victory and all things will be made new.

We now consider Ezekiel 38–39. These chapters describe Israel's purification to prepare for the temple's restoration in chapters 40–48. Thus, Ezekiel 38 envisions Gog's defeat, while chapter 39 features Gog's disposal.

Premillennial dispensationalists—believing that God fulfilled Ezekiel 37 when Israel became a country on May 14, 1948—explain Gog as the military leader who will launch an invasion of the Jewish state. The prophet describes Gog as "the chief prince of Meshech and Tubal" (Ezekiel 38:2 ESV). The Hebrew word translated "prince" is *rosh*—a term premillennial dispensationalists believe refers to Russia. How would this apply to Ezekiel's audience, since the Romanov dynasty didn't begin ruling over a united Russia until 1613?

It's therefore better to understand that Gog's identity derives from Gyges, the name of a Lydian king mentioned in six inscriptions of the Assyrian king Ashurbanipal (668–631 BC). Magog, for its part, is a reference to the territory of Lydia in western Anatolia. Meshech is also known from Assyrian sources and is portrayed in Psalm 120:5–7 as a barbaric enemy. Likewise, Tubal is mentioned in Assyrian documents and was the territorial designation of the interior Anatolian kingdom bounded on the west by Meshech. What is the prophet doing by using these names that derive from the north of Israel? Ezekiel employs them to symbolically describe evil and their wicked ways. In other texts, Israel's enemies also derive from the north (e.g., Jeremiah 1:13–15; 6:22; Zechariah 2:6).

Therefore, unlike the foreign nations in Ezekiel 24–32, the references in Ezekiel 38–39 are employed as cyphers of great wickedness. Contrary to the Egyptians, Assyrians, and Babylonians, with whom Judah had frequent contact, people in the distant north were shrouded in mystery. This combination of mystery and brutality made Gog and his confederates perfect symbols for Israel's ultimate enemy.

John confirms this interpretation in Revelation 20:7–10. Toward the end of the NT era—and just before Christ's second coming—God will, for a short time (Revelation 20:3), permit Satan to make one final, all-out attack against the church. Satan will deceive the nations. He will gather people from throughout the world who despise God's Word and reject God's gracious offer of life and salvation through Jesus Christ. Gog and Magog—symbols of evil—will lead this great uprising of nations. The battle, though, won't last long. Just as God destroyed Gog (Ezekiel 38:17–23), so divine fire will consume the enemies of the church (Revelation 20:9).

Let's review. The premillennial dispensational reading of Ezekiel 37–48 follows this sequence: Israel will return to the land in 1948 (Ezekiel 37); Russia will invade the Jewish state (Ezekiel 38–39); Christ will reign on earth for a thousand years, when Jerusalem's temple will be rebuilt and animal sacrifices will be offered according to OT regulations.

Is this premillennial dispensational reading how Ezekiel intends us to read his last nine chapters? Not at all.

The prophet's vision in chapters 40–48 is similar to Solomon's temple presented in 1 Kings 6–8. Perhaps most striking is the threefold structure described in Ezekiel 40:48–42:20: first comes the vestibule, then the nave, and finally the inner room—the Most Holy Place.

But there are discontinuities as well. Most significantly, the prophet reworks Solomon's great bronze sea of 1 Kings 7:23 so that it becomes a river flowing from the temple (Ezekiel 47:1–12). Ezekiel describes it as a surging river that flows into the Dead Sea, which is 1,400 feet below sea level and has a saline content of 35 percent. Ever since divine fire torched Sodom and Gomorrah, the two cities near the Dead Sea, the entire area had become the ultimate symbol of death (cf. Genesis 19:24–25).

But no longer. Ezekiel stands on a riverbank and sees both sides covered with a great number of trees. These, he is told, will miraculously bear fruit every month and always yield leaves that heal. The prophet's guide points eastward and tells Ezekiel that the river from the temple will transform the Dead Sea into a freshwater lake. Fishermen will spread their nets and haul in their catches. "Wherever the river flows, everything lives" (Ezekiel 47:9).

Premillennial dispensationalists read Ezekiel's rebuilt temple and river of life as events that will happen while Christ reigns on earth for a thousand years. Amillennialists, however, interpret these chapters as they do all OT prophecy: Ezekiel is pointing to Jesus (e.g., Luke 24:27, 44).

John's Gospel shows us how. The evangelist interprets Ezekiel's temple and river. It begins with just a trickle when Jesus tells Nicodemus, "No one can enter the kingdom of God unless he is born of water and the Spirit" (John 3:5). Christ then tells the Samaritan woman, "I give you living water" (John 4:10). This is followed by a surge: "Whoever believes in Me, streams of living water will flow from within him" (John 7:38).

Then, in one ironic twist for the ages, this raging river of life is reduced to just a drop—until it completely dries up. Christ cries out, "I thirst" (John 19:28). Here is Jesus, crushed and cursed by the sin of the world. Yet, just as the glory of the Lord returned to Ezekiel's temple (Ezekiel 43:4–5), that same glory returned when Jesus stepped out of Joseph's tomb alive on the third day.

DANIEL

There are four sections in the book of Daniel that premillennial dispensationalists use to promote their understanding of OT prophetic passages. The first is in Daniel 2. Nebuchadnezzar—the great Babylonian king who reigned from 605–562 BC—sees a statue composed of four metals, each one representing a different kingdom. On this, all Christians agree. What is uncommon, though, is the premillennial dispensationalist emphasis on the two legs and ten toes in the iron section of the statue (Daniel 2:33). They maintain that the two legs signify two different Roman empires. The last one will be marked by a ten-nation confederacy, which they believe is the current European Union. They further argue that it is during this time that God's kingdom will come upon earth. However, it is dubious to interpret two legs as two separate Roman eras with a long gap between the two.

Moreover, the premillennial dispensational interpretation depends on *two* legs and *ten* toes, though nowhere in Daniel 2 are the number of legs or toes mentioned. In Daniel's interpretation of Nebuchadnezzar's dream, he never mentions the number of legs or toes or indicates that they would have any significance. Far from being a literal interpretation as premillennialists claim, their interpretation is imaginative and symbolic. In their view, the two legs are not literal legs, nor are the ten toes literal toes.

Daniel 7 relates the prophet's vision of four fierce animals followed by the coming of the Son of Man (Jesus) to stand before the Ancient of Days (God the Father). In this chapter, the fourth creature in Daniel's vision devours everything remaining from the onslaught of the first three beasts. This animal is different from the others as it has ten horns (Daniel 7:7). Most agree that the fourth creature represents the Roman Empire, which ultimately fell in the fifth century AD. What is unique about the premillennial dispensational interpretation is the argument that the Roman beast will be revived at a future time. This interlude of time allows for a gap in God's work with Israel, which they call the church age. In their words, this is a parenthesis. Just as a parenthetical comment in a sentence might interrupt the main flow of the sentence, so the church is seen as interrupting God's real work through ethnic Israel.

However, this incorrectly teaches that God's coming kingdom is postponed until Christ's thousand-year reign on earth. How so? Jesus Himself announces, "The time is fulfilled, and the kingdom of God is at hand; repent and believe in the gospel" (Mark 1:15 ESV). Moreover, the problem with the premillennial interpretation of Daniel 7 is that this vision (along with Nebuchadnezzar's dream in Daniel 2) unfolds in a continuous manner, without any gaps. Again, we see that far from being a literal interpretation of the text, the premillennial approach is imaginative in that it inserts a gap, or parenthesis, where none exists in the text.

The vision in Daniel 8 consists of a ram (representing Persia) and a goat (representing Greece). The little horn that comes out of the goat (see Daniel 8:9–14) is a prophecy about Antiochus Epiphanes, who reigned over the Seleucid Empire from 175 BC until his death in 164 BC. Antiochus instituted Greek reforms that sought to destroy Judaism, and this, in turn, brought about the successful revolt of the Jewish Maccabees.

Premillennial dispensationalists, though, overinterpret God's directive to Daniel: "Behold, I will make known to you what shall be at the latter part of the indignation, for it refers to the appointed time of the end" (Daniel 8:19). Understanding "end" as an absolute end, a premillennial dispensational reading denies any connection with Antiochus and pushes the prophecy toward a future antichrist, who will appear at the end of the church age and before the seven-year tribulation.

However, when the angel Gabriel told Daniel that the vision "concerns the time of the end" (Daniel 8:17), this must be understood according to the context of the vision itself. Daniel was told that the vision's emphasis was on 2,300 evenings and mornings (Daniel 8:14)—meaning 2,300 evening and morning sacrifices, or 1,150 days. This is a prediction of the length of the cessation of sacrifices in Jerusalem's temple during Antiochus's persecution of the Jews, which lasted a little over 1,100 days. (On the OT's prediction of time periods as approximate, see the previous discussion in chapter 10). Thus, the "end" is the end of the 2,300 evenings and mornings and is confirmed in Daniel 8:19, where this is called "the latter part of [God's] indignant anger" and "the appointed time of the end." The prediction is confirmed in Daniel 8:26, where Daniel's vision is called "the vision of the evenings and mornings." Once again, the premillennial dispensational interpretation, though claiming to be literal, ignores the actual context and proposes a novel reading that disregards the literal markers in the text that indicate this passage is not speaking of the absolute end of time.

Daniel 9:24–27 is a difficult section to interpret, but based upon what we are learning about the premillennial dispensational reading of Daniel, it should not surprise us that they twist the passage in order to delay God's coming kingdom—maintaining that the first sixty-nine weeks (Daniel 9:24–26) were completed in Christ's first coming, while the seventieth week (Daniel 9:27) has yet to be fulfilled. Driving this interpretation is the need to create a parenthesis for the church that will then be raptured (i.e., taken out of the world) before the tribulation.

It is important, though, to see that two passages in Jeremiah speak of the seventy years of captivity. The first is Jeremiah 25:11–12, a prophecy given in 605 BC, the year Daniel was taken to Babylon. The second, Jeremiah 29:10, is part of a letter Jeremiah wrote in 597 BC to Babylonian captives. Jeremiah's missive urged exiles to settle in Babylon because they would not return to Jerusalem until seventy years were completed. Daniel saw that in both of these prophecies, God would bring captivity to an end by punishing Babylon (Jeremiah 25:12) when seventy years were completed (Jeremiah 29:10).

Since there are no gaps in Jeremiah's seventy years, why should we suppose that there is an interlude in Daniel's vision? Daniel 9:27 reads:

> And he shall make a strong covenant with many for one week, and for half of the week he shall put an end to sacrifice and offering. And on the wing of abominations shall come one who makes desolate, until the decreed end is poured out on the desolator. (ESV)

The premillennial dispensationalists' argument is tied to their belief that Daniel 9:26 and Daniel 9:27 are phrased in prose that describes events in a chronological order. There is, they hold, a two-thousand-year gap, which they term "the church age," between verses 26 and 27. Once the church is raptured, the tribulation will commence with the events described in Daniel 9:27.

All of this means that the "he" of Daniel 9:27 cannot be Christ, who is described as the "anointed one" who is "cut off" in Daniel 9:26. Rather, it is argued that the "he" in Daniel 9:27 is the antichrist, who makes a covenant with the Jews at the beginning of the tribulation. Halfway through this period, though, "he shall make an end to sacrifice and offering" and set up "the abomination of desolation" to persecute the Jews for the remaining three and a half years. This, premillennial dispensationalists hold, is the antichrist's decision to outlaw temple sacrifices. When the antichrist breaks his covenant with the Jews, this leads to the "great tribulation" that will end with the advent of Christ's millennial kingdom on earth.

Amillennialists, on the other hand, embrace the idea that the relationship between Daniel 9:26 and 27 is not a linear progression but repetition with intensity. Hebrew authors frequently express their thoughts by stating an idea, then they build upon it. This means, then, that the "He" of Daniel 9:27 is Christ, described in Daniel 9:26. It is Jesus, who on Good Friday "put an end to sacrifice and offering" (Daniel 9:27), thus fulfilling and abolishing the OT sacrificial system (cf. Hebrews 9:11–28). There is therefore no time gap between Daniel 9:26 and 27.

The premillennial dispensational reading of Daniel misrepresents texts to make them fit into their preconceived end-times scenario, which moves the focus away from the life, death, and resurrection of Jesus to a millennial reign on earth. God's kingdom, then, for premillennial dispensationalists, is not primarily an announcement of forgiveness, salvation, and eternal life in Christ. It is instead a future earthly kingdom of power and glory. However, when Daniel is properly understood, we are invited to see how God's kingdom comes to us now in Christ, even as we await its consummation when He comes again.

AMOS

Amos is an eighth-century-BC shepherd from Tekoa who predicts fires, earthquakes, locusts, drought, famine, disease, and an army bent on the complete annihilation of Israel. Amos 1:2–9:10 burns and buries the world of power politics and phony religion, as these were known in the prophet's day.

Would there be a future after such devastation? Yes. The prophet announces restoration in Amos 9:11–15. The night of judgment will soon be over, and a new day will dawn. Yahweh has a plan for the entire created order. God will first "rebuild David's fallen tent" (Amos 9:11). The "remnant of Edom" will then be restored (Amos 9:12). Finally, the mountains and hills will drip with new wine (Amos 9:13).

Premillennial dispensationalists believe these promises envision Israel's restoration to the land in 1948. God's chief concern, after all, is the Jewish people. What will happen to the church? According to premillennial dispensationalists, the church is God's alternate plan, or a parenthesis. The church age must end with the rapture before God can reestablish His primary work with the Jews and the culmination of history with Christ's thousand-year reign on earth.

The problem with this interpretation is that it ignores how James explains Amos in Acts 15. James, the half brother of Jesus, employs Amos 9:11–12 to vindicate the universality of the Gospel and the church's Gentile mission. If premillennial dispensationalists argue that this is spiritualizing the OT, then they should acknowledge that it is James, under the inspiration of the Holy Spirit, who does so. Instead, James saw that the rebuilding of David's fallen tent was accomplished by Jesus, the ultimate Son of David. His life, death, and resurrection ushered in God's eternal kingdom and allows all humanity—both Jew and Gentile—to seek the Lord by believing in Christ and being incorporated into His church (Amos 9:12).

By using Amos 9:11–12 to teach a predetermined chronological and futuristic plan for national Israel, premillennial dispensationalists take away the heart of the passage, which implicitly focuses on Christ's work at Calvary as the reason Gentiles were turning to God (Acts 15:26).

ZECHARIAH

Passages in Ezekiel, Daniel, and Amos are viewed differently by premillennial dispensationalists and amillennialists. So is Zechariah 9–14. This section of the book consists of two parts, chapters 9–11 and 12–14. Each section begins with the term "oracle" (Zechariah 9:1; 12:1). The first envisions a new king (Zechariah 9:9–10) with a new kingdom that reunites Israel and Judah (Zechariah 9:1–8; 10:1, 3–12). The second part, chapters 12–14, offers two perspectives of the same war. The result is God's kingship over all the earth (Zechariah 14:9, 16).

Zechariah 14:1–5 reflects divine warfare motifs, while Zechariah 14:6–11 envisions a new creation. The change in perspective is dramatic. The darkness of warfare gives way to a new day of never-ending light. Creation, as well as Jerusalem, will be transformed. The polarities of the first creation will cease to exist (day and night, cold and heat, summer and winter). There will also be an immense display of light. The pinnacle of this renewal is the new Jerusalem.

Zechariah 14:10–16 is both particular and global. Jerusalem is the center of the nations—the conduit through which Yahweh will channel His blessing to the world. How shocking this must have sounded to Zechariah's contemporaries. In his day, the great cities were Babylon, Susa, and Memphis—certainly not Jerusalem. Yet the prophet announces that the city of David will be elevated and unassailable by any enemy. While Jerusalem had long been considered a sacred mountain—high and lifted up (e.g., Psalm 48:2)—now, with a flat area surrounding it and its elevation heightened, there will be no doubt about its importance. Jerusalem's lofty status will draw many nations (Isaiah 2:2–4; Micah 4:1–4; cf. Zechariah 8:20–23).

By geography, Jerusalem is not in an advantageous position. The city has no major source of water, and it is surrounded by desolate hills. It is not on a major trade route, and foreign armies regularly overrun it. All of this will change, though, in the coming age. The city will have a perpetual and overflowing source of water (Zechariah 14:8), its elevation will be a bulwark of protection (Zechariah 14:10–11), and the nations will come to it and enrich its economy (Zechariah 14:14). In the end, from Yahweh's house in Jerusalem, He will restore the entire world to its perfect state of holiness (Zechariah 14:20–21).

Premillennial dispensationalists neglect the poetic and symbolic features of Zechariah 14. Instead, they read it literally. They argue that this is what the earthly thousand-year reign of Jesus will look like. Amillennialists, however, use the NT to explain Zechariah's last chapter. It provides John with a map to articulate his vision in Revelation 20–22. The connections are as follows:

- Zechariah 14:2; Revelation 20:7–9—Nations gather against Jerusalem.
- Zechariah 14:5; Revelation 20:12–13—God resurrects people.
- Zechariah 14:7; Revelation 21:25; 22:5—Night is banished.
- Zechariah 14:7; Revelation 21:23–24; 22:5—God gives eternal light.
- Zechariah 14:8; Revelation 21:6; 22:1–2, 17—God gives living water.
- Zechariah 14:9, 16, 17; Revelation 21:5—God reigns forever.
- Zechariah 14:10; Revelation 21:10—The holy mountain is established.
- Zechariah 14:11; Revelation 22:3—Curses are removed.
- Zechariah 14:20–21; Revelation 21:2, 27; 22:15—Jerusalem becomes holy.

John teaches us that Zechariah's point is theological, not geographical. To become overly concerned about specific locations in chapter 14 misses the prophet's thrust—Yahweh's gift of a perfectly beautiful and unassailable city, the new Jerusalem. No wonder Jerusalem goes by the names "the holy city" (Isaiah 52:1), "the City of Yahweh" (Isaiah 60:14), "the Zion of the Holy One of Israel" (Isaiah 60:14), "the throne of Yahweh" (Jeremiah 3:17), and "Yahweh Is There" (Ezekiel 48:35).

CONCLUSIONS

How shall we understand OT prophecies? Is it through the lens of current events or through the inspired writers of the NT? We believe the books of Matthew through Revelation teach that Israel's prophetic corpus points to the person and work of Jesus. Colossians 2:16–17 provides an excellent example: "Therefore do not let anyone judge you by what you eat or drink, or with regard to a religious festival, a new moon celebration or a Sabbath day. These are a shadow of the things that were to come; the reality, however, is found in Christ." OT prophecies are shadows of Jesus, not prognostications of the modern state of Israel—much less, the rapture of the church, the great tribulation, and Christ's millennial reign on earth.

Until the day of Pentecost, the disciples had an expectation of a glorified kingdom of Israel, not unlike the premillennial dispensationalist expectation of a thousand-year kingdom of Christ (cf. Luke 24:21; Acts 1:6). But after the coming of the Holy Spirit, they began to use OT language in new ways. Peter, for instance, speaks of our inheritance, which, unlike the land of Palestine, "can never perish, spoil, or fade" (1 Peter 1:4). The book of Hebrews is filled with examples of how the NT reinterprets the OT. Note, for example, that in Hebrews 11:13–16, the central Gospel motif is the land. The pilgrimage of faith is set in three scenes: (1) the land of the patriarchs, (2) their nomadic wandering, and (3) their hoped-for homeland that is a better, indeed a heavenly, city. Abraham, Isaac, and Jacob did not pin their hope on an earthly Canaan but upon the new Jerusalem depicted in Revelation 21–22.

Note also that when Jesus speaks about the land (e.g., Luke 19:41–44), He makes no reference to it ever being restored to the Jews. Rather, He taught His disciples to look forward, not to a Jewish return to the land but to the coming of the Son of Man in His glory on the Last Day (e.g., Luke 21:25–28).

Paul, for his part, teaches that Christians inherit the promises to Abraham (Galatians 3:29). Present-day Jews without faith in Christ do not. God didn't promise the land to the Jews. Instead, those baptized into Christ Jesus are heirs of the world (Romans 4:13)—indeed, a renewed heaven and earth where righteousness dwells (2 Peter 3:13). This end-time hope inspires us to sing: "Christians, this Lord Jesus shall return again in His Father's glory, with His angel train; for all wreaths of empire meet upon His brow, and our hearts confess Him King of glory now" (*LSB* 512:6).

Yet premillennial dispensationalists argue that redemptive history takes a U-turn during Christ's thousand-year reign on earth. Everything returns to the types and shadows of the OT. The future is a restoration of the past. This interpretation views God's ultimate reality not in Jesus but in the types and shadows of the OT. Christ, however, says that all of Israel's texts point to Him (John 5:39).

Premillennial dispensationalists treat the OT as a self-contained entity to be understood apart from Christ and the NT. Denying the unity between the testaments almost amounts to treating the OT as a non-Christian Jewish book. To teach, for instance, on the basis of Ezekiel 40–48 that the temple in Jerusalem will be rebuilt during Christ's millennium rule and that the sacrificial system will be reinstituted is to raise questions about Scripture's teaching that Jesus Himself is the new temple (Matthew 12:6; John 2:12–22) and that

His sacrifice on the cross is fully sufficient for all people of all time (Hebrews 10:18).

However, when we allow the NT to interpret the OT, it becomes clear that the modern state of Israel is not a prophetic realization of Christ's kingdom. Furthermore, we should not anticipate a day in which this kingdom will manifest Jewish distinctives, whether by its location in the land of Palestine, its capital in Jerusalem, or its ceremonial institutions and practices. "The testimony of Jesus is the spirit of prophecy" (Revelation 19:10 ESV).

DISCUSSION QUESTIONS

1. How does Ezekiel 37:14 summarize the chapter?
2. What is the history of premillennial dispensationalism?
3. Contrast premillennial dispensationalism with amillennialism.
4. Why is Revelation 19:10 the best way to interpret OT prophets? Can you give an example?
5. What are some verses in the NT that support a focus on Christ in the OT instead of the 1948 state of Israel?

CHAPTER 13

DOES GOD CHANGE HIS MIND IN THE OLD TESTAMENT?

"Return to Yahweh your God,
for He is gracious and compassionate,
slow to anger and abounding in steadfast
love; and He relents concerning evil."
(Joel 2:13)

Clearing his throat first thing in the morning, a father announces with great gusto, "We're going to the game tonight!" Then, when picking up his children after school, he sheepishly says, "I changed my mind. It won't work for us to go to the game tonight."

None of us like it when people flip-flop. We get frustrated when a parent, spouse, employee, or teammate says one thing and then does the other. Fickle people rub us the wrong way. So why does the OT teach us that Yahweh changes His mind?

Just five chapters after announcing that His creation is "very good" (Genesis 1:31), we learn that "Yahweh regretted [*nacham*] that He had made man on earth, and it brought Him heart-piercing sorrow" (Genesis 6:6). Is Yahweh an inconsistent God who can't always be counted on? Does He start off in one direction and then go in another? What's going on?

God changes His course of direction at some of the key junctures in Israel's Scriptures—not only at the flood story (Genesis 6:6) but also at Mount Sinai (Exodus 32:12, 14), as well as at the institution of the monarchy (1 Samuel 15:11, 29, 35). The idea is even incorporated into Israel's creedal statements about Yahweh (Joel 2:13; Jonah 4:2). Both of these verses declare that Yahweh is gracious and merciful, slow to anger, and abounding in steadfast love, and that He relents (*nacham*) over disaster. Yahweh's willingness to pivot comes within a list of His Gospel characteristics. He delights in showering mercy and grace upon His people.

NACHAM

The King James Version translates the Hebrew word *nacham* as "repent." Contemporary translations employ other words, with the most common being "regret," "retract," "think better of," "change one's mind," and, most commonly, "relent." There are two ways to interpret verses when God is the subject of *nacham*.

The first is to designate descriptions of God's change as anthropomorphic. We encountered this idea in the chapters titled "Does God Suffer in the Old Testament?" and "What About Divine Anger and Vengeance in the Old Testament?" You may recall that the anthropomorphic argument goes like this: God describes His relationship with people in ways we can understand, Yahweh condescends to our level, He accommodates Himself to us in ways that make sense, but God doesn't actually suffer pain or feel anger. Neither does He change His mind. Instead, when OT writers speak like this, they're using language that describes Yahweh using human ideas and categories. These anthropomorphisms don't describe God as He really is.

Those who promote this interpretation believe that if God actually changes, then all is lost. A God who reverses His Word provides no solid foundation for faith. A changing God is no help in life's most vexing moments. We don't need a God who shifts like sand or changes like shadows. Like David, we need a God who is likened to a rock (2 Samuel 22:2–3; Psalm 18:2)—a God who is constant, dependable, and always faithful.

This interpretation is built upon ancient Greek philosophy—a system of thought that believes God is perfectly immutable and absolutely transcendent. God never changes.

In this chapter, we argue that the OT embraces both the

authenticity of Yahweh's relenting (it's not anthropomorphic or symbolic language), as well as Yahweh's dependability (His divine characteristics never change). He is eternal, all-knowing, all-present, all-powerful, and completely holy. The statement "I, Yahweh, do not change" (Malachi 3:6) refers to God's character, not His ability to respond to what happens in the world. Several OT passages confirm this understanding of God's change of mind and not of His character. Let's look at them.

EXODUS 32

In Exodus 32:11–14, Yahweh forthrightly tells Moses that, because the Israelites worshiped a golden calf, He is going to destroy the nation. Moses responds by offering a series of reasons as to why Yahweh should reconsider. Then Moses prays, "Turn aside from Your burning anger and relent [*nacham*] from this evil against Your people. Remember Abraham, Isaac, and Israel, Your servants" (Exodus 32:12–13). Moses commands Yahweh to calm down and reconsider, to recall His unconditional promises to the patriarchs. And God does just that. "Yahweh relented [*nacham*] from the evil He had spoken of bringing on His people" (Exodus 32:14). When pressed by Moses, Yahweh's desire is for life, not death.

Divine change, therefore, announces the priority of grace in all of Yahweh's dealings with the world. To be affected and to interact genuinely doesn't mean some imperfection in Yahweh. His move from judgment to mercy indicates that the world isn't in the hands of an iron fate or an impersonal power. In Exodus 32, Yahweh shows Himself not only to be perched high upon His throne but also interacting with His people.

WHEN YAHWEH DOESN'T RELENT

There are, however, places in the OT where Yahweh doesn't relent on previous decisions. This happens in eight verses. Of these, five describe His refusal to change the decision about employing the Babylonians to execute judgment on Judah and Jerusalem in 587 BC (Jeremiah 4:28; 20:16; Ezekiel 24:14; Hosea 13:14; Zechariah 8:14). One verse speaks of Yahweh's unwillingness to modify His commitment to Melchizedek's eternal priesthood (Psalm 110:4). The remaining two verses appear to place God's refusal to change as a standard principle: "God is not man, that He should lie, or a son of man, that He should change His mind" (Numbers 23:19 ESV; cf. 1 Samuel 15:29).

NUMBERS 23 AND 1 SAMUEL 15

Numbers 23 describes the interaction between Balaam (a pagan prophet) and Balak (a Moabite king). They join forces in order to curse Israel. In his first oracle in Numbers 23:7–10, Balaam paradoxically blesses God's people. Balak becomes furious but invites Balaam to try again. These words then appear within Balaam's second oracle: "God is not man, that He should lie, or a son of man, that He should change His mind [*nacham*]" (Numbers 23:19 ESV). Balaam seems to say that God will never change His mind—period. End of discussion.

Because Balaam's statement comes within the context of Balak hiring him to curse Israel, the prophet's point is that God won't let that happen. Yahweh has pledged to protect Abraham and his descendants (Genesis 12:2–3). This is an everlasting covenant, sealed in circumcision (Genesis 17:7, 11). Israelites, then, can't be cursed. On this, Yahweh will never *nacham*. That's what Balaam is saying.

God's unwillingness to change His course of direction appears again in 1 Samuel 15. In this chapter, Yahweh directs Saul to strike down the Amalekites because of how they had treated His people when they came out of Egypt (1 Samuel 15:1–2; cf. Exodus 17:8–16). Saul is to utterly destroy these ancient enemies (1 Samuel 15:3). Yet, because he fails to follow orders, Yahweh says, "I changed My mind [*nacham*] that I made Saul king" (1 Samuel 15:11). Then Saul pleads with Samuel to allow him to continue serving as Israel's monarch. Samuel responds, "He who is the Glory of Israel does not lie or change His mind [*nacham*], for He is not a man, that He should change His mind [*nacham*]" (1 Samuel 15:29). The chapter ends with these words: "Yahweh changed His mind [*nacham*] that He made Saul king over Israel" (1 Samuel 15:35).

Do you see the discrepancy? Two times, Yahweh announces that He has changed His mind. Once, He says that He doesn't change His mind. Which is it?

In the first ten verses of 1 Samuel 15, Saul rebels against God's Word spoken through Samuel; only after that does God express His regret. God's regret follows Saul's sin. God changes when Saul changes.

But then we read these words in 1 Samuel 15:29: "God is not man, that He should lie, or a son of man, that He should change His mind [*nacham*]." Like the passage in Numbers 23, this observation is connected to Yahweh's refusal to revise one specific decision. In this case, His choice of David as Israel's new king (1 Samuel 13:14).

Like God's covenant with Abraham, His covenant with David is also unconditional and everlasting (cf. 2 Samuel 23:5). What, then, are we to make of these two verses, Numbers 23:19 and 1 Samuel 15:29?

Though Yahweh can and does change from Law to Gospel (or vice versa), He will never revoke His promises to Abraham and David—the two covenants that form the backbone of the NT (e.g., Matthew 1:1; Luke 2:4; Galatians 3:29). God's unchanging intention is to bless all the families of the earth (His pledge to Abraham) through Jesus Christ (His pledge to David). Unlike the times when we change, Yahweh isn't capricious when He distributes or revokes blessings and curses. No one and nothing will ever remove God's promises to Abraham and David. The NT announces that this includes all the baptized. The deal is sealed. On this, God will never change His mind.

Yahweh is thus both constant and changing. He is constant with respect to His covenants to Abraham and David. He's eternally resolute with respect to these promises. At the same time, Yahweh changes in view of changing circumstances in the lives of those He is in relationship with.

Yahweh isn't fickle. Far from it. Yahweh is ever faithful, ever true, ever committed to His people. Therefore, there is no need to fear arbitrary change. We may live in the freedom of God's unswerving goodness and grace in Christ Jesus.

JEREMIAH

No other book in the OT contains as many references to Yahweh's changes of previous decisions as does Jeremiah. The foundational passage comes in Jeremiah 18:7–10, with the most comprehensive statement in the Bible to explain divine relenting. While in specific circumstances Yahweh is willing to change from Law to Gospel (e.g., Jonah 3:6–10), as well as from Gospel to Law (e.g., Genesis 6:6–7; 1 Samuel 15:11, 35), Jeremiah 18:7–10 announces God's willingness to change for all people of all time:

> If at any time I speak about a nation or a kingdom, that I will pluck up and throw down and destroy, and if that nation, about which I have spoken, turns from its evil, I will relent [*nacham*] of the evil that I intended to do to it. And if at any time I speak about a nation or a kingdom that I will build and plant it, and if it does evil in My sight, not listening to My voice, then I will relent [*nacham*] of the good that I had intended to do to it. (Jeremiah 18:7–10)

Jeremiah 26 illustrates these hypothetical events. The chapter is set in 609 BC, shortly after the death of King Josiah. Josiah's son Jehoiakim is the new Judean king. Through Jeremiah, Yahweh announces the possibility that He could change from judgment to grace: "Perhaps they will turn from their evil ways, then I will relent [*nacham*]" (Jeremiah 26:3). However, if the people don't repent, the prophet continues, God will make Jerusalem like Shiloh (Jeremiah 26:6). (Yahweh destroyed Shiloh, where the tabernacle was located, during the days of Samuel when the Philistines confiscated the ark of the covenant.)

This is too much for Jerusalem's priests, prophets, and citizens. Jeremiah must die! The prophet won't back down: "Now reform your ways and your actions and trust Yahweh your God. Then Yahweh may relent [*nacham*] and not bring the evil He has pronounced" (Jeremiah 26:13).

With Jeremiah inches from death, some of Jerusalem's leaders protect the prophet. They quote from Micah, who, during the days of Hezekiah (715–686 BC), prophesied, "Zion will be plowed like a field; Jerusalem will become a heap of ruins, and the mountain of the house a wooded height" (Jeremiah 26:18; cf. Micah 3:12). King Hezekiah prayed to Yahweh with the result that "Yahweh relented [*nacham*] concerning the evil" (Jeremiah 26:19). Micah's prophecy of doom didn't happen, because Yahweh changed from Law to Gospel. And Jeremiah? This vindicated his message that Yahweh is a God who relents.

ISAIAH

Hezekiah, the Judean king, is involved in another event when Yahweh pivots from an earlier decision. At one point in his life, Isaiah says to the king, "This is what Yahweh says, 'Put your house in order, because you are going to die: you will not recover'" (Isaiah 38:1). After the king weeps bitterly and prays about his impending doom, God tells Isaiah, "Go back and tell Hezekiah, 'Thus says Yahweh, the God of your father David says, "I have heard your prayer and seen your tears; I will add fifteen years to your life"'" (Isaiah 38:5). Had the king not prayed, he would have died. Yahweh turned from a prior decision because Hezekiah prayed. Mercy triumphs over judgment.

JOEL

The book of Joel furthers our understanding of Yahweh's change of direction. The oracle against Judah in Joel 2:1–17 has two sections.

Verses 1–11 contain a description of an invasion and destruction of Judah that is likened to the "day of Yahweh." The graphic tone of these verses emphasizes the certainty and finality of Judah's coming destruction. Yet, even as Joel envisions the final phase of the attack, he recognizes the possibility that Yahweh might change His decision. Why? If His people repent.

To convey this hope, Joel uses Exodus 34:6, a verse that Joel 2:13 repeats almost word for word. The first term Joel employs is the adjective "gracious." In the OT, only Yahweh is described as gracious. The prophet doesn't pin his hope upon people but solely upon Yahweh and His grace.

The next part of Exodus 34:6 that Joel employs is the term "merciful"—a word linked with the emotional bond that a mother has for her child in utero. Such is Yahweh's affection for His people. Next Yahweh is depicted as "slow to anger"—a motif we cover extensively in chapter 9. Finally, in Joel 2:13, the prophet describes Yahweh as possessing great steadfast covenantal love. By placing *nacham* alongside these remarkable Gospel characteristics, Joel confesses that Yahweh has such great love that He's willing to relent, forgive, and extend mercy.

One more point needs to be made about divine change in Joel. Right after the prophet expresses his hope in Yahweh, he asks, "Who knows?" (Joel 2:14). Note Joel's humility. It's the same posture that the Ninevite king takes in Jonah 3:9, when the monarch petitions Yahweh to change a previous decree uttered by Jonah: "Forty days and Nineveh will be overturned" (Jonah 3:4). Nineveh's king, just like Joel, follows his request for Yahweh to *nacham* with "Who knows?" Those who pray this way are asking Yahweh to pivot from condemnation to salvation, for it's in His heart to do so. But these people don't force the issue. Instead, they leave the matter in God's hands.

Yahweh is willing to back up from a prior decision. He's responsive to what is happening and adjusts His ways. Yahweh isn't immutable when it comes to interacting with people. This is one reason for Israel's disgust with the unchangeable nature of idols (cf. Psalm 115:5–7; Jeremiah 10:4–5). By prohibiting idolatry, the OT confesses Yahweh's relatedness, not only His transcendence. One of the characteristics of the gods of the nations is that they can't be moved or affected (cf. 1 Kings 18:27–29). Yahweh can and does.

ISAIAH 40–48: YAHWEH KNOWS THE FUTURE

The passages we've considered so far feature Yahweh's decisions to modify His plans. Does this mean He doesn't have a full grasp of the future? Do God's midstream changes indicate His inability to know what will happen next?

Not at all. In fact, there are 164 verses in the OT that explicitly affirm God's foreknowledge and 271 verses that teach other aspects of His omniscience (either of past, present, or future events). Yet, like nowhere else in the OT, Isaiah 40–48 announces that Yahweh knows everything about everything—past, present, and future.

The prophet's literary court scene in Isaiah 41:1–7 demonstrates how Yahweh works in history. *He predicts it in advance.* Acting like a bailiff crying out "Hear ye, hear ye," God calls the nations and their gods into His chambers. It's really Israel, however, who is on trial. Isaiah addresses sixth-century BC Israelite captives in Babylon, many of whom are convinced that Babylonian deities are more powerful than Yahweh—that they, not Yahweh, know and orchestrate history. Thus, Isaiah composes a mock trial where Yahweh and Babylonian gods testify.

In Isaiah 41:1–7, the prophet focuses on Cyrus, whom Yahweh would use to free His people from Babylon as well as to reconstitute life in Judah and Jerusalem. While Cyrus is foregrounded in this trial scene, Abraham is in the background. The point? Yahweh has decided, planned, and executed the lives of Abraham and Cyrus. Babylonian gods didn't do this. Babylonian gods *can't* do this. Yahweh alone knows and controls history.

In another mock trial, Isaiah again sets forth God's ability to predict the future (Isaiah 41:21–29). The test of true divinity is the capacity to predict both future events as well as bring them to pass. Of all the so-called gods and lords in the ancient Middle East, Yahweh alone does this. The conclusion of this trial indicates that Babylonian gods are impotent (Isaiah 41:29). The upshot? The nations (Isaiah 41:1, 4, 11–12), their idols (Isaiah 41:6–7, 24), and their counselors (Isaiah 41:28) are nothing but sinful delusions. Yahweh is the only Savior because He alone knows, directs, and controls history for the sake of His people.

Isaiah 44:24–45:13 continues this argument and is the central section of Isaiah 40–48, bringing together Yahweh's calling of Cyrus (likened to Abraham), His overthrow of Babylon, and His restoration of Israel. While Isaiah 41:2 describes "a victor from the east" and Isaiah 41:25 announces "one from the north," this human helper in now named—Cyrus (Isaiah 44:28; 45:1).

Creational ideas bracket Isaiah 44:24–45:13—thus the prophet's blending of creation and history comports with Isaiah 40:12, 22, 26, 28. In Isaiah 44–45, the prophet interweaves Yahweh's creational power with statements in Isaiah 40:15–17, 22–24, which describe Yahweh's mastery over the nations.

Isaiah 40–48 thus presents a contrast between Yahweh and false gods. Pseudodeities don't know or control the future. Yahweh does both. The OT therefore embraces Yahweh's change of mind *and* His omniscience. Yahweh's ability to change a course of action doesn't negate His complete foreknowledge of the future. "Who can fathom Yahweh's Spirit? Who can instruct Yahweh as His counselor?" (Isaiah 40:13; cf. Romans 11:33–36).

THE NEW TESTAMENT

While the NT doesn't directly address Yahweh's change of mind, there are several passages that express the idea. The Canaanite woman is a good example (Matthew 15:21–28). She persists in prayer, trusting that Jesus will pivot from rejection to heeding her plea. Christ finally grants her request; her daughter is healed. The Canaanite woman's boldness stands in the tradition of Moses, Hezekiah, and Joel. They keep praying and never give up (cf. Luke 18:1).

Add Paul to the lineup. At one point in his life, the apostle asks Christ to remove the thorn in his flesh—not once, but three times (2 Corinthians 12:7–10). In this case, Jesus denies Paul's petition. The apostle had to learn to live in pain. God didn't relent, though Paul pleaded for Him to do so.

CONCLUSIONS

The OT doesn't employ anthropomorphic or symbolic language when it describes Yahweh changing a previous decision. Yahweh's pivots are real. At the same time, He also has an exhaustive foreknowledge of everything that will ever happen. Both attributes of God stand side by side. Divine change doesn't diminish Yahweh's foreknowledge. When God relents, it doesn't mean He's saying, "Oops! I didn't see that one coming. I have to go back and reconsider."

Yahweh is "perfect in knowledge" (Job 37:16), and His "understanding has no limit" (Psalm 147:5). He keeps track of our tears (Psalm 56:8) and knows our innermost thoughts (Psalm 139:2). His omniscience covers all knowledge, including future events. He foreknew Cyrus two centuries in advance. God knows the future—exhaustively and perfectly.

The OT invites us to confess both God's immutability and His mutability as essential divine attributes, each in their own sphere. Yahweh is immutable in terms of His omnipotence, omniscience, omnipresence, and the like. He's mutable in His ability to change from Law to Gospel, as well as from Gospel to Law.

Two extremes, therefore, need to be avoided—either that Yahweh is immutable in any absolute sense or that He is mercurial, capricious, and unstable. To be affected and to interact genuinely doesn't mean Yahweh is imperfect. In fact, not being able to respond or interact, not being open and vulnerable, or refusing to change are signs of imperfection. God shifts from anger and judgment to mercy and grace. His pivot from Law to Gospel is still part of one unchanging divine will.

While there are similarities between how God and people step back from earlier decisions, there is also one fundamental difference. Within the context of veering from wrath to redemption—"I will not execute My burning anger; I will not destroy Ephraim" (Hosea 11:9)—Yahweh announces, "I am God and not a man, the Holy One among you" (Hosea 11:9). When Yahweh modifies His intentions, He doesn't forfeit His holiness. He doesn't change like we change. Yahweh is holy, separate, and distinct from us and from all creation—and in the most fundamental of ways. He knows everything; we see but through a mirror dimly (1 Corinthians 13:12).

Yahweh is personal. He is loving. He is relationally tied to us. Yahweh is also sovereign. He is also transcendent. He is unimaginably holy. Yahweh knows the end from the beginning, and all things are at His disposal. There is, no doubt, a hushed mystery in all of this.

This much, though, is clear. Yahweh is a person relentlessly operative through His Word. He is changeless in His attributes and purposes. In His relationships with people, He can—and sometimes does—change a prior plan or decision. We must resist the idea that for God to respond to the prayers of His people is somehow beneath Him. "Thou art coming to a King, large petitions with thee bring; for His grace and pow'r are such none can ever ask too much" (*LSB* 779:2).

Finally, we note that God's constant availability for changing decisions stands in the service of His unchanging divine intention to bless all the families of the earth through Jesus Christ.

DISCUSSION QUESTIONS

1. How does Joel 2:13 summarize this chapter?
2. What are the two options when it comes to understanding verses when Yahweh relents [*nacham*]?
3. What verses in the OT best shed light on this topic?
4. How does the NT contribute to your understanding of God's propensity to change from Law to Gospel?

CHAPTER 14

WHERE IS GOD IN SONG OF SONGS AND ESTHER?

"May Yahweh our God be with us,
as He was with our ancestors.
May He not leave us or forsake us."
(1 Kings 8:57)

There are three books of the Bible in which women play roles as prominent or perhaps more prominent than men: Ruth (Ruth and Naomi), Song of Songs (the Shulammite), and Esther (Esther). Interestingly, in two of these books, God is not mentioned—neither by Hebrew terms for God nor by His covenant name, Yahweh. They are Song of Songs and Esther. This lack of direct attention paid to God was noticed already in antiquity and has called for explanation even to the present day. Are these religious books worthy of inclusion in the OT? Why is God seemingly absent from these books? Has He abandoned Israel in these ancient writings or is something else hinting at His presence even when He is not mentioned? Is there a way to understand God as present even when He is not a primary, overt focus of a biblical book?

FINDING GOD IN SONG OF SONGS

Love between a man and a woman was designed to include sexual expression (Genesis 2:20–25). Ancient and modern readers have noticed that Song of Songs features the most open depiction of sexual attraction between a woman and a man in all of the OT. Although this dimension of God's plan for humans has been corrupted by the fall into sin, sexuality nevertheless remains part of God's blessing in marriage. Song of Songs depicts the main characters—the Shulammite woman (Song of Songs 6:13) and her beloved—as rejoicing in the gifts of love, emotional and physical intimacy, and companionship. This also reminds Christians of God's loving relationship with His people (see Isaiah 62:5; Jeremiah 2:2; Ephesians 5:22–33; Revelation 19:7; 21:2, 9; 22:17). Yet, where is God in all this? Was the sexual attraction depicted in the Song too overt so that Solomon was embarrassed to mention God?

Even a quick and casual reading of Song of Songs leads readers to notice that the woman in the poem at times directly addresses her friends as the daughters of Jerusalem (Song of Songs 1:5; 2:7; 3:5; 5:8, 16; 8:4), or, once, the daughters of Zion (Song of Songs 3:11). In three of these addresses, she urges her friends to take an oath. The first two are identical:

> I place you under an oath, daughters of Jerusalem, by the gazelles or by the does [i.e., female deer] of the field, that you do not awaken and you do not arouse this love until it desires. (Song of Songs 2:7; 3:5)

The third is similar but contains some important differences:

> I place you under oath, daughters of Jerusalem: Why would you awaken and why would you arouse this love until it desires? (Song of Songs 8:4)

Notice that at Song of Songs 8:4, not only are the gazelles and does missing but the "that you do not awaken and you do not arouse" becomes "*why* would you awaken and *why* would you arouse?" This draws attention to the mention of the gazelles and does and also leads readers to wonder the reason for transforming the statements about awakening and arousing love into rhetorical questions.

Let us first consider the rather strange oath sworn by gazelles and does. While we are used to solemn oaths sworn in the name of God, calling on wild animals like gazelles and deer seems quite bizarre. In fact, Song of Songs 2:7 and 3:5 are the only examples in the entire Bible of animals called to witness oaths. It was common in biblical times to take an oath in the name of God or, in the case of pagans, the gods (see Ruth 1:17; 1 Samuel 3:17; 19:6; 2 Samuel 2:27; 1 Kings 17:12; 18:10; 2 Kings 6:31; Job 27:2; Jeremiah 44:26; Amos 8:14). As noted in Hebrews 6:13, occasionally oaths were sworn by a superior human authority: Pharaoh (Genesis 42:5), the high priest Eli (1 Samuel 1:26), the crown prince Jonathan (1 Samuel 23:3), or the prophet Elijah (2 Kings 2:4, 6). As Hebrews 6:13 observes, God, who has no superior, swore oaths by Himself as witness (Numbers 14:21, 28; Deuteronomy 32:40; Isaiah 49:18; Jeremiah 22:24; 46:18; Ezekiel 5:11; 14:16; Zephaniah 2:9).

So why does the Song call for an oath with wild animals as witnesses? Some scholars have suggested that it was common for shepherds to use objects in their environment to attest to their oaths. Not only is this speculation—as there is no evidence for this—but it also does not account for the specific animals. Why gazelles and does when Song of Songs mentions many animals, including doves (Song of Songs 1:15; 2:14; 4:1; 5:2, 12; 6:9), turtledoves (Song of Songs 2:12), goats (Song of Songs 4:1; 6:5), and ewes (Song of Songs 6:6). Song of Songs also mentions many plants that were in pastoral settings in Israel, but the oath specifically focuses on gazelles and does.

Other scholars have highlighted specific features of gazelles and does as the reason for them being chosen. The suggestions include the following:

- Gazelles and does are easily frightened, indicating that one cannot force love upon others.
- Gazelles and does wait until mating season to couple, indicating that humans, too, should wait for the proper time for love.

- Gazelles are beautiful, vigorous, and sexually active, thereby making them a favorable comparison to the Shulammite.

- Gazelles and does are lovely and free, and they roam the hills. They should not be disturbed, just as love should not be disturbed.

Note the arbitrariness of this type of explanation. The interpreter picks characteristics of the animals and then seeks an explanation that fits. Moreover, the characteristics are not exclusive to gazelles and does. Other animals are skittish, others are said to be beautiful, others have a mating season, and so forth.

A third explanation is that the Hebrew word for "gazelles" is identical to the Hebrew word for "armies." This would imply that the oath was taken in the name of "Yahweh of armies," often translated "Yahweh of hosts," or perhaps by the angels, His heavenly army. (Note that the NT lists instances of swearing an oath by things associated with God: heaven, earth, Jerusalem's temple. See Matthew 5:34–35; James 5:12.) While this explanation at least acknowledges that oaths were often taken in God's name, it makes for a rather awkward translation: "I place you under an oath, daughters of Jerusalem, by the *armies* or by the does of the field . . ." Why would deer be mentioned alongside God or His angels?

In addition, the oath is not only sworn by gazelles and does, but by "the gazelles or does *of the field*." The addition of the phrase "of the field" is unusual. Elsewhere in the OT, this term is used only with generic words for animals. The phrase "animal of the field" occurs twenty-nine times and often indicates wild animals (e.g., Exodus 23:11; Hosea 2:12). At times, it seems to distinguish earthbound animals from birds in the sky (see Genesis 2:19–20). In one instance, the similar phrase "beast of the field" is used to characterize wild animals (1 Samuel 17:44). Therefore, "gazelles and does of the field" appears to be somewhat awkward and nonsensical. It cannot be distinguished between wild gazelles and does and domesticated gazelles and does, since those animals were never domesticated.

However, another suggestion accounts for all of the features of the phrase "by the gazelles and does of the field." In Hebrew, "by the gazelles or does of the field" (*bitsevaoaoth o beayloth hasadeh*) sounds similar to "by Yahweh of armies or by God Almighty" (*beyahweh tsevaoth o beel shaday*). This is a circumlocution—a substitution of a direct reference to something with a longer, indirect reference to that thing. This is done in modern expressions of shock or surprise to avoid using God's name by using a phrase that is somewhat incongruous. For instance, "gosh" for "God," "holy cow" instead of "Holy Christ," or the French *sacré bleu* ("holy blue") for *sacré dieu* ("Holy God"). In the case of Song of Songs, note that not only is swearing an oath with animals as a witness illogical but also adding "of the field" makes little sense.

But why would Solomon feel the need to use a circumlocution to avoid directly mentioning God? The answer may lie in the Israelite's reluctance to mention God in a book in which sexual matters are very prominent. After all, the OT never uses a Hebrew word that precisely corresponds to the English word *sex*. It always uses indirect phrases such as "know someone" (Genesis 4:1, 25) or "lie with someone" (Genesis 19:33–34) or "go to" [a woman's room for sexual intercourse] (Genesis 16:2). This reluctance to speak openly about sexual matters may have led Solomon to use a circumlocution rather than link God directly with an oath that included the sexual aspects of love between men and women. Notice that immediately before the Shulammite addresses the daughters of Jerusalem, she pictures the beginning of a sexual encounter with her beloved:

- His left hand is under my head, and his right hand embraces me! (Song of Songs 2:6 ESV)
- I found the one whom my soul loves. I held on to him and would not let him go until I brought him into my mother's house and into the chamber of the one who conceived me. (Song of Songs 3:4)

Then she tells the daughters of Jerusalem to swear not to awaken "the love," meaning "this kind of love," until it desires (Song of Songs 2:7; 3:5).

Throughout Song of Songs, the Shulammite is teaching others—signified by the daughters of Jerusalem—about her love for her beloved and the appropriate time for the expression of that love (see Song of Songs 1:5; 3:11; 5:16). By placing them under oath that is intended to invoke Yahweh of armies, God Almighty, she is signaling the seriousness of not arousing love until "it desires"—that is, until the appropriate time according to God's plan for humans, within the bonds of holy marriage.

When we turn to the third time that the Shulammite places the daughters of Jerusalem under an oath, we see that she changes her words to form questions: "Why would you awaken and why would you arouse this love until it desires?" (Song of Songs 8:4). These questions should be read as exclamations that ask rhetorical questions. In essence, the Shulammite is asking, "*Why in the world* would you awaken and *why in the world* would you arouse this love until it desires?" In this way, this final invitation to take an oath emphasizes the foolishness of the misuse of love, especially in its physical expressions. It also anticipates topics in the rest of Song of Songs 8 that encourage love being expressed within marriage:

- Song of Songs 8:5—Love has been awakened between the Shulammite and her beloved. It leads to mutual dependence and satisfaction between the two. She leans on him, and he is awakened (!) by her.
- Song of Songs 8:6–7—Love is stronger than death and is a blazing flame that cannot be extinguished. So do not fool around with it until it desires.
- Song of Songs 8:7—Money cannot buy love, so do not treat it lightly.
- Song of Songs 8:8–12—Chastity is desirable, so do not misuse love's physical expression. Instead, in your chastity, your beloved will find peace.
- Song of Songs 8:13–14—When love is appropriately awakened, you will find joy in your beloved.

In the final address to the daughters of Jerusalem, the Shulammite does not invoke the gazelles and does, even though by now the reader expects them to be mentioned in order to hint that God approves and encourages the proper expression of love within marriage. So, where is God's presence in this oath refrain? It lies just two verses later:

> Love is as relentless as death; ardor is as relentless as Sheol, its flames are flames which is the fiercest blaze. (Song of Songs 8:6)

The Hebrew noun for "fiercest blaze" is a compound word—a fairly rare occurrence. It uses the word for "blaze" and a suffix that can intensify the meaning. Other examples occur at Jeremiah 2:31 ("thick darkness") and Jeremiah 32:19 ("mighty deeds"). This suffix is very similar—but not identical—to the shortened form of God's name Yahweh, which is sometimes used in poetry. (The suffix is *ya[h]*, whereas the shortened form of God's name is *Yah*.) Once again, Solomon is using a circumlocution for God by implying His holy name in connection with the fierce blaze. Some English versions make this explicit by translating "fiercest blaze" as "flame of Yahweh" (see ESV, CSB footnote, NIV footnote).

God is the one who blesses marriage with love in all its varied expressions, something that Solomon is hinting at through the words of the Shulammite. In turn, this allows Christians to also ponder God's relationship to His people, as He loves them like a loving husband (see Ephesians 5:25–27; Revelation 19:7–8; 21:2, 9).

GOD AS THE HIDDEN HAND GUIDING ESTHER AND MORDECAI

Esther appears to be the most secular book of the Bible. It never mentions overt religious practices such as prayer, sacrifice, or worship. Perhaps the only hint of religion is Esther's request of Mordecai: "Go, gather all the Jews to be found in Susa, and hold a fast on my behalf, and do not eat or drink for three days, night or day. I and my young women will also fast as you do. Then I will go to the king, though it is against the law, and if I perish, I perish" (Esther 4:16 ESV). Since fasting was usually accompanied by prayer and pleas to God for favor (Ezra 8:21–22, 31; Daniel 9:3), this request implies that Esther was seeking God's favor before approaching King Ahasuerus. However, apart from this one passage, the author never reveals any religious faith or practice of Esther, Mordecai, or the Jews in the Persian Empire.

In some ways, Esther appears to present a story from a secular perspective, with no mention of the Israelite faith in the one true God or the beliefs of the Persians in their gods. This appearance is bolstered by ten feasts and celebrations that have no explicit religious components:

- Esther 1:3–4—Ahasuerus's 180-day feast for his officers and nobles
- Esther 1:5–8—A seven-day banquet for all the people in Susa
- Esther 1:9—Vashti's feast for the women
- Esther 2:18—The banquet celebrating Esther's elevation to the status of queen
- Esther 3:15—The king and Haman sitting down to drink following Haman's decree that permitted Jews to be attacked
- Esther 5:1–8—Esther's first banquet for Ahasuerus and Haman
- Esther 7:1–10—Esther's second banquet for Ahasuerus and Haman (mentioned already in Esther 5:8, 12, 14; 16:4)
- Esther 8:17—Jews celebrating the defeat of their enemies

- Esther 9:18—Jews in Susa celebrating on the fifteenth day of Adar

However, these verses do not mean to suggest that God is absent from the book, even though He is never mentioned. In fact, the author of Esther has several ways of leading his readers to suspect that God is the major—though unmentioned—character in the story. One of these ways is by repeated use of what at first seems to be happenstance: coincidences that drive the plotline of the story. These appear to be beyond the control of the people they affected. For instance, Esther happened to please Hegai, so he hastened her beauty treatments and gave her servants to aid her (Esther 2:8–9). Mordecai happened to overhear the plot to assassinate Ahasuerus (Esther 2:21–23). When Haman cast lots to determine when to hold his campaign to exterminate the Jews in the empire, the lot fell "on the twelfth month," eleven months in the future, giving plenty of time for his plot to be foiled (Esther 3:7). When Ahasuerus had a sleepless night, his servants chose to read the account of how the plot to kill the king was thwarted by Mordecai's report of it (Esther 6:1–2). When Ahasuerus returned to the banquet that Esther prepared for him and Haman, he happened to enter the room when Haman was pleading for his life on the queen's couch, and Ahasuerus assumed Haman was molesting Esther (Esther 7:8).

These instances of happenstance are far too many and far too coincidental to be mere flukes of the flow of human events. They point to someone who is purposely kept out of the sight of the readers, unmentioned by the narrator, and only intimated by Mordecai's warning at Esther 4:14. The careful reader will come to the conclusion that, despite first appearances, God was controlling all the events, even when neither the people in the story nor the storyteller himself acknowledged Him.

A number of scholars have noted another feature of the narrative technique of Esther's author that leads readers to conclude that God is in control of all the events: unexpected reversals and turns in the plot. In literary terms, this technique is called peripety, and the author uses it to great effect. Some of the more prominent reversals are noted in the following chart.

SITUATION	REVERSAL
Haman's High Rank	*Mordecai's High Rank*
After these things King Ahasuerus promoted Haman the Agagite, the son of Hammedatha, and advanced him and set his throne above all the officials who were with him. And all the king's servants who were at the king's gate bowed down and paid homage to Haman, for the king had so commanded concerning him. But Mordecai did not bow down or pay homage. (Esther 3:1–2 ESV)	All the officials of the provinces and the satraps and the governors and the royal agents also helped the Jews, for the fear of Mordecai had fallen on them. For Mordecai was great in the king's house, and his fame spread throughout all the provinces, for the man Mordecai grew more and more powerful. (Esther 9:3–4 ESV) For Mordecai the Jew was second in rank to King Ahasuerus, and he was great among the Jews and popular with the multitude of his brothers, for he sought the welfare of his people and spoke peace to all his people. (Esther 10:3 ESV)

Haman's Vestiture	*Mordecai's Vestiture*
So the king **took his signet ring** from his hand **and gave it to** Haman the Agagite, the son of Hammedatha, the enemy of the Jews. (Esther 3:10 ESV)	And the king **took off his signet ring**, which he had taken from Haman, **and gave it to** Mordecai. And Esther set Mordecai over the house of Haman. (Esther 8:2 ESV)
Mordecai's Mourning Clothes and Lament	*Mordecai's Royal Clothes and Acclaim*
When Mordecai learned all that had been done, Mordecai tore his clothes and put on sackcloth and ashes, and went out into the midst of the city, and he cried out with a loud and bitter cry. (Esther 4:1 ESV)	Then Mordecai went out from the presence of the king in royal robes of blue and white, with a great golden crown and a robe of fine linen and purple, and the city of Susa shouted and rejoiced. (Esther 8:15 ESV)
Jews Lament	*Jews Celebrate*
And in every province, wherever the king's command and his decree reached, there was great mourning among the Jews, with fasting and weeping and lamenting, **and many** of them lay in sackcloth and ashes. (Esther 4:3 ESV)	**And in every province** and in every city, **wherever the king's command and his edict reached**, there was gladness and joy among the Jews, a feast and a holiday. **And many** from the peoples of the country declared themselves Jews, for fear of the Jews had fallen on them. (Esther 8:17 ESV)

Haman Advised to Execute Mordecai	*Haman Advised That Mordecai Will Prevail*
Then his wife Zeresh and all his friends said to him, "Let a gallows fifty cubits high be made, and in the morning tell the king to have Mordecai hanged upon it. Then go joyfully with the king to the feast." This idea pleased Haman, and he had the gallows made. (Esther 5:14 ESV)	And Haman told his wife Zeresh and all his friends everything that had happened to him. Then his wise men and his wife Zeresh said to him, "If Mordecai, before whom you have begun to fall, is of the Jewish people, you will not overcome him but will surely fall before him." While they were yet talking with him, the king's eunuchs arrived and hurried to bring Haman to the feast that Esther had prepared. (Esther 6:13–14 ESV)
Haman Constructs a Gallows for Mordecai	*Haman Hangs on the Gallows Made for Mordecai*
Then his wife Zeresh and all his friends said to him, "Let a **gallows fifty cubits high** be made, and in the morning tell the king to have Mordecai hanged upon it. Then go joyfully with the king to the feast." This idea pleased Haman, and he had the gallows made. (Esther 5:14 ESV)	Then Harbona, one of the eunuchs in attendance on the king, said, "Moreover, the **gallows** that Haman has prepared for Mordecai, whose word saved the king, is standing at Haman's house, **fifty cubits high**." And the king said, "Hang him on that." So they hanged Haman on the gallows that he had prepared for Mordecai. Then the wrath of the king abated. (Esther 7:9–10 ESV)

Haman Seeks His Own Honor	*Haman Forced to Honor Mordecai*
So Haman came in, and the king said to him, "**What should be done to the man whom the king delights to honor?**" And Haman said to himself, "**Whom would the king delight to honor** more than me?" And Haman said to the king, "For the man whom the king delights to honor, let royal **robes** be brought, which the king has worn, and the **horse** that the king has ridden, and on whose head a royal crown is set. And let the robes and the horse be handed over to one of the king's most noble officials. **Let them dress the man whom the king delights to honor, and let them lead him on the horse through the square of the city, proclaiming before him: 'Thus shall it be done to the man whom the king delights to honor.'**" (Esther 6:6–9 ESV)	So Haman took the **robes** and the **horse**, and **he dressed Mordecai and led him through the square of the city, proclaiming before him, "Thus shall it be done to the man whom the king delights to honor."** Then Mordecai returned to the king's gate. But Haman hurried to his house, mourning and with his head covered. (Esther 6:11–12 ESV)

Another case of reversal involves irony focusing on the Persian king's supposedly unchangeable decrees (Esther 1:19). To overcome the proclamation issued by Haman in Ahasuerus's name, Esther requested that Ahasuerus issue a decree reversing Haman's decree (Esther 8:3, 5). Such a directive—also supposedly irreversible—is issued (Esther 8:8). The Hebrew verb roots for "pass over/across" or "turn/return" are used in each case. This makes it appear as if the decrees of the Persian rulers are not as inflexible as claimed but remain subject to an implied higher authority. The author's use of similar wording to draw attention to such reversals demonstrates his intention to use the art of narrative so that the reader concludes that God is involved deeply in the events.

In at least two cases, the author deliberately notes the reversal of circumstances:

- Now in the twelfth month, which is the month of Adar, on the thirteenth day of the same, when the king's command and edict were about to be carried out, on the very day when the enemies of the Jews hoped to gain the mastery over them, *the reverse occurred*: the Jews gained mastery over those who hated them. (Esther 9:1 ESV; emphasis added)

- As the days on which the Jews got relief from their enemies, and as the month that *had been turned* for them from sorrow into gladness and from mourning into a holiday; that they should make them days of feasting and gladness, days for sending gifts of food to one another and gifts to the poor. (Esther 9:22 ESV; emphasis added)

The Hebrew verbs translated "the reverse occurred" and "had been turned" are from the same verb root, again calling attention to the reversal. Moreover, both are in the passive voice, which does not reveal the agent who caused the turnaround—implying that the real power in the chain of events is God Himself.

In addition, these reversals and God's control of them is heightened by the author's use of this same literary technique elsewhere. Irony—the deliberate inclusion of contradictory items that are incongruous—is found throughout Esther:

- Esther 1:17–19; 5:1–2, 8—Vashti was deposed as queen for disobedience, while Esther was disobedient twice and was rewarded.
- Esther 6:11–12; 3:2; 8:1–2—Haman was humiliated by having to obey the king's command, while Mordecai deliberately disobeyed a royal command but was rewarded.
- Esther 3:15—The city was in turmoil while the king and Haman enjoyed drinks.
- Esther 6:6–9—Haman, who sought to prescribe royal honors that he would enjoy, actually prescribed the honors given to his enemy Mordecai.
- Esther 7:9–10—Haman's body was hanged on the gallows that he had intended for Mordecai.

For readers who are carefully following the story, the cumulative effect of this series of reversals, heightened by numerous ironies combined with a series of coincidences that seem too good to be true, leads to the conclusion that God's providence and care for His people lie behind all these events. The author of Esther is using peripety as it has been used elsewhere in the OT:

- Genesis 39–45—Joseph's rise from slave to lord of Egypt (especially 45:8–9)

- Exodus 14–15—Israel's deliverance from Pharaoh's army at the Red Sea (especially 15:9–10)
- 1 Samuel 1–2—Hannah's elevation in her rivalry with Peninnah (especially 1 Samuel 2:5)
- 1 Samuel 17—David's victory over Goliath
- Daniel 6—Daniel's rescue from the lions' den and his enemies thrown into the den

For Bible readers familiar with these earlier stories, Esther's multiple cases of peripety surely lead to the conclusion that the same God who rescued His people in these earlier events was also behind the defense of the Jews in the Persian Empire.

As has often been noted, the most important passage hinting at God's work behind the scenes in Esther is found in Mordecai's warning to Esther when she displayed reluctance to appeal to Ahasuerus on behalf of her people:

> For if you keep silent at this time, relief and deliverance will rise for the Jews from another place, but you and your father's house will perish. And who knows whether you have not come to the kingdom for such a time as this? (Esther 4:14 ESV)

How could Mordecai be so confident that Esther was placed in a position to deliver the Jewish people? His words imply that he had faith in God's promises. God would bless those who bless Israel and curse those who curse them (Numbers 24:9; cf. Genesis 12:3; 27:29). In addition, God had promised that all nations would be blessed through Israel (Genesis 12:3; 18:18; 22:18; 26:4; 28:14; cf. Galatians 3:8). This last promise was to be fulfilled in Christ (Galatians 3:14). God's promise to save the world through the promised Messiah would only be fulfilled through Israel. Thus, Israel would be delivered from Haman so God's chosen OT people could bring forth the world's Redeemer. Mordecai recognized that God had placed Esther in the correct position to protect Israel from extermination and to further God's plan of salvation.

None of this, however, is stated explicitly by any person in the story of Esther—not Esther nor Mordecai nor any other Jew. Instead, the author skillfully arranges his narration of events to lead the reader to the conclusion that even when God's actions are veiled or hidden, He is not inactive. Instead, He is working to defend and provide for His people and to bring about the salvation of all humankind in the promised Savior.

The message to readers today is also clear: God's work is often hidden from our eyes, and at times, the world seems to be spinning out of control. Nevertheless, God is in charge of all that happens, and He still watches over His people by directing the course of human events. This is why we sing, "Lord, enthroned in heav'nly splendor, first-begotten from the dead, You alone, our strong defender, lifting up Your people's head" (*LSB* 534:1).

DISCUSSION QUESTIONS

1. In what ways does the use of circumlocutions for God's name in Song of Songs bring you a greater appreciation of God's role in marriage's most intimate moments?
2. How does the treatment of love in human marriage in Song of Songs help you appreciate more deeply God's love for His Bride, the Christian Church?
3. In what ways does the book of Esther's avoidance of mentioning God make its message more powerful for modern readers?
4. How is Mordecai and Esther's society similar to your modern and highly secularized society? In what ways are they different?

FOR FURTHER READING

CHAPTER 1: WHAT MAKES PORTIONS OF THE OLD TESTAMENT SEEM SO DIFFICULT TO UNDERSTAND?

Dougherty, Raymond Philip. *Nabonidus and Belshazzar*. Yale University Press, 1929. An exploration of the early archaeological evidence for Belshazzar as a historical figure.

Engelbrecht, Edward A., ed. *Concordia's Complete Bible Handbook*. 2nd ed. Concordia Publishing House, 2013. A book-by-book Bible guide that often explains the historical and cultural background of biblical times.

Engelbrecht, Edward A., ed. *Lutheran Bible Companion*. Vol. 1, *Introduction and Old Testament*. Concordia Publishing House, 2020. A guide to the Bible that often explains noteworthy events, people, and places.

Silzer, Peter James, and Thomas John Finley. *How Biblical Languages Work: A Student's Guide to Learning Hebrew and Greek*. Kregel, 2004. A concise introduction to the way that Hebrew and Greek function as languages, emphasizing each language's unique features.

Vardaman, Jerry. "A New Inscription Which Mentions Pilate as 'Prefect.'" *Journal of Biblical Literature* 81.1 (1962): 70–77. The seminal article on inscriptional proof of Pontius Pilate as a historical person.

CHAPTER 2: WAS THE UNIVERSE REALLY CREATED IN SIX DAYS?

Ashton, John S., ed. *In Six Days: Why Fifty Scientists Choose to Believe in Creation*. Master Books, 2018. An evangelical evaluation of creation from a scientific perspective.

Ham, Ken, and Bodie Hodge, eds. *The New Answers Book One: Over 25 Questions on Creation/Evolution and the Bible*. Master Books, 2006. A concise debate between reading Genesis 1–2 literally and Darwinian evolution.

Lennox, John C. *Seven Days That Divide the World: The Beginning According to Genesis and Science*. Zondervan, 2011. A comparison and contrast between the traditional reading of the Genesis creation account and Darwinian evolution.

Moreland, J. P., Stephen C. Meyer, Christopher Shaw, Ann K. Gauger, and Wayne Grudem, eds. *Theistic Evolution: A Scientific, Philosophical, and Theological Critique*. Crossway, 2022. A series of essays exploring the weakness of theistic evolution in several different disciplines.

CHAPTER 3: DOES THE OLD TESTAMENT TEACH US ABOUT THE HOLY TRINITY?

Beckwith, Carl L. "The Trinity and the Old Testament: YHWH, Our Elohim." In *The Holy Trinity*, vol. 3 of *Confessional Lutheran Dogmatics*, edited by Gifford A. Grobien. Luther Academy, 2016. A nice exploration of Christian doctrine relating to the Holy Trinity.

Gerhard, Johann. *On the Nature of God and on the Trinity.* Theological Commonplaces: Exegesis II–III, translated by Richard J. Dinda, edited and annotated by Benjamin T. G. Mayes. Concordia Publishing House, 2007. A classic Lutheran exposition of the Christian doctrine concerning the Holy Trinity that defends the proposition that both the OT and NT witness to the Trinity.

Hamilton, Victor P. *The Book of Genesis: Chapters 1–17.* New International Commentary on the Old Testament. Eerdmans, 1990. A commentary on Genesis by a respected American evangelical scholar.

Steinmann, Andrew E. *Genesis*. Tyndale Old Testament Commentaries. InterVarsity Press, 2019. A commentary on Genesis by one of the authors of this book.

Thomas, Heath A. "Old Testament." In *The Trinity in the Canon: A Biblical, Theological, Historical, and Practical Proposal*, edited by Brandon D. Smith. B&H Academic, 2023. A nice essay on the evidence for the Trinity in the Old Testament.

CHAPTER 4: WHY DID SOME MEN LIVE SO LONG?

Steinmann, Andrew E. "A Comparison of the Text of Genesis in Three Traditions: Masoretic Text, Samaritan Pentateuch, Septuagint." *Journal of the Evangelical Theological Society* 64 (2021): 25–43. This essay is in two parts: a comparison of the textual traditions behind three ancient forms of the text of Genesis and an application of the findings to the genealogies in Genesis 5 and 11.

Steinmann, Andrew E. "Genesis Genealogies and the Messianic Promise." *Bibliotheca Sacra* 176 (2019): 343–59. A study that argues that the primary purpose of the Genesis 5 and 11 genealogies is to teach about the Messiah's descent from Adam and not to present information to construct a chronology from Adam to Abraham.

Steinmann, Andrew E. "Challenging the Authenticity of Cainan, Son of Arpachshad." *Journal of the Evangelical Theological Society* 60 (2017): 697–711. This article argues that the mention of Cainan in the Septuagint version of Genesis 10:24 is a late addition.

Steinmann, Andrew E. "Gaps in the Genealogies in Genesis 5 and 11?" *Bibliotheca Sacra* 174 (2017): 141–58. A study that explores reasons to believe that one cannot use Genesis 5 and 11 for chronological purposes.

Wenham, Gordon J. *Genesis 1–15*. Word Biblical Commentary. Zondervan, 1987. Especially helpful for Wenham's discussion of several ancient and modern attempts to explain the perceived chronological difficulty of Genesis 11:10. See especially page 250.

CHAPTER 5: WHAT ABOUT ALL THE VIOLENCE IN THE OLD TESTAMENT?

Copan, Paul. *Is God a Moral Monster? Making Sense of the Old Testament God.* Baker, 2010. The most comprehensive study on divine violence in the OT from an evangelical perspective.

Cowles, C. S., Eugene H. Merrill, Daniel L. Gard, and Tremper Longman III. *Show Them No Mercy: Four Views on Canaanite Genocide.* Counterpoints: Bible and Theology, edited by Stanley N. Gundry. Zondervan, 2003. Four evangelical scholars debate the events recorded in the book of Joshua.

Longman, Tremper, III, and Daniel G. Reid. *God Is a Warrior*. Zondervan, 1995. An evangelical interpretation of divine warfare in the Bible.

CHAPTER 6: HOW SHOULD WE UNDERSTAND FIGURATIVE NUMBERS IN THE OLD TESTAMENT?

Bazak, Jacob. "Numerical Devices in Biblical Poetry." *Vetus Testamentum* 38 (1988): 333–37. A brief discussion of several numerical devices, including numbers as symbols, as well as the graded numerical saying.

Berlin, Adele. "When Five Is Not 5: The Bible's Nonliteral Use of Numbers." In *Ve-'Ed Ya'aleh (Genesis 2:6)*. Vol. 1, *Essays in Biblical and Ancient Near Eastern Studies Presented to Edward L. Greenstein*, edited by Peter Machinist, Robert A. Harris, Joshua A. Berman, Nili Samet, and Noga Ayali-Darsha. The Society of Biblical Literature, 2021. A brief survey of figurative use of numbers in the Bible.

Dell, Katharine J., and Tova Forti. "'Two Are Better Than One': The Conceptual and Thematic Use of Numbers in Ecclesiastes." *Hebrew Union College Annual* 94 (2023): 1–19. An examination of numbers employed symbolically in Ecclesiastes.

Gevirtz, Stanley. *Patterns in the Early Poetry of Israel*. University of Chicago Press, 1963. This book contains a valuable discussion of the graded numerical saying in the Bible.

Roth, Wolfgang M. W. "The Numerical Sequence X/X+1 in the Old Testament." *Vetus Testamentum* 12 (1962): 300–311. A classic discussion of graded numerical sayings in the OT.

Steinmann, Andrew E. "The Graded Numerical Sayings in the Book of Job." In *Fortunate the Eyes That See: Essays in Honor of David Noel Freedman in Celebration of His Seventieth Birthday*, edited by Astrid B. Beck, Andrew H. Bartelt, Paul R. Raabe, and Chris A. Franke. Eerdmans, 1995. An examination of the use of the graded saying in Job, noting that it occurs at important junctures in the book.

CHAPTER 7: DOES GOD SUFFER IN THE OLD TESTAMENT?

Fretheim, Terence E. *The Suffering of God: An Old Testament Perspective*. Fortress Press, 1984. A penetrating study of divine pathos in the OT that sometimes borders on open theism—the belief that God doesn't know everything about the future.

Ngien, Dennis. "The God Who Suffers." *Christianity Today*. February 3, 1997. A practical and pastoral overview of the Bible's teaching about divine suffering.

Schlimm, Matthew Richard. "Different Perspectives on Divine Pathos: An Examination of Hermeneutics in Biblical Theology." *Catholic Biblical Quarterly* 69 (2007): 673–94. A scholarly evaluation of leading twentieth-century theologies of God's pain and suffering.

Tada, Joni Eareckson, and Steven Estes. *When God Weeps: Why Our Sufferings Matter to the Almighty*. Zondervan, 1997. A practical approach to divine pathos and its implications for our lives.

CHAPTER 8: ARE OLD TESTAMENT SEXUAL LAWS STILL BINDING?

Gagnon, Robert A. J. "Are There Universally Valid Sex Precepts? A Critique of Walter Wink's Views on the Bible and Homosexuality." *Horizons in Biblical Theology* (2002): 72–125. An insightful debate between an evangelical and liberal theologian.

Gagnon, Robert A. J. *The Bible and Homosexual Practice: Texts and Hermeneutics*. Abingdon Press, 2001. An evangelical treatment of sexual practice that is detailed and comprehensive—looking at both OT and NT texts.

Gagnon, Robert A. J., and Dan O. Via. *The Bible, the Church, and Homosexuality*. Fortress Press, 2003. A thorough study on how the church has interpreted biblical texts that address same-sex intimacy.

CHAPTER 9: WHAT ABOUT DIVINE ANGER AND VENGEANCE IN THE OLD TESTAMENT?

Baloian, Bruce Edward. *Anger in the Old Testament*. Peter Lang, 1992. An exhaustive study of divine wrath in the OT.

Lessing, R. Reed. *Lamentations*. Concordia Commentary. Concordia Publishing House, 2024. See especially pages 257–68. A theological evaluation of OT and NT laments.

Peels, H. G. L. *The Vengeance of God: The Meaning of the Root NQM and the Function of the NQM-Texts in the Context of Divine Retribution in the Old Testament*. Brill, 1995. The most thorough study of divine vengeance to date.

CHAPTER 10: PREDICTING THE FUTURE: HOW MANY YEARS?

Ogden, Graham S. "'Within Sixty-Five Years . . .'—Problem or Emphasis? (Isaiah 7.7–9)." *The Bible Translator* 51.4 (2002): 445–47. Demonstrates that the reference to sixty-five years is not a late intrusion into the text, as suggested by many scholars, but an integral part of Isaiah 7:7–9.

Renz, Thomas. "Proclaiming the Future: History and Theology in Prophecies Against Tyre." *Tyndale Bulletin* 51.1 (2000): 17–58. Examines Isaiah's and Ezekiel's prophecies against Tyre and concludes that the prophecies are intentionally vague concerning any chronology of the fulfillment of these prophecies.

Steinmann, Andrew E. *Daniel*. Concordia Commentary. Concordia Publishing House, 2008. Contains an extended discussion of the meaning of the seventy weeks of Daniel 9 on pages 452–76.

Steinmann, Andrew E. *From Abraham to Paul: A Biblical Chronology*. 2nd ed. Concordia Publishing House, 2024. Includes a discussion of the chronological issues related to the various prophecies discussed in this chapter.

Steinmann, Andrew E. "The Shape of Things to Come: The Genre of the Historical Apocalypse in Ancient Jewish and Christian Literature." PhD diss., University of Michigan, 1990. A discussion of apocalypses and their prophecies, including Daniel and later works that use *seventy* and *weeks* in symbolic depictions of history or in future predictions.

CHAPTER 11: IS THERE ANY VALUE IN OLD TESTAMENT LAMENTS?

Allen, Leslie C. *A Liturgy of Grief: A Pastoral Commentary on Lamentations*. Baker Academic, 2011. A wonderful application of Lamentations for the church.

Bayer, Oswald. "Toward a Theology of Lament." In *Caritas et Reformatio: Essays on Church and Society in Honor of Carter Lindberg*, edited by David M. Whitford. Concordia Publishing House, 2002. A Lutheran view of biblical laments.

Eklund, Rebekah. *Practicing Lament*. Cascade, 2021. A comprehensive and pragmatic approach to the Bible's lament passages.

Lessing, R. Reed. *Lamentations*. Concordia Commentary. Concordia Publishing House, 2024. A thorough look at the lament genre in Lamentations as well as in the rest of the Bible.

CHAPTER 12: DO OLD TESTAMENT PROPHETS PREDICT CURRENT EVENTS?

Lessing, R. Reed. *Amos*. Concordia Commentary. Concordia Publishing House, 2009. See especially the discussion on Amos 9.

Lessing, R. Reed. *Zechariah*. Concordia Commentary. Concordia Publishing House, 2021. See especially the discussion on Zechariah 14.

Riddlebarger, Kim. *A Case for Amillenialism: Understanding the End Times*. Baker, 2003.

Steinmann, Andrew E. *Daniel*. Concordia Commentary. Concordia Publishing House, 2008. See especially the discussions of Daniel 2, 7, 8, and 9, as well as the examination of dispensational premillennial interpretation on pages 51–62.

CHAPTER 13: DOES GOD CHANGE HIS MIND IN THE OLD TESTAMENT?

Fretheim, Terence E. "The Repentance of God: A Key to Evaluating Old Testament God-Talk." *Horizons of Biblical Theology* 10 (1988): 47–70. A helpful discussion that points out how Greek philosophy has skewed our understanding of God's relenting.

Lessing, R. Reed. *Jonah*. Concordia Commentary. Concordia Publishing House, 2009. See especially pages 324–41. A Lutheran interpretation of Yahweh's mutability.

Roy, Steven. *How Much Does God Foreknow? A Comprehensive Biblical Study*. InterVarsity Press, 2006. An insightful defense for God's immutability set within the framework of divine relenting.

CHAPTER 14: WHERE IS GOD IN SONG OF SONGS AND ESTHER?

Goldman, Stan. "Narrative and Ethical Ironies in Esther." *Journal for the Study of the Old Testament* 15 (1990): 15–31. A good treatment of the narrative technique of the author of Esther.

Gordis, Robert. *The Song of Songs and Lamentations: A Study, Modern Translation and Commentary*. Rev. and augmented ed. Ktav, 1974. See especially pages 27–28 for a discussion of the oath refrain in Song of Songs.

Steinmann, Andrew E. *Esther*. Christian Standard Commentary. Holman Bible Publishers, 2024. See especially pages 22–27, which discuss the features of Esther that demonstrate God's control of the events narrated in Esther.

Steinmann, Andrew E. "Gazelles, Does, and Flames: (De)Limiting Love in Song of Songs." *Journal for the Evangelical Study of the Old Testament* 2.1 (2013): 25–39. A treatment of the purpose of human sexual attraction and God's involvement in it through the oath refrain and other passages.

Wiebe, John M. "Esther 4:14: 'Will Relief and Deliverance Arise for the Jews from Another Place?'" *The Catholic Biblical Quarterly* 53 (1991): 409–15. A short but comprehensive study of some of the most discussed passages in Esther.